ADVENTURES
on & off
INTERSTATE 80

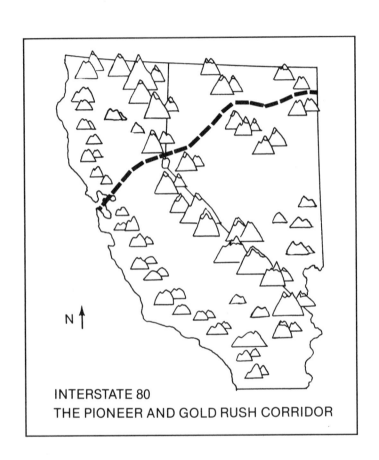

N

INTERSTATE 80
THE PIONEER AND GOLD RUSH CORRIDOR

ADVENTURES
on & off
INTERSTATE 80

Natural and human history
along the pioneer
and gold rush corridor from San Francisco's Pacific shore
to Nevada's desert sands

By Eleanor Huggins and John Olmsted

Illustrations by Carolyn L. Ryan and Andrea Hendrick

Text design by Judy Olson

Library of Congress Cataloging in Publication Data

Huggins, Eleanor M. (Eleanor Mitchell), 1929–
Adventures on & off Interstate 80.

Bibliography: p.
Includes index.
1. California—Description and travel—1981–
Guide-books. 2. Nevada—Description and travel—
1981–   —Guide-books. 3. Interstate 80—Guide-books.
I. Olmsted, John, 1938–   II. Title. III. Title:
Adventures on and off Interstate 80.
F859.3.H83 1985   917.94   84-23967
ISBN 0-935382-53-4

© 1985 Tioga Publishing Company.
P.O. Box 98
Palo Alto, California 94302

Distributed by William Kaufmann, Inc.
95 First Street
Los Altos, California 94022

10 9 8 7 6 5 4 3 2 1

We dedicate this book to the hundreds of students, teachers, and parents who for thirteen years have participated in California Institute of Man in Nature trips along the I-80 corridor. These educational excursions laid the foundation for the adventures that follow.

There are few places in the world where one can dip feet in the ocean at breakfast, drive across fertile valleys to feast at noon on fruit grown by the roadside, walk through pine and oak forests at four, stand on a snowy summit before dinner, and finally descend to watch the last rays of the sun paint the desert pink.

Contents

Chapter 7. THE GREAT BASIN

xi

List
of Maps

Foreword

You can know all about Henry James and the Art of the Fugue, but unless you know the world under your feet and before your eyes, you are not truly civilized.

—Kenneth Rexroth

The first few times I drove Interstate 80 east from San Francisco, it seemed mostly a boring stretch of road on the way to someplace else.

It was mile after mile and hour after hour of dry barren ranges, Kansas-flat prairie, dusty foothills, monotonous forests, and sterile parched deserts hot as the hinges of Hades.

Dullsville.

Shut the car windows, turn on the radio, and try to avoid somnolescence by figuring the driving time to the Nut Tree for rest and refreshment.

By accident rather than intention, I slowly began to pick up a little information over a period of years, and the drive was gradually transformed.

I learned to identify the pear trees with their upswept branches and to anticipate the sweet juicy Bartletts that swell on the boughs in late summer and early fall. I watched for the tall groves of walnuts, the aristocrats of orchard trees.

I found out that the great flat expanse of fields that form a freshwater sea in winter just west of Sacramento was the Yolo Bypass, where the Sacramento River overflows like the Nile to create the rich farm soil for spring planting. I learned about innumerable parks and pleasure grounds where you can stop and relax en route and side roads to historic locations.

These are the kind of gold nuggets of information you will find in this book, which is about the 300-mile stretch of Interstate 80 east of the

Golden Gate—not merely the roadside but the region through which it passes.

You will be able to visualize the pioneers and the wagon trains that came this way during one of the great migrations of history and left their wheel prints on the rocks. You will learn about John Muir and Mark Twain and John Sutter and how they saw these landscapes.

You will see where the Argonauts panned gold, and perhaps you'll do some panning yourself. You will be able to identify the giant piles of rock left by gold dredges and the huge open pits created by the hydraulic miners.

You will see gold towns and silver towns and ghost towns where John Wayne or Tom Mix or William S. Hart might stride out of a saloon any minute.

You will be able to pick out old cattle trails on the hills and great green outcrops of that extraordinary mineral, serpentine—the California state rock, which has flowed up through fissures in the earth.

You will learn how these hills and mountains were raised by the million-year collision of the Oceanic and Continental tectonic plates of the earth's crust.

You will know how to find vernal pools where successions of wild-flowers create contracting concentric rings of color in the spring.

You will see the site of a great train robbery and a great train snow-in, where a transcontinental luxury train was buried for three days.

You will see billiard-ball boulders as big as your car on mountain ridges where they were left by the melting ice. You will be able to identify such extraordinary high-country trees as the gnarled junipers and the graceful mountain hemlocks.

You will see where the wagon trains paused while their leaders made the fateful decision on crossing the dread Forty-Mile Desert. You will be able to identify Ice Age landscapes as you drive across the dry bed of vast Lake Lahontan, formed by the melting glaciers in the time of the Big Thaw.

You will follow the most varied, spectacular, and dramatic portion of the cross-section of the continent traversed by this great national artery. You will read this landscape like a book that you can't put down.

A terrain that appears dull to the ignorant becomes to the knowledge-able a revelation of multiple wonders.

As we approach the twenty-first century, Americans are beginning to find again their roots in this continent. This book—far more comprehensive and illuminating than the conventional fragmentary, mileage-keyed guidebook—offers invaluable ways to experience our geologic and historic past, our rich present, and our promising future, and to learn something about where we came from, who we are, and what we may become as we discover the meaning of the land under our feet and before our eyes.

And it offers enough fun on the road for a lifetime of weekends. I hope there will ultimately be a book like this about every highway in America.

Harold Gilliam
San Francisco, August 1984

ACKNOWLEDGMENTS

We wish to thank the staffs of the Oakland Museum, the Placer County Historical Museum, and the Nevada Historical Society who read various drafts of this manuscript so that our historic information was both correct and informative. Special thanks also to the geologists and naturalists who helped us clarify the complicated story of California's and Nevada's natural history.

We appreciate the efforts of the publishing staff at William Kaufmann, Inc., who helped turn our computer manuscript into this eminently usable book.

We are indebted to the following for their expertise:

Bob and Nils for guiding us through computer processing of the manuscript.

Sally for her help with the disability access information.

Bill Clark for his assistance with acquisition of the Muir letter and for sharing his knowledge of Sierra ski history.

John Corbett and the Truckee Historical Society for providing historic photos from their collection.

Mabel Crittenden for her no-nonsense vision of how botany can be learned by looking.

Harold Curran and Great Basin Press for quotes from emigrant diaries.

Tim Hall for his ability to simplify the complicated geologic history of California while guiding us on a geologic trip along the corridor. His drafts of the geology introduction provided the basis for the text.

Dorothy Harding for the photograph of the Emigrant Train from *Harper's Weekly*.

Diane Hart for her editorial guidance and comments.

Dr. Elizabeth Hone for her understanding of the interrelationships of living things.

Ted Huggins for his on-the-spot stories of Golden Gate Bridge construction and for his fine photo of opening day.

Malcolm Margolin for reviewing the Ohlone history and for educating thousands about the fascinating story of these early residents of the Bay Area.

Bert Wiley for directing us to emigrant wagon tracks in the granite and for diary quotes from his publication "The Overland Emigrant Trail in California."

Prelude to Your Adventures

As you open this book you are about to embark on a 300-mile guided tour along one of America's principal east-west highways. Your journey will take you through a remarkably diverse landscape and give you colorful glimpses into the events that shaped the history of California and Nevada. The first several pages provide background information to help you understand what you will see and visit.

Each of the seven chapters begins with a **Trip Planner** that previews each stop along the way. Symbols alert you to major attractions and facilities.

   Museum

   Gentle or paved walking path or trail

   Picnic tables

   Restrooms

Following, the natural history and historical events of that particular geographic region are detailed. The **Exploring** section is the heart of each chapter as it follows the interstate from west to east interpreting the features of the landscape and recounting tales of the past. Each stop along the interstate begins with an "open seat belt" symbol ▧ ▨ to alert you to look for the exit.

Restful Parallels leave the freeway for several miles of a quieter pace on remnants of old U.S. 40, the two-lane transcontinental forerunner of Interstate 80.

Alternate Loops leave from the interstate and return some miles further. Some will not add significantly to your travel time, whereas others take several hours. Each loop has a historical emphasis within a scenic setting and includes visits to spots not on the usual tourist routes.

Favorite Diversions are for travelers with up to half a day to spare. Some of these side trips explore country roads; several visit trails or structures known only to locals; a couple appear in print for the first time; and others describe special tours of Sacramento, Truckee, and Reno.

The footsteps of those who traveled this way have disappeared, but their memories remain in diaries, stories, and poetry. You can participate in their travails, their joys, and their tragedies when you read the selections in **Yesterday's Voices.**

The book concludes with a list of the many **Plant Communities** and suggestions to **Read On.**

A special feature is the **Disability Access Guide** that follows. Our hope is that it will allow a wide range of people to enjoy adventures along the interstate.

Disability Access Guide

Facilities listed meet legal disability access standards or are usable by a majority of persons with limited mobility. Marginally accessible exhibits, trails, or restrooms that require persons in wheelchairs to be assisted are marked with an asterisk. Most picnic tables are not marked but are marginally accessible.

A survey of other accessible facilities along I-80 in California specifies wheelchair access, trail characteristics and measurements, and opportunities for hearing- and sight-impaired persons and is available at nominal cost from Sequoya Challenge, Box 1026, Nevada City, CA 95959.

Chapter 1

Fort Funston	overlook, trail, picnic, restrooms
Ocean Beach	steep paved ramp to sand*
The Cliff House	overlook, exhibit, restaurant, restrooms on request
Golden Gate Bridge Overlook	overlook, bridge sidewalk, restrooms*
Golden Gate Park	exhibit, trails, restrooms
Mission Dolores	ramp
The Historic Waterfront	exhibit, restaurant, pier, restrooms*
Alcatraz Island	boat trip*, exhibit, trail*
North of the Golden Gate	
Bay Model	exhibit, restrooms
GGNRA Rodeo Beach	ramp to sand, picnic, restrooms
Mt. Tamalpais Peak	overlook, trail*, picnic, restrooms
Audubon Canyon Ranch	exhibit, bird blind*, restrooms
Point Reyes Seashore	visitor center, exhibit, trails*, picnic, restrooms

Chapter 6

Chapter 7

The Landscape

Beautiful, dramatic, incredibly varied—all are descriptions of the scenery of California and Nevada, where the unexpected is the rule. The Interstate 80 corridor across these two states is a year-round, memorable showcase of natural beauty and diversity. Seen from aloft, the features of this corridor become etched in mind and memory: the rocky Pacific shoreline, the thin scar of the San Andreas earthquake fault, the coastal mountain ranges ringing twin-armed San Francisco Bay, the elongated Central Valley resembling an immense earthen bathtub, subtle shades of green ascending the slope of the Sierra Nevada, snow-capped peaks surrounding lakes large and small, and the pastel washboard of Nevada's basins and ranges. This introduction explains the geology and ecology of this countryside.

THE LAND

For 200 million years California and Nevada have been formed by the opposing forces of mountain building and erosion. Mountain building is the result of *tectonic* forces that push the outer skin of the earth upward as heat escapes from deep inside the earth. Wind, water, and ice produce erosion, wearing away high places and filling in low spots. The landscape we see, dull or dramatic, depends upon which set of forces temporarily holds sway. In the eastern and central United States, erosion has all but won. In California and Nevada, mountain building still outpaces erosion.

Whereas erosion is easily observed and has been understood for a long while, the causes of mountain building have been a mystery until recently. Within the last twenty years a revolutionary theory called *plate tectonics* has shed new light on the origin of mountain formation. To get a sense of this new idea, imagine cutting the skin of a ripe peach into a dozen or so irregular shapes. Next, picture yourself sliding the pieces around on the fruit and watching the edges where they meet. Sometimes they wrinkle, and at other times one piece moves over or under another.

The earth's skin or crust is similarly broken into pieces that earth scientists call *plates*. These plates do not correspond exactly to the continents; most include some ocean floor as well as land masses. Nearly all of Canada, the United States, and the western portion of the Atlantic Ocean make up the North American Plate. Scientists have recently discovered that tectonic or mountain building activity occurs along plate boundaries. The spectacular scenery of California and Nevada is the result of such dynamic interactions, a geologic story still being written by nature and deciphered by geologists.

The Dance of the Plates

Plate movement can be compared to a dance with three steps: apart, together, and slide. Around its edges a plate can do any or all of these steps at a time. With plates moving only an inch or two a year, the dance is a ponderously slow one by human standards.

Apart: When plates push away from each other, continents may be split apart and ocean basins created. Such is the movement along a zigzag line in the middle of the Atlantic Ocean floor. At this *spreading ridge*, molten rock seeps up between two plates, causing the North American Plate to move westward so that New York and London dance slowly away from each other. Halfway around the world, the East Pacific spreading ridge has caused millions of years of geologic tumult at the edge of California. Spreading may now be occurring beneath Nevada, causing the land to stretch and break into great blocks. Indeed, someday in the geologic future it may be fashionable to swim in the Nevada Ocean and to sail from Utah to California.

Together: When an ocean plate and a continental plate meet, a process called *subduction* can occur. The thin but heavy plate of ocean floor slides under the lighter, higher-riding continental plate and is remelted in a crustal recycling scheme. The resulting molten rock may rise to the surface in volcanic eruptions. Evidence of such activity is found in the Sierra Nevada and the Cascade Range to the north. Eruptions of Mt. Lassen, Mt. Shasta in California, and Mt. Saint Helens in Washington continue this process. If the subducted molten material remains underground as it cools, it forms rocks like granite. Such a massive unit of granite rose slowly over millions of years to become the batholith of crystalline rock that formed the Sierra Nevada.

For about 150 million years the western edge of the North American Plate rode over a subducting slab of an oceanic plate. The veneer of ocean floor sediments was scraped off and welded onto the battered edge of the adjacent continental plate. The rocks of California's coastal

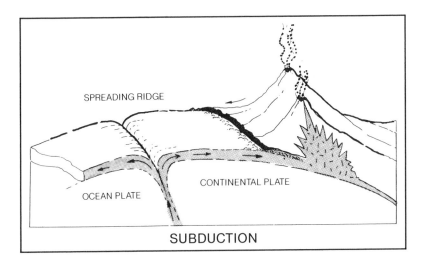

SPREADING RIDGE

CONTINENTAL PLATE

OCEAN PLATE

SUBDUCTION

ranges thus were formed from the scrapings of the Pacific Ocean floor. These jumbled, folded, and broken rocks look as though they had been "mixmastered."

Then, about 30 million years ago, a complex series of plate movements began that are not yet completely understood. The North American Plate collided with the East Pacific spreading ridge and perhaps overrode part of it. Eventually a strip of California and the west coast of Mexico became fused to the Pacific Plate and began sliding in a northwesterly direction toward Alaska. This long, narrow block of land that includes Baja California, Los Angeles, Monterey, and Point Reyes—but not San Francisco—is separated from the North American Plate by a 700-mile-long series of cracks and fractures known to us as the San Andreas fault system.

Slide: Movement along an active plate boundary like the San Andreas fault is the slide step in the tectonic dance. This third type of plate dance occurs when two plates move past each other, neither creating nor destroying crust in the process. Movement occurs along zones of weakened rocks called *faults*. Normally, friction along the edges prevents plates from sliding smoothly. The rocks bend and store up tremendous amounts of energy. The strain builds until rocks along the boundary snap and slide into new positions, causing earthquakes that rearrange our dishes and, over time, the appearance of the land.

Zones of weakened rocks occur in many places, not just along plate boundaries. California and Nevada are laced with faults where the earth has slid sideways or jolted up and down. This latter vertical movement is responsible for the dizzying heights of the Sierra Nevada and Nevada's basins and ranges. After subduction had produced volcanoes and set the

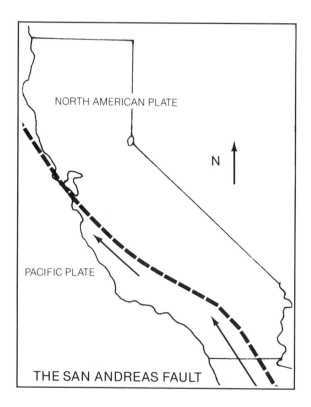

NORTH AMERICAN PLATE

PACIFIC PLATE

N

THE SAN ANDREAS FAULT

granite batholith in place, the earth began to tremble on a fault line along
the eastern edge of the ancient Sierra range. The huge block of granite
was slowly uplifted until the peaks reached into the clouds. The resulting
range rose steeply along its eastern boundary and sloped gently westward toward the Central Valley.

Whereas Sierran rocks are the result of subduction and associated volcanoes, Sierra scenery is the result of stream erosion, uplift, and glaciation. Some three million years ago uplift began, and the earth became
cooler and entered the Ice Ages. Glaciers, some thousands of feet thick,
surrounded Sierra mountaintops and flowed slowly downhill. In the
process they reshaped the mountains, carving deep river canyons into U-
shaped valleys. When the ice melted for the last time, the exposed
granite was polished smooth and the landscape was dotted by lakes of
every size filling ice-carved bowls. During the time of melting glaciers,
erosion of the range reached a climax, particularly along the western
slope. Rivers rushed seaward carrying quantities of rocks and sand,
carved deep canyons into the range's western flank, and filled the Central Valley trough with sediment.

These processes—spreading, subduction, faulting and erosion—have created the landscape seen today. California's and Nevada's most prominent features are a series of north-south-trending mountains: the Coast Ranges, the Sierra Nevada, and the Basin and Range Province. The processes are still at work today, giving periodic reminders of their power in the form of volcanic eruptions and earthquakes.

WATER ON THE LAND

Because the mountain ranges of both California and Nevada trend from north to south, they serve as effective barriers to storms blowing in from the Pacific Ocean. How different the rainfall along the Interstate 80 corridor would be if the winds blew unobstructed across flat plains. Instead, clouds crash against the ranges and drop their moisture first along the seaward side of the Coast Ranges and then near the top of the western slope of the Sierra. By the time storms reach the Sierra summit they are nearly depleted. The eastern side of each range is in a rain shadow, and the farther east you go into Nevada, the drier the landscape.

The interstate corridor is affected by an unusual interplay between land and water. Summers are nearly stormless, but along the Pacific coast a huge fog bank builds up offshore as warm, moist winds blow over cold ocean water. The San Francisco Bay provides the only sea-level gap in the Coast Range mountains. Fog pouring through the Golden Gate brings summer cooling to the hills around the Bay's edge and creates intriguing inland weather patterns.

Much of California enjoys a climate with long months of warm, rainless days similar to the climate of the Mediterranean, Chile, South Africa, and western Australia. Little rain falls from March to November. Total precipitation is moderate, occurring mainly during a half-dozen memorable storms in December, January, and February. The highest amounts

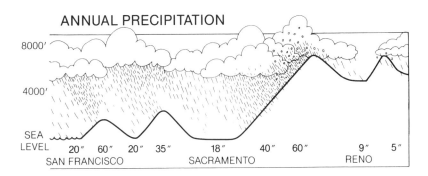

ANNUAL PRECIPITATION

of precipitation occur in certain coastal canyons and near the Sierra summit. Freezing temperatures are unusual, except in the higher mountains, but subzero weather can occur throughout the winter months in Nevada.

Our route passes through three major climatic regions. The narrow coastal band is characterized by balmy temperatures, six or more rainless months, frost-free winters, and intermittent summer fog. The interior of California has very hot and cloudless summers, some frost, and localized winter fog. As one ascends the western Sierra slope, the temperature becomes cooler. For each thousand feet of elevation gain the temperature goes down about five degrees Fahrenheit. Winter rain turns to snow near the Sierra crest, and summer thunderstorms are not uncommon. The third climatic region, Nevada's Great Basin, is known for its extreme heat and cold, minimal precipitation, and drying winds.

Watersheds are drainage areas, part of the circulatory system of the land. Each of the three climatic regions happens to correspond with a major watershed system. Streams and rivers on the western slopes of the Coast Ranges drain into the Pacific. California's Central Valley collects water from the Inner Coast Ranges and from the Sierra Nevada. The principal rivers of the Valley, the Sacramento and the San Joaquin, meet at the southern edge of our corridor where their combined flow reaches the Pacific via San Francisco Bay. East of the Sierra crest lies the "dying" watershed of the Great Basin, where rivers have no outlet to the sea and end in lakes and marshy sinks.

LIFE ON THE LAND

Our 300-mile journey from ocean to desert passes through an amazing array of vegetation that clothes the earth in many shades of green and gold. Seaside bush lupines give way to stately redwood forests, lone oaks,

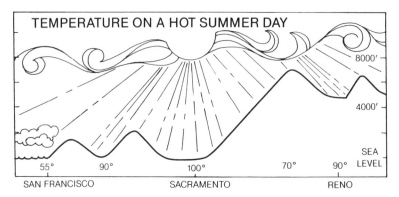

TEMPERATURE ON A HOT SUMMER DAY

8000'

4000'

SEA LEVEL

55°   90°   100°   70°   90°

SAN FRANCISCO   SACRAMENTO   RENO

open grasslands, colorful rings of wildflowers, towering conifers, and endless sagebrush. One can drive less than 100 miles from our path to the tallest, oldest, largest or shortest tree species in the world. In the remaining distance across America—ten times as far—there are long stretches of sameness, for the scenery has less variety in both climate and topography.

"Plants and animals live where they do because they can!" This seemingly simple concept states the most fundamental fact about the adaptations of living things and helps explain why such diversity can be found along our corridor. Each species requires certain special conditions while being able to tolerate others. Over time, as conditions change, plants either adapt or die. Soil, precipitation, wind, altitude, temperature, exposure to the sun, and availability of water all play a part in providing either a livable or an inhospitable environment.

Plants and animals having similar needs cluster together into *natural communities*. Over twenty such communities can be found from the Pacific Ocean to the Great Basin. The plant list at the back of the book lists the communities along with the indicator species in each. Although most plants seen along the way survive the long, dry summers, local water conditions offer special opportunities. Water-loving plants cluster along rivers and lakes, providing a lush landscape in the most unexpected places. Certain tough plants have adapted to harsh, salty conditions, such as those on ocean cliffs, in salt marshes, and in desert alkaline flats.

Some natural communities are not confined to one place; like old friends, they reappear. Heat-tolerant chaparral plants may be found on coastal hills or in the Sierra. An interesting symmetry exists in the hills around the Central Valley where different natural communities circle the Valley like rings of a bathtub.

Belts of plant communities occupying different *lifezones* march up mountain slopes. Some plants near the Central Valley floor are reminiscent of those in Mexico, and others near the Sierra crest are tundra plants of the Arctic. In a climb of 10,000 feet in just 100 miles from west to east from the Central Valley to the Sierra crest, it is as if you have traveled northward over much of North America.

The communities have not always been where we find them, nor will they stay exactly as we see them. Humans and nature alter the land and growing conditions change through fire, lumbering, mining, or by natural catastrophes such as volcanic eruptions or landslides. The first plants to establish themselves after such a change are called *pioneers*. As natural conditions change, the pioneer species may give way to others until the area is populated by a *climax* species, which remains dominant until the next catastrophe begins the process again.

In addition to its many different and specialized plant communities, California has incredible variety within single plant families. One-tenth of all known conifers, or cone-bearing trees, are found here. Of all the species of pine growing in the United States, half are found in this state. Among them are the tallest pine (some 225 feet), the pine with the longest cone, and the one with the heaviest cone. Almost half of all the species of oak growing throughout the United States are found in this one state. Oak leaves, which range from soft and deciduous to leathery and evergreen, give clues to ways that they have adapted to the dry climate.

It is difficult to conclude a discussion of California's trees without superlatives. The coastal region supports the redwood, the world's tallest tree. Old-growth giants attain heights of over 350 feet. In comparison, above treeline in the Sierra there are tiny willows that do not grow more than two inches high. A few isolated areas on the western slope of the Sierra are home to the giant sequoia, the world's largest living thing. It takes twenty people, hands outstretched, to reach around the base of the really big trees. The Great Basin mountains of California and Nevada have scattered groves of the bristlecone pine, the oldest living tree. The growth rings of the Methuselah tree record wet and dry periods for the past 4600 years. Other dead specimens go back 7000 years, long before Egyptians built their pyramids.

One of the joys of driving in the West is to come across the splash of color from spring wildflowers, some lasting only a week. And what variety! Of California's 2500 wildflower species, 1000 are found nowhere else. Especially loved are yellow-orange poppies, mariposa lilies, pentstemons (relatives of garden snapdragons), and members of the phlox family. California and Nevada shrubs also come in many kinds and shapes. There are several dozen species each of wild lilac, red-barked manzanita, and saltbush.

Over time, changes in the landscape and climate have allowed plants to migrate to and around California. Our interstate corridor roughly marks where certain plants from the north and from the south meet and go no farther. The Bay Area is near the southern limit of the redwood, and most desert dwellers and south Coast Range species fade out to the north. Many of the deciduous trees such as oaks and buckeyes as well as the pines remind travelers from other temperate parts of the world of the vegetation at home.

Botanists could spend a lifetime discussing just what is a native plant. How long must a plant be in an area to get old-timer status? California has been particularly receptive to plants from other places, and it seems as if most plants we call weeds have come as foreign immigrants. It is no accident that many are from the Mediterranean. Spaniards brought the seeds here in animal feed, and some—like wild oats and mustard—

adapted beautifully to a climate much like home. Nor is it a surprise to learn that eucalyptus, which thrives in California, has come from warm, dry Australia.

Although the California and Nevada landscapes allow for immense plant diversity, the original mammal populations were not exceedingly varied. Rather, the land could and did support large numbers of a few grazing species. When Europeans arrived and introduced cattle and annual grasses, the herds of grassland dwellers diminished. Today only a few protected herds remain, and predators like the grizzly bear and wolf have been hunted to extinction. Other unique California species also appear doomed: there are now less than twenty wild condors and a few hundred tule elk.

A Historical Overview

CALIFORNIA BEFORE THE GOLD RUSH

In 1510 a Spanish novelist wrote a fable about an Amazon queen named Calafia who ruled an island abounding in gold and precious stones. This wondrous land was called California. Two hundred years after publication of the story, Spanish explorers sailed north from their Mexican province and discovered Queen Calafia's fabled land; they called it Alta California.

By the time Americans living along the eastern seaboard had declared their independence from Great Britain, Spanish soldiers had built forts called *presidios* along the California coast, and the Catholic Church had sent priests to found a string of missions between San Diego and Sonoma. The road connecting these missions was named El Camino Real, "the king's highway." The presence of the Crown and the Church in these far-off places attracted settlers who found the climate wonderfully similar to that of Spain. The Spanish monarch granted these new arrivals huge tracts of land, and soon cattle herds measured in the thousands roamed freely on mammoth ranchos. All of these ranchos and presidios were located near or on the coast, and the great plain of the Central Valley and the Sierra Nevada remained almost unknown to the Spanish inhabitants.

Momentous events were taking place in the rest of the world that would change the course of California history. In 1803 the United States purchased a huge area of the land in the Mississippi Valley from France. The Louisiana Purchase opened up the vast interior of America to a breed of who sought to explore the rivers, ranges, deserts, and valleys west of the Mississippi. Soon restless farmers, including many newcomers who had just gotten off the boats from Europe, moved westward to settle land they could call their own.

Mexico rebelled against Spain in 1821 and became an independent republic with dominion over Alta California. But a weak Mexican government lost control of its California province, allowing presidios to fall into ruin and dismissing former Spanish soldiers. The United States began to think of California as a ripe plum ready for harvest, and the U.S.

government supported several expeditions to map its western territories and find routes to the continent's western coast. California's Spanish era ended less than fifty years after the last mission was erected.

THE PIONEER AND GOLD RUSH CORRIDOR

The story of California's Spanish past is found along the coastal highways between San Diego and San Francisco. The state's American history, however, unfolded along the east-west corridor that became Interstate 80. Many significant events that contributed to the development of the nation's richest and most populous state occurred near this transcontinental route.

California was a magnet to the adventurous, the restless, the discontented, and the dreamers. Soon after Alta California became part of Mexico, American and European immigrants began to arrive. Many were sailors who found California a sunny paradise after scurvy-ridden months in cramped sailing ships. They jumped ship in San Francisco and disappeared inland or found a Mexican señorita to marry.

Land routes to Oregon were opened in 1840, and restless farmers rounded up their cattle, put their families in wagons, and blazed a trail west. Some decided that California's beneficent climate and seemingly limitless supply of fertile acres were more attractive, and in 1841 a small group left the Oregon Trail and struck off across the deserts of Utah and Nevada to open a trail to California. No one is exactly sure which route they used to cross the Sierra Nevada, but they arrived wagonless at a ranch near Mt. Diablo with little but the clothes on their backs. Not until 1844 did the first wagons open the route that we know as Donner Pass. By 1848 several hundred wagons had made the fearful crossing and struggled over the forbidding Sierra Nevada to open the way to California.

Events far away were changing the course of California history. American politicians with expansionist ideas dreamed of a United States from the Atlantic to the Pacific, and war with Mexico ensued. The United States prevailed and in early 1848 signed a treaty adding the territories of Utah, New Mexico, Arizona, Nevada, and California to the United States. The stars and stripes were hoisted in the former Mexican outposts of Monterey and San Francisco while the residents awaited the establishment of an American government and wondered about the changes to come.

GOLD IS DISCOVERED AND A STATE IS BORN

Gold on the American River! The cry of gold in the Sierra foothills soon emptied the coastal towns, and sailors lucky enough to be in port during 1848 abandoned ship, lured by dreams of easy wealth. When rumors of the riches were confirmed by President Polk the California gold rush was on in earnest. Hordes of Americans left eastern farms and factories to take part in one of history's greatest migrations. In the spring of 1849, 40,000 men gathered on the banks of the Mississippi River preparing to dash across America's western wilderness. The first to leave were guided only by the faint twin traces of earlier pioneer wagons. By the end of the summer the route across the plains and deserts became a maze of deep ruts. When these gold seekers reached the Sierra, groups often had to wait in line to haul their wagons over the Donner Summit. Elsewhere in the world thousands of men boarded ships bound for San Francisco and from there, by whatever conveyance possible, to Sacramento and the gold fields.

This influx of would-be miners created instant towns in the foothills and swelled the populations of San Francisco and Sacramento. The population of coastal areas south of San Francisco remained as it had been during Spanish and Mexican times. The corridor between San Francisco and the gold country, however, became home for several hundred thousand newcomers, and only six in ten were Americans.

Not all the West's mineral wealth was on the California side of the Sierra Nevada. High on a mountainside in western Nevada, prospectors found a gigantic deposit of gold mixed with silver-bearing blue muck and called it the Comstock Lode. In 1859 a reverse migration took place. Thousands of disappointed California miners crossed the Sierra hoping to strike it rich near the Comstock boomtown of Virginia City.

By 1870 California and Nevada mineral wealth was being tapped at a furious rate. Miles of tunnels were bored deep under Virginia City where miners worked in intolerable heat to load the rock and blue muck into carts. In California, too, gold mining had become big business when new techniques were discovered to extract the wealth. Hydraulic and deep rock mines were earning millions of dollars for their investors, and new waves of experienced miners flocked to fill the jobs that paid three dollars per hour. San Francisco had become the financial center of the region, and Sacramento had used its proximity to the gold to declare itself the state capital.

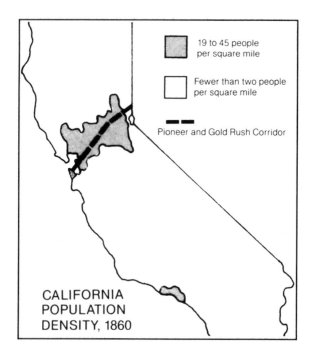

19 to 45 people
per square mile

Fewer than two people
per square mile

Pioneer and Gold Rush Corridor

CALIFORNIA
POPULATION
DENSITY, 1860

ROADS AND RAILROADS

As the populations of both California and Nevada increased, reliable transportation of goods and people across the Sierra Nevada became of paramount importance. Old wagon routes were turned into private toll roads, and enterprising teamsters founded stagecoach companies. But no matter how good the road, twenty-foot snowdrifts on the Sierra's rocky heights shut down most traffic between California and Nevada for six months of the year. During winter and spring, wagons became mired in mud on the dirt tracks between the Sacramento Valley and the port of San Francisco.

The only solution seemed to be a railroad, but over which pass could such a rail line be constructed, and with whose money? Fortunately for the growing state of California and for the nation there were four Sacramento merchants and an engineer who believed that a transcontinental railroad could be built across the Sierra. With the Civil War in progress, these men joined together to form the Central Pacific Railroad Company and lobbied President Lincoln and the Congress to pass the Pacific Railroad Act in 1862. The legislation granted railroad builders federal loans as well as sections of land along the route. Soon the Central Pacific Railroad began building its line eastward from Sacramento. The tracks crossed the Sierra at the exact spot on Donner Pass where pioneers had dragged the first wagons into California two decades earlier. Our route on Interstate 80 also crosses nearby.

Five years after the first rails were laid in Sacramento, a golden spike was driven into the final rail at Promontory Point, Utah, to signify completion of the iron link between east and west. A year after that historic occasion, a continuation of the line was begun between Sacramento and San Francisco. Wishing to increase traffic and revenues, the Central Pacific advertised California's fertile land and balmy weather to lure settlers and tourists. And west they came to farm, to start new businesses, and to tap California's seemingly limitless resources. Sierra lumber companies sprang up as fast as men could build a crude road into the forest. The Central Valley turned green as homesteaders hurried to plant the fertile soil with fruit trees. Huge tracts of cheap land were tilled and planted with wheat, whose plump kernels were shipped around the world.

The state's population grew in fits and starts however. After the Civil War many left the financial uncertainties of the East or the devastation of the South and emigrated to California. Six decades later, when the Oklahoma and Kansas fields turned to dust during the 1930s, midwestern farmers and their families flocked to the Central Valley to pick crops. And when World War II ended, soldiers and sailors returned to the sunny shores near their former bases. The airfields built in the flat Central Valley to defend our western shores remained in service after the war and were expanded. When the silicon chip was born in the 1970s, a new gold rush began, bringing a burgeoning computer industry to the state. The first Silicon Valley was just south of San Francisco, but as land has become expensive new sites have been sought near Sacramento.

Growth brought prosperity and time for leisure activities. Just as the ancients traveled into the mountains to escape summer heat and to hunt and fish, so millions of flatland citizens have turned the Sierra Nevada into their summer and winter playground. Old gold towns and former lumber camps are now tourist meccas.

Interstate 80 has become the gateway to mountain pleasures as well as a vital link to the rest of the nation. The onetime Indian path and wagon route is now a commercial lifeline for California as well as the shortest drive between San Francisco and points east. Thousands of travelers are able to whiz across the 7000-foot pass with little idea that their now-effortless journey once took several weeks. Nor do many realize how much history is to be discovered along this corridor. Recognizing the importance of this route across California, the legislature has designated it the Pioneer and Gold Rush Corridor. This book is an attempt to increase your enjoyment by introducing you to people, places, and events that molded the gold and silver states.

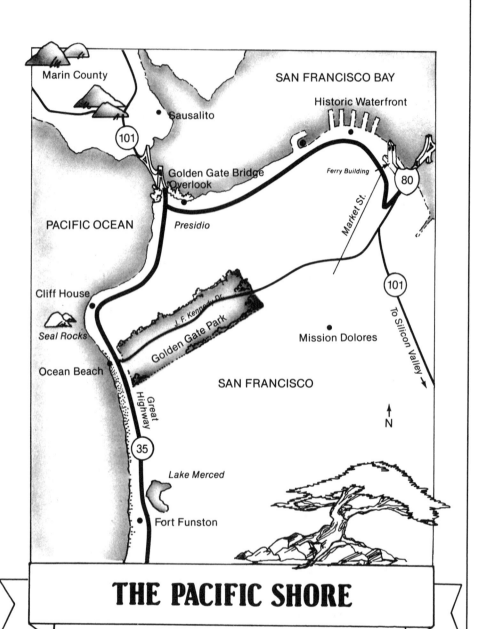

THE PACIFIC SHORE

1

THE PACIFIC SHORE
Fort Funston to the S.F.- Oakland Bay Bridge

Trip Planner

EXPLORING

Exploring the eighteen-mile drive around the perimeter of San Francisco keeps the ocean and bay in sight. A city map is recommended. When at the water's edge, give the power of the breakers the respect they deserve. Year round, be prepared for windy and often foggy days. This route joins Interstate 80 at the San Francisco-Oakland Bay Bridge.

Fort Funston is an old military site turned into a park where you can watch hang gliders take off from the cliffs over the Pacific Ocean. Breathtaking views of coastline, whale watching in season, and trails through coastal native vegetation are featured.

Ocean Beach offers beachcombing along San Francisco's window on the Pacific.

The **Cliff House** is one of the most visited attractions in San Francisco, partly due to the views of Seal Rocks. Less well known is an exciting walk through a sandstone tunnel.

The **Golden Gate Bridge overlook**, with its expansive views of bridge and bay, is a must for all visitors. Start here to walk across the bridge or to visit Fort Point.

FAVORITE DIVERSIONS

Golden Gate Park offers an alternate approach to Interstate 80 through this 1000-acre city park. Museums, aquarium, and arboretum invite closer inspection of California's plant and animal diversity.

Mission Dolores is an easy side trip from Golden Gate Park. It is the oldest building in San Francisco and one of the twenty-one Spanish missions in the state. The mission birth registry has been kept since 1776, and a cemetery garden has gravestones of the earliest inhabitants of the city.

The **Historic Waterfront**, as it is called in this book, is near Ghirardelli Square. Old sailing and steam ships, early ferries, and exhibits of San Francisco's maritime history are located within walking distance of Fisherman's Wharf.

North of the Golden Gate traverses the wilderness portions of Marin County. The drive visits the tall redwoods of Muir Woods, climbs to the top of Mt. Tamalpais, and goes on to Point Reyes National Seashore.

THE GOLDEN GATE REGION

To orbiting astronauts, San Francisco Bay is the most prominent feature of the California coastline. The ocean seems to be invading the land through the narrow opening of the Golden Gate. Though often hidden by fingers of summer fog, the Gate has inspired poets, painters, and photographers. San Francisco, "the City by the Golden Gate," occupies a dramatic peninsula bordered on three sides by ocean and bay. North of the Gate the headland cliffs of Marin County drop into the ocean.

The birthing process of the Coast Ranges was complex. For millions of years during subduction of the Pacific Ocean floor, its rocks were scraped off and stuffed onto the North American Plate to form the rocky underpinnings of the Bay Area. Then the San Andreas fault began to dance, moving pieces of coast northwestward like a long conveyor belt, bringing pieces of Mexico up the coast to northern California. During the famous earthquake of 1906, some of the land on this plate lurched sixteen feet closer to Alaska, reminding us that the dance of the plates is not completed. It's only a matter of time, albeit millions of years, until Los Angeles (sitting on the Pacific Plate) sails past the Golden Gate. **Yesterday's Voices** at the end of this chapter includes Mark Twain's tongue-in-cheek reaction to earthquake fears.

California's coast displays three distinctive landforms. Precipitous cliffs north of the Golden Gate plunge nearly 1000 feet to the breakers' edge. South of San Francisco, wave-cut terraces provide flat areas for homes, parks, and fertile fields. Gentle beaches and sand dunes exist where present and past rivers have met the ocean.

The geologic history of the region can be read in the pebbles and sand on beaches. Native bedrock is called the Franciscan Formation. Beachcombers can find reddish pieces of chert and veined graywacke sandstone as well as granite pebbles. Even rocks containing ancient fossil seashells can be found. Beach sands are gifts of cliff erosion and of the last glacial period when the melting glaciers rushed seaward, bringing their loads of sand and pebbles. The rising sea pushed great quantities of sand onshore to create a sandy necklace around the city. Now, 10,000 years later, sand is in diminishing supply. Heavy surf from winter storms pulls sand out to sea where it is destined to reappear on beaches to the south or disappear forever into ocean trenches. New beaches form and old ones become rocky shelves.

The Golden Gate region has been shaped by the confrontation of many forces. Powerful waves drive against the rocks and sands of the continent. Ocean tides pulse back and forth twice daily, creating strong currents and circular eddies. This turbulence along with dense fog have driven many ships onto coastal rocks, leaving the ocean floor littered with ship skeletons.

The dramatic landscape of San Francisco and its neighboring coast is matched by a spectacular climate. During winter, days of incredible clarity alternate with rainstorms sweeping inland off the world's largest ocean. Spring winds continue sculpting the dunes as rain diminishes and the sunny days begin. With the Mediterranean-style climate, little rain falls between April and November.

Summer visitors arrive unprepared for San Francisco's brand of moist air conditioning. A shivering Mark Twain complained that "the coldest winter I ever spent was summer in San Francisco." Fog pours in from the ocean and may linger all day in some sections of the city. This strange weather is caused by a meeting of opposites. Warm winds blow eastward across the Pacific. Several miles offshore this moist air encounters the upwelling of cold waters from the north. Moisture is condensed into waves of fog that roll across the coastal mountains, dwarfing stately redwood trees. Fog streamers flow silently through spider cables of the Golden Gate Bridge and reach inland across the Bay.

Rocky hills, coastal valleys, varying soils, sun, and fog create corners that are both nature's and a gardener's delight. Blessed by the boon of frost-free winters, city dwellers have filled their gardens with colorful pockets of plants from the temperate and subtropical regions of the world. Orchids grow near camellias, and cacti and roses thrive nearby; however, very little of San Francisco's native vegetation remains.

San Francisco of yesteryear was largely shifting sand dunes. These were stabilized in some places by plants of the *coastal strand* community, deep-rooted verbena and silver beachweed that could survive the desertlike setting. On foggy, windswept bluffs and coastal hills, compact, low-growing species of the *coastal scrub* community thrived and presented a springtime carpet of brilliant reds and yellows. Intermittent streams were lined with thick growths of vines, shrubs, and broadleafed trees. A large lake, now Lake Merced, was ringed with tules and other plants of the *freshwater marsh* community. Groves of coastal live oaks grew in a few locations. (A few of the remaining ones are now protected in Golden Gate Park at the corner of Arguello and Fulton streets.)

Across the Golden Gate, beaches, seaside bluffs, steep mountains, and forested canyons are still essentially in their natural state. It is as if nature threw her book of possibilities here and natural communities accepted the challenge and flourished.

Where land meets sea a broad zone of marine plants live under water for varying amounts of time. These *intertidal* communities provide food and shelter for many species of tidepool animals, presenting a multicolored spectacle between high and low tides. Land plants on the open

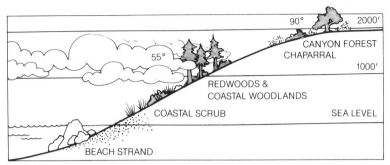

90° 2000'

55° CANYON FOREST
CHAPARRAL
1000'

REDWOODS &
COASTAL WOODLANDS

COASTAL SCRUB SEA LEVEL

BEACH STRAND

OUTER COAST RANGE PLANT COMMUNITIES

slopes above the tidal zone often have succulent leaves and are subjected to drying winds carrying traces of salty spray.

Redwoods that once clothed wider areas of these mountains still nestle in damp canyons. High and dry above the fog that nourishes the *redwood* and *coastal woodland*, *chaparral* and *canyon forest* communities are subjected to a six-month dry season and hot summer days. The coastal mountains rise from the sea, offering a staircase of very different natural habitats.

THE CITY BY THE BAY

Spanish exploration of the California coast began in 1542, when Joao Rodriguez Cabrilho (a Portuguese explorer whom the Spanish renamed Juan Cabrillo) sailed north from Mexico on a voyage of discovery. He never found San Francisco Bay, as adverse winds and currents along the coast north of Santa Barbara kept his expedition well out to sea until he was 200 miles north of the Golden Gate.

In July of 1579 the English explorer Sir Francis Drake beached his ship, the *Golden Hinde*, near San Francisco and claimed California for Queen Elizabeth I. He gave the world the first description of the California Indians who had inhabited the area for at least 5000 years. His exact landing spot, however, continues to be the subject of debate among historians and archeologists, one side claiming that he was inside the Golden Gate; the other that he was on Point Reyes Peninsula, north of the Gate. Whichever is true, no other seaward approaches to San Francisco Bay were discovered for the next 200 years.

Spanish colonization of California began in 1769 with the establishment of a military outpost in San Diego. Shortly thereafter, Gaspar de Portola rode north in search of a land route to the beautiful Monterey harbor described by several seagoing explorers. The descriptions were so exaggerated that Portola failed to recognize the harbor when he found it, and he continued north to become the first Spaniard to see San Francisco Bay.

Despite Portola's discovery, the Spanish government in Mexico elected not to develop an official harbor at San Francisco. Instead, Monterey was chosen as the colony's capital and major harbor with an official customs office. Still, Father Junipero Serra saw to it that his string of California missions included one near the Bay of Saint Francis.

In the 1770s Juan Bautista de Anza led a small band of soldiers, two priests, and a few settlers across the mountains north from Monterey. Two weeks later they straggled onto a sandy, windswept bluff overlooking the entrance to the Bay, where soldiers lost no time in constructing a presidio. The mission priests selected a site a few miles to the south near a stream and began to round up the local Indians to instruct them in the ways of the Church. Spanish life at this windy, sandy outpost had begun.

Curiously, the garrison at the Presidio did not have its own boats. Instead, Indian-skippered tule boats became ferries across the Bay. Both the Presidio and the new mission depended on land transportation for communication and supplies from the south. The trail connecting missions and presidios became known as El Camino Real, "the king's highway"; it was virtually impassable during the rainy season which isolated the San Francisco outpost.

After Mexico became a republic in 1821, San Francisco's mission was secularized, and the Indians fled to their former villages. Over the next few years the Presidio was manned by fewer and fewer regiments until it was finally abandoned in 1835.

In 1822 an Englishman, Captain William A. Richardson, arrived in San Francisco and immediately saw the commercial advantages of such a protected harbor. He obtained permission from the Mexican governor to settle permanently and build a trading post in a cove bounded by today's Montgomery Street. He named his harbor after a pungent local herb called yerba buena, "the good herb," which was brewed into tea and used as the local Lydia Pynkham's tonic. Richardson was a master mariner, and his services soon earned him enough to build a fine house above Yerba Buena Cove. His trading post attracted ships filled with cargoes of European silks and Mexican silver, which were sold to Mexican ranch owners for their cattle hides and grain. Curiously, few Mexican or Spanish artisans ever settled in California, so that by the 1830s most Californians were wearing shoes made in Boston from hides they had sold to Boston ship captains.

Believing that California would soon be part of the United States, a number of Americans were emboldened to settle in the village by the Bay during the 1840s. Early arrivals included a colony of Mormons who gave San Francisco its first "prayer-meeting," first jury trial, first local advertising, and first newspaper, the *California Star*. By 1848, when California was annexed to the United States, the forgotten Mexican outpost had been transformed into a town of 800 inhabitants, three-fourths of whom had arrived within the previous two years.

In April of 1848 rumors of gold in the Sierra foothills were confirmed and San Francisco emptied. But not for long. The cry of "Gold!" echoed and reechoed along docks around the world. Soon ships were arriving, first from Oregon and then from South America and the Far East. The city's population grew and diminished daily as new arrivals departed for the diggings as soon as they could gather food and implements. An early history of San Francisco described the 1849 scene.

> Many ships with valuable cargoes had arrived in the bay, but the seamen deserted. The goods at great expense had somehow been landed, but there was nobody to take care of them, or remove them from the wharves where they lay exposed to the weather. Merchants who remained were in a feverish bustle. They were selling goods at high prices, but could get no hands to assist them in removing and delivering the articles. The common laborer, who had formerly been content with his dollar a day, now proudly refused ten. It was certainly a great country . . . every subject was as lofty, independent, and seemingly rich as a king.

A few of the earliest gold seekers found fortunes. Some smart ones carried their wealth back home and returned with their families to start a business or buy land. But others lost their fortunes as quickly as they were made. Gamblers fleeced miners by night, and by day merchants charged exorbitant prices for everything from a head of cabbage to a mule. Even keeping clean was expensive. Aquatic Park was then Washerwomen's Lagoon, but the price for laundering was so high that some people sent their dirty clothes to the Sandwich Islands (Hawaii), preferring a two-month wait to excessive prices. Yerba Buena was quickly transformed into San Francisco, an international port and bawdy "city of sin." Men outnumbered women six to one, and nearly everyone was under the age of forty. Large numbers of foreigners gave the new city a cosmopolitan flavor. Scotsmen formed an exclusive club for native Scots, Germans congregated along present-day Pine and Bush streets, and the first Chinese laundry was established at Washington and Grant.

Many San Franciscans became rich by mining the miners—making their fortunes feeding, clothing, and providing tools and services for the gold seekers. Among those early entrepreneurs was Levi Strauss, who arrived by ship from New York in 1853 bringing with him tent canvas to sell to miners. When one miner told him, "Should have brought pants, cause pants don't wear a hoot up in the diggins," Strauss found a tailor to make his canvas into pants. The Levi Strauss Company continues to make Levi's for people the world over who depend on these hard-wearing, practical pants.

"Born of gold but ravaged by fire" might be an apt description of early San Francisco. The young city of tents and wooden houses burned six times in the eighteen months between 1849 and 1850, and when three times the normal rain fell, some streets became canals. Everyone battled dysentery, and an army of fleas seemed determined to get rid of the human invaders.

San Franciscans also had to contend with rowdy criminals who bullied, burglarized, and killed. These lawbreakers were protected by corrupt officials, and by 1856 the city was under a reign of terror. The citizens were finally aroused from apathy to form vigilance committees that rid the city of its worst elements and elected honest people to office.

From the early days of the gold rush, most of the mining wealth gravitated to San Francisco. By 1860 gold and silver from the Comstock Lode in Nevada was added to fortunes made from gold and trade, fueling a cycle of boom and bust on the fledgling Pacific Stock Exchange. Instant millionaires became instant paupers, and most of the wealth remained in the hands of solid merchants and those smart enough to leave the stock market to the gamblers. The Bank of America and the Bank of California were founded to manage the California and Nevada millions. By the late 1800s San Francisco was well on its way to becoming the major west coast financial center.

Disaster struck once again in 1906 when a violent earthquake rocked the Bay Area. The earthquake itself did not destroy San Francisco, but fires ignited by broken gas lines swept through half the city, leaving thousands of citizens homeless. Undaunted by disaster, San Franciscans pitched their tents on the recently planted fields of Golden Gate Park and went about the business of rebuilding.

The city that rose from the ashes of 1906 has continued to attract people from around the world. Linked to the east coast by rail since 1869, thousands of early tourists were lured west when new travel guides extolled California's splendid weather and brilliant scenery. Since then, San Francisco itself—with its bridges, cable cars, wharves, and cultural attractions—has become one of the world's best-known tourist cities.

Exploring

THE SAN FRANCISCO SHORELINE

A visit to the coast is a sensory symphony. Screeching, wheeling gulls and broken lines of scurrying shorebirds perform ballets across a coastal stage. Brightly hued marine life moves in and out of focus in tidal pools beneath flower-strewn headlands. Crashing waves, rumbling pebbles, and whispering winds complement the visual spectacle.

Fort Funston, Ocean Beach, and the Cliff House are windows on the 1200-mile California coastline. All are part of the thousands of acres of the Golden Gate National Recreation Area (GGNRA). Its beaches and trails form a thirteen-mile, continuous band along San Francisco's shoreline. Across the Golden Gate is a wilderness open space protected by county, state, and federal governments. Twenty million people visit these sites each year, making it the most visited park complex in the United States.

FORT FUNSTON

Located on Skyline Drive four miles south of Golden Gate Park, this park is on the southwest corner of the City and County of San Francisco.

This park is hang gliders' paradise. Viewing platforms hundreds of feet above the beach offer breathtaking views of the coastline and of whales during winter and spring migrations. A level, paved path leads through coastal plant communities. The adventurous can climb down the cliff on a sand ladder to explore the beach. This is an urban park, and the National Park Service suggests that trails always be hiked with a companion and only between sunrise and sunset.

The U.S. government has owned this piece of land since 1900, and a series of army battalions have been in residence here. The fort is named for Frederick Funston, commander of the Presidio during the quake and fire of 1906. As late as 1957, Nike antiaircraft missiles were housed in silos under today's parking lot. In 1972 the military abandoned the site, enabling the National Park Service to open the land to the public. The silos and bunkers were sealed and trails built. The old army buildings now house an environmental education center.

From the viewing platform located west of the parking area, an almost limitless ocean horizon lies before you broken only by three distant small triangles—rocks of the Farallon Islands twenty-two miles away. Bird researchers have replaced lighthouse keepers on these islands that were once raided by entrepreneurs who stole seabird eggs for San Francisco breakfasts.

California gray whales migrate past these shores in December and January on their southward journey to Baja California to breed. In March and April, whale families swim north to their rich feeding grounds in Arctic waters. These fifty-foot mammals can be spotted by their plumes of spray: exhaled, water-laden air.

From the platform you can pick out the thirty-five-mile shoreline, a crescent beginning at San Pedro Point to the southwest, curving inland to Ocean Beach and out toward the rim of Point Reyes far to the northwest. Fort Funston sits near the juncture of two great tectonic plates. The uninhabited hills forming the southern tip of this crescent are on the Pacific Plate, which has been inching in a northwesterly direction past the North American Plate upon which you are standing. To the dismay of San Franciscans, this inexorable movement will place Los Angeles off Fort Funston in about fifteen million years. The mile-wide San Andreas fault zone lies beneath the waves due west of Fort Funston, having left the land two miles south, directly beneath the houses on the cliff.

The park is on a wave-cut terrace that at one time was beneath the ocean. One hundred thousand years ago, flounders and stingrays lay where you are now standing. Uplift of the land raised that terrace to its present height. Fifteen thousand years ago, marshes and sand dunes were where the waves are breaking today. At that time, ocean water was locked up in the icy glaciers covering much of the earth, and the ocean lay several miles to the west. The westerly winds blew sand inland, piling it up against the rocky hills of the city until "they were islands in a sea of sand."

Two trails leave the parking lot. The Sunset Trail goes north along the flat terrace. It is paved for easy strolling through a coastal garden. In several hundred yards the trail enters an old bunker built in 1938 to house huge guns installed to protect the western edge of the continent. The yellow- and pink-blooming ice plant (sea fig) and dune grass were planted by the army to stabilize the sand. Both plants almost succeeded in crowding out native shrubs and ground covers; the National Park Service is replanting colorful natives. Plants with silvery leaves are heat-resistant members of the coastal strand community, adapted both to hot sand dunes and glaring beaches. Among the spreading tentacles of wild strawberry are relatives of desert sagebrush. In spring you can surely

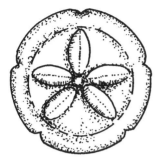 

FOSSIL SAND DOLLAR   LIVING SAND DOLLAR

identify candles of yellow flowers above the many-fingered, gray-green leaves of bush lupine, a cousin to the garden sweet pea and member of the coastal scrub community.

The Philip Burton Trail, named after the local congressman who authored the bill to create the GGNRA, leads from the parking lot toward the cliff. It descends on steep sand ladders that offer shaky footing over the disintegrating cliff to the beach below. The degeneration of this cliff face has taken place during the winter storms of the early 1980s. Geologists believe that the supply of shore sand left from the melting glaciers is nearly depleted. Each winter, thundering storm waves climb the beach to wash away sand. With little sand to break the onslaught of the waves, cliff rocks are weakened and fall into the ocean. Those who do descend to the beach may be rewarded by finding rocks containing ancient fossils. Look but do not collect. This strand is part of Ocean Beach, which ends at the Cliff House. You can start here on a long hike to Fisherman's Wharf.

Exiting Fort Funston one must turn south on Skyline Drive. At the first light, make a U-turn to begin driving north toward Ocean Beach. At this light, the closed road on the ocean side used to lead to the entrance to the now-defunct Thornton Beach Park. The old Cabrillo Highway crossed part of the San Andreas Fault Zone and was washed away during numerous winter storms. As the cliff continues to vanish, one wonders which houses now perched perilously close to the edge will suffer the same fate as the old highway.

North of Fort Funston, Skyline Drive passes Lake Merced, a natural lake. Here you turn left onto the Great Highway at the traffic light. The ocean view is dominated by a long pier used to upgrade San Francisco's sewage disposal system. Four and one-half miles of pipe were laid into the ocean to carry treated sewage beyond onshore currents. Sloat Boulevard takes you to the San Francisco Zoo.

Driving north on the Great Highway one senses the constant movement of the sand dunes. When Golden Gate Park was constructed, timbers were laid and then filled with concrete to create a sea wall. The Great Highway is on this dike, which reduced but failed to eliminate blowing sand that periodically buries the highway and the landscaping of nearby homes. The forest of Monterey cypress was planted a century ago between the two windmills that mark the corners of Golden Gate Park. At the northwest corner you can take J. F. Kennedy Drive to begin our **Favorite Diversion** through Golden Gate Park and on to Mission Dolores.

OCEAN BEACH

Park in the open area of the intersection of J. F. Kennedy Drive and the Great Highway, near the reconstructed windmill.

This beach at the city's edge beckons walkers, joggers, and beachcombers, but brisk westerly winds discourage sunbathing. Swimming is not recommended due to a strong undertow.

The resounding waves and wide arch of sky are half a wilderness at the edge of a city. Beyond the horizon are birds not often seen by land-locked people. Long-winged albatrosses and gull-like petrels and fulmars follow the ships offshore. Gliding perilously close to the crests of breaking waves are lines of giant brown pelicans.

Like a clean-up crew with "litter stickers," the scurrying, long-legged shorebirds follow the foaming wave line and probe the sand with stiletto bills in search of clams, worms, and mole crabs. You might try digging down where dimples in the sand are close to retreating waves. If you dig far enough, your reward may be a wiggling mole crab. Farther up the beach, sand fleas and beach hoppers leap from rotting kelp.

Gulls strut up and down the beach or stand one-legged on the sea wall. It is difficult to distinguish the different species, as all immature ones are brown. Not until their third year do gulls begin to wear gray or black topcoats over their white suits. The California gull is smaller than most and has greenish yellow legs. Each spring, the adult California gulls fly east to raise their young at Mono Lake east of Yosemite Park or at Pyramid Lake beyond Reno.

As you drive north toward the Cliff House notice the gray, contorted cliff on the right. This is graywacke sandstone, one of the several types of

Adolph Sutro's Cliff House about 1890. The resort has continued to be popular with San Franciscans in all seasons. (*California Historical Society, San Francisco*)

ocean sediments that have been scrunched together and then uplifted to form the California Coast Ranges. Don't be fooled by the layer of concrete that has been laid on to help control erosion.

THE CLIFF HOUSE

Parking lots are located on Point Lobos Avenue just east of the Cliff House.

The Cliff House complex houses several restaurants, gift shops, and an observation deck. All are part of the Golden Gate Recreation Area (GGNRA). The visitor center keeps a telescope trained on Seal Rocks. An old-fashioned arcade features nineteenth- and twentieth-century mechanized and electronic games. Trails lead to tidepools and fascinating sand caves.

Three Cliff Houses have perched on this rocky tip of San Francisco's shoreline. The first was built in 1863 and catered to the wealthy. Adolph Sutro, a millionaire, bought this house in 1881, remodeled it, built a railroad across the city's sand dunes, and welcomed all people to his resort. This first structure lasted until 1894 when it was destroyed by fire. Sutro then constructed the second, more grandiose building, pictured here.

This eight-story chateau housed several dining rooms, art galleries, and observation towers. The building survived the 1906 earthquake only to burn to the ground the next year. Sutro's daughter built the third and present Cliff House, which was purchased by the National Park Service in the 1970s.

Sutro invested his fortune gained from Nevada's Comstock Lode in San Francisco. Besides the Cliff House and Sutro Heights, a park on the cliff across from the building, he built the Sutro Baths, whose ruins lie below the Cliff House. He also served as mayor of the city.

Take the stairs to the lower level observation deck. Here at the very edge of the continent you feel the power of ocean waves crashing against the cliffs below. Orange-billed diving ducks called scoters flirt with disaster as each incoming wave threatens to dash them upon the rocks. Looking northward you can see the ascending ridges of Mt. Tamalpais in Marin County. Our **Favorite Diversion** takes you to Muir Woods nestled in a canyon of this imposing mountain.

In the visitor center you can purchase maps of the GGNRA, learn about ocean mammals or local Indian tribes, and scrutinize old photographs. A free telescope is trained upon the winter colony of sea lions lounging on the rocks offshore. Sutro wanted to protect this special attraction at his Cliff House, so he used his considerable influence to have an act of Congress passed to preserve Seal Rocks.

Although the name implies that seals use the rocks, only sea lions can be seen. Larger than seals and having external ears, these California sea lions use their flippers adeptly to clamber over the rocks. During April and May you may spot the lounging hulk of a 1000-pound Steller sea lion.

CALIFORNIA SEA LION

At the south end of the lower deck is a curious wooden structure that houses a replica of Leonardo da Vinci's camera obscura, a precursor to the movie camera. The minimal entrance fee buys a few minutes to view a changing, 360-degree mirrored image of the Cliff House, sea, and beach.

Children of all ages will enjoy the nineteenth-century game arcade located to the right of the stairs returning to the street. A nickel to a quarter will buy any number of interesting animated shows. One is a farmyard complete with pecking chickens, knitting grandmas, bucking horses, and scratching dogs.

Walking up the sidewalk toward the parking lots, look over the wall. Below are the ruins of the Sutro Baths, once a playground for thousands. Imagine a magnificent structure resembling a Greek temple. Glass domes protected six saltwater tanks, one freshwater plunge, nine springboards, seven slides, three trapezes, one high dive, and thirty swinging rings. In addition, a dining room seated 1000; art galleries, a natural history display, and other delights cost just twenty-five cents. These pleasures were located at the end of a five-cent train ride from downtown!

Sutro Baths with activities for 10,000 people. (*California Historical Society, San Francisco*)

Fifty yards up the sidewalk by a small restaurant, a short, paved trail leads to the ruins and tidepools below. The trail descends through coastal scrub and the coastal strand community of succulents and salt-resistant trees and shrubs. The closed-coned Monterey cypresses fringing the walk were planted as a windbreak. Dwarfed and twisted by the continuous onslaught of wind and salt spray, their form is similar to that of alpine-dwelling conifers. Near the overlook you can walk through eerie tunnels in the sandstone. At the edge of the thundering surf an unusually big wave can roll in from the Pacific, so stay well away from danger.

This overlook offers the best available display of rocky *intertidal* marine communities on our route. All tidepool animals are protected. Observe but do not remove! A light-gray band above the waves at high tide is habitat for marine animals of the uppermost zone. Here acorn barnacles feed by opening armored trap doors and waving hair-fringed feet or plankton rakes through sea foam to strain out breakfast or lunch. In the calm summer sea, there are only a few mealtimes each week.

Visitors at low tide will see the middle and lower zones. Tightly packed beds of mussels and gooseneck barnacles intertwined with brown kelp called rockweeds occupy the middle level. Bivalve mussels are anchored securely to the rocks. Their shell halves open only when filtering seawater. Brown, yellow, or orange starfish use their five armored legs to pry open the mussels, and then they turn their stomachs inside-out to feast on their prey.

The next lower tidal zone is under water about three-fourths of the time. Here purple sea urchins nestle into baseball-sized craters they have carved into the rocks. The urchins have inch-long spines and tentacles that help convey bits of kelp to their five-jawed mouths. Think of them as plant-eating starfish adapted to defend themselves against their meat-eating cousins.

The lowest zone is actually the underwater life of rocky shores. It extends to many feet below low tide. Its inhabitants are not adapted to life out of water and will die after only a few hours' exposure. The indicator species are feather boa kelps, bottlebrush algae, orange or yellow sponges, and large red or black urchins up to eight inches across. The Franciscan urchin is a favorite food of the sea otter.

Continue the drive around the edge of San Francisco on Point Lobos Avenue, which becomes Geary Boulevard. Turn left at 34th Street to Lincoln Park, where a replica of the French Palace of the Legion of Honor houses a fine collection of art. The semicircular drive lined with sculptures was the beginning of U.S. 40, the first paved transcontinental highway. Looking from the steps, the view through giant cypress trees extends across the Bay to Mt. Diablo. The pointed tip of the Transamerica tower and the rectangular, black Bank of America building dominate the cityscape.

Continue on El Camino del Mar, "the way of the sea," where you will be greeted by unusual views of the Golden Gate Bridge filtered through the cypress trees. You will soon pass the stately houses of Seacliff that are bordered by green lawns and magnificent gardens. Signs to China Beach, noted on most maps as Phelan Beach, lead to the only swimming with summer lifeguard service in the area. Wheelchair access is provided.

Our route becomes Lincoln Boulevard as it enters the Presidio. The original Spanish fort stood near today's Fort Point. The run-down barracks of the Spanish Presidio were renovated by the Americans in the 1850s. Fearing possible Confederate invasion from the sea during the Civil War, the fort was improved. During World War II the Presidio was a major military installation. Driving through the lush green landscape it is hard to imagine the scene described by Richard Henry Dana in his 1840 book *Two Years Before the Mast.*

> To the westward of the landing-place were dreary sandhills, with little grass to be seen and few trees, steep and barren, their sides gullied by the rain. Some five or six miles beyond, to the right, was a ruined Presidio, and some three miles to the left was the Mission of Dolores, as ruinous as the Presidio, almost deserted, with but a few Indians attached to it.

At the crest of a hill about a mile into the Presidio, you may stop at the pullout on the ocean side of the road. You will be rewarded with an especially fine view of the bridge and the Marin side of the Golden Gate. The name *Golden Gate* was conferred upon the opening by the explorer, John C. Fremont, who wrote in his memoirs: "To this gate I gave the name of Chrysopylae, or Golden Gate; for the same reason that the harbor of Byzantium [afterward Constantinople] was called Chryso-ceras, or Golden Horn." The name appeared on an official map that accompanied Fremont's geographical memoir addressed to the U.S. Senate in 1848.

In the 1880s, before the bridge was built, William Rhodes wrote of the Golden Gate:

> Its glittering bars are the breakers high,
> Its hinges are hills of granite:
> Its bolts are the winds, its arch is the sky,
> Its corner-stone a planet!

Point Bonita lighthouse lies along the Marin coast to the northwest. Until 1982 it was occupied and maintained by the Coast Guard; now, computers have replaced the keeper.

Until the Golden Gate Bridge was completed in 1937, the scene below was filled with ferries, barges, and frigates. The Pacific Ocean, San Francisco Bay, and the Sacramento River were California's highways. Today one sees huge container ships slicing through the waves heading for Asia or the Panama Canal, and on weekends a rainbow display of yachts grace the waves below.

In the morning and evening two kinds of commuters utilize the Golden Gate. Fishing boats steam seaward at dawn while wavering lines of black cormorants pass beneath the bridge to fish inside the Bay. In the evening the fishing commute is reversed: the boats return to harbor and long lines of cormorants return to their white, guano-covered cliffs northwest of the Gate.

THE GOLDEN GATE BRIDGE OVERLOOK

The turnoff to the Golden Gate Bridge Overlook comes just after you drive through an underpass. Turn left into the parking lot.

Climb the stairs to the base of the flagpole for excellent views of the bridge and bay. An unmarked trail leads from the statue of Joseph Strauss, the bridge's designer, to Fort Point, a Civil War fortification and now a living history museum. For those prepared for a windy hike, the sidewalk on the city side of the bridge span is open to walkers and bicyclists. On a clear day there is no better view of San Francisco and its bay than on this one-mile round trip to the center of the bridge.

Follow the garden path past the statue of Strauss and climb the stairs to the flagpole. In summer the wall above the garden is punctuated by the four-foot-high, purple candles of pride of Madeira. This tree forget-me-not symbolizes the many plant treasures that accompanied passengers arriving through the Golden Gate from temperate continents and islands of the world. Most of these plant visitors have thrived in the benign coastal climate of the Bay Area.

The panorama of the Bay fills the eastward horizon, where you see two prominent islands. The larger, tree-covered one is Angel Island, named by Juan Manuel de Ayala, the first Spaniard to enter the Bay in 1775. He anchored in a cove and christened the spot Isla de los Angeles, "island of the angels." For many years, all incoming Asians were detained on this island until they were cleared for entry. Immigration buildings and several Civil War structures are currently being restored. A five-mile bicycle route circumnavigates the island, and a trail leads up Mt. Livermore.

The small island in the foreground is Alcatraz, its fortress a lonely reminder of the prison that no one was able to escape. In the middle of this century the prison was closed because it was so expensive to operate. It is now a National Park Service museum. Boats to both islands leave from Fisherman's Wharf.

The second span of the Oakland Bay Bridge can be seen leaving Yerba Buena Island. Formerly called Goat Island, it is a rocky mountain in the middle of the Bay. Alcatraz and Angel Island are similar promontories. During glaciation, when the Bay was still an inland valley, these islands thrust their rocky heights above a sandy valley.

The south tower of the Golden Gate Bridge looms above you. In the late 1920s San Francisco was in danger of becoming an isolated peninsula unless convenient access could be provided for the newfangled automobiles. It seemed that everyone owned cars, and waiting times exceeded one hour for ferries.

Influential business executives began to promote a bridge from San Francisco to Marin County, noting competition from the San Francisco-Oakland Bay Bridge, which was already planned. Many people were opposed to construction of any structure across the Golden Gate, afraid that a beautiful view would be destroyed. Undaunted by the criticism, a group of citizens from nine counties was formed to find the money. Many of the bonds were bought by the Bank of America, a signal to the community of its faith in the project.

Most engineers declared that a bridge could not be constructed across that windy gap. Joseph Strauss, a talented designer who had just completed a bridge over the Columbia River at Longview, Washington, was invited to review the problem. He was hired when he stated that he would build a bridge so beautiful it would enhance the view, not detract from it.

Begun in 1933, the bridge took four years to complete. First the north tower was planted on the rocky shore of Marin County, a relatively easy task because the footings were on solid rock. The south shore presented a difficult problem. The support towers were to be poured in deep water amid swirling currents and high winds. A concrete breakwater was built to protect a caisson. This underwater structure had an airtight chamber in which the men were supposed to work. The first night after the caisson was moored in place, heavy surf threatened its destruction. The very next day Strauss ordered the caisson towed out to sea and sunk. He believed in the project so strongly that he decided to use deep-sea divers to excavate for the piers and pour concrete beneath the water. The Golden Gate became one of the first bridges constructed by divers.

Opening Day of the Golden Gate Bridge, May 28, 1937.
"The Bridge looms mountain high; its great steel arms
link shore with shore, its towers pierce the sky."
(*California Historical Society, San Francisco*)

Joseph B. Strauss was not an ordinary engineer. A worshiper of redwoods and lover of music and poetry, he wrote a poem to commemorate completion of his masterpiece, which has been reprinted in **Yesterday's Voices**. Strauss died one year after completing his dream—a bridge that would glorify the view. Today, the Golden Gate Bridge remains one of the most photographed bridges in the world.

Drive over the bridge to our Marin County **Favorite Diversion** to Muir Woods, Mt. Tamalpais, and Point Reyes. Here wilderness peaks, beaches, and the earthquake fault await you. Stop at the vista point on the north side of the bridge for another spectacular view of the city.

To continue the shoreline route around San Francisco to the Bay Bridge, drive through the underpass west of the parking area. Follow signs to downtown San Francisco. Be sure to stay on Doyle Drive as it bears left to the marina. The light brown dome of the Palace of Fine Arts appears to the right. This colonnaded structure was built for the 1915 Panama Pacific Exposition, but it was allowed to fall into disrepair. Civic leaders rescued it in the 1960s. It now houses a theater and the Exploratorium, where children of all ages can explore scientific and natural phenomena in a seemingly endless array of hands-on exhibits. The turnoff is well marked at the first stoplight.

Nearby is Marina Green. During lunch hour and on any sunny day, this spacious park lawn is filled with sun worshippers, kite flyers, joggers, exuberant children, and others content just to sit and enjoy the special ambience of bay and city. The St. Francis Yacht Club slips are filled with sleek racing machines.

The headquarters for the Golden Gate National Recreation Area is at Fort Mason. These old military buildings now bustle with the activity of an amazing variety of cultural and environmental organizations. Parking here is free, and there is an easy walk east over the hill to Aquatic Park, the Maritime Museum, and Fisherman's Wharf. To reach this area by car, follow the green signs to Fisherman's Wharf. Turn left on Polk. Turn right in one block on North Point Street, one of the less-traveled roads through this busy corner of San Francisco. Parking structures anywhere along this road are convenient to our **Favorite Diversion**, a walk along San Francisco's Historic Waterfront where ships of all ages, including modern fishing boats, are moored.

At the end of North Point, turn right on the Embarcadero, which leads to the Bay Bridge and Interstate 80 East. As you drive along the Embarcadero—which is Spanish for wharf or pier—open your window to take in the sounds and smells of the docks. Imagine the hustle and bustle when San Francisco was a port of world importance. Before gold created a metropolis out of this former Spanish outpost, all people and goods traveling from the wider world to California's interior passed through this waterfront. Nearly every kind of vessel has plied the waters of the Bay, and until the bridges were built in the 1930s, ferries provided the only link to Oakland and Marin County. The transcontinental railroad tracks ended in Oakland, where passengers changed to ferries that docked at the Ferry Building located at the foot of Market Street. Today the stately clock atop the Ferry Building is all but lost in a tangle of freeway overpasses.

The Embarcadero winds in and out of supports for the elevated and much-criticized Embarcadero Freeway. We recommend that you drive three blocks past the Ferry Building to Harrison Street and take the First Street ramp to the Oakland Bay Bridge. Note the tantalizing smells of roasting coffee from the Hills Brothers factory nearby.

The first piers of the Bay Bridge are built over an old tidal slough, which during the gold rush was hastily filled with abandoned ships, unsold goods, rocks, and sand. During the 1906 earthquake, before the bridge was built, this unconsolidated material shimmied and shook, causing severe damage to the buildings. Refilled and further developed in recent decades, the land continues to subside so that many buildings have front doors below street level. Geologists worry about the stability of the bridge when another major earthquake hits.

Halfway across the Bay Bridge, the interstate passes through a tunnel in Yerba Buena Island. In 1939 the Golden Gate International World Exposition buildings were constructed upon landfill dumped north of Yerba Buena Island. This artificial peninsula was called Treasure Island. Imagine the splendor of Ferris wheels, lighted walkways, and even a ski jump. Members of a ski club from Auburn in the Sierra foothills contracted with Union Ice Company to blow snow over an eighty-five-foot tower. Jumpers awed the visitors with their daring flights, and thereafter locals were lured to the Sierra to participate in this developing sport. Today the island is a naval installation; the Navy, Marine, and Coast Guard museum is open daily. If you wish to visit the museum or picnic nearby, exit from the left lane just before the tunnel.

Favorite Diversions

GOLDEN GATE PARK

Take J. F. Kennedy Drive from the Great Highway at Ocean Beach. Take the second left after entering the park, which brings you to the museum complex, where parking is available. This route leads easily to an approach to the San Francisco-Oakland Bay Bridge via Oak Street, which joins Interstate 80 at the Laguna Street on-ramp. On Sundays the eastern portion of Kennedy Drive is closed to vehicles.

Twenty years after the gold rush populated the City by the Bay, a 1000-acre park was being designed. What vision the originators must have had as they gazed across endless sand dunes stretching west of the city. Their goal was to create a counterpart to New York's Central Park. Sand dunes were stabilized, and curved plantings of pines, Monterey cypress, and eucalyptus were planted to break the Pacific winds and to outline lawns and lakes edged with flowering plants from around the world.

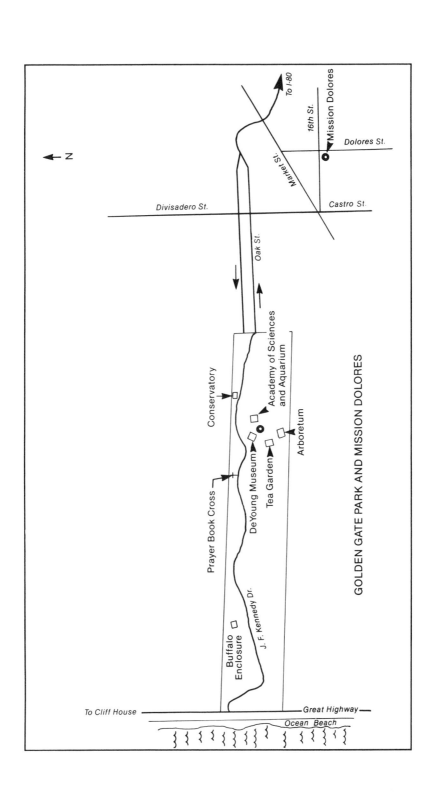

GOLDEN GATE PARK AND MISSION DOLORES

The Dutch windmill on the northwest corner of the park was built in the 1900s. It and the Murphy windmill to the south were used originally to pump well water for the park. When the city water system began to serve the park, the mills rusted and deteriorated. In the 1960s the McLaren Society and the Navy Seabees carefully restored the looks but not the function of the Dutch mill.

After the first stop sign, look on the left for a herd of buffalo standing in a paddock. These shaggy, barrel-chested beasts are a reminder of the animals that once dominated the Great Plains. Also on the left, aficionados race sleek, miniature yachts and remote-control motorized boats on Spreckels Lake. After the underpass, a waterfall cascades through folded rocks of red chert. A pleasant walk leads to Prayer Book Cross.

Parked cars signal the museum complex; park anywhere on Kennedy Drive. Sunday concerts in the mall serenade summer picnickers. The De Young Museum, with its renowned collection of Asian art and nearby Japanese Tea Garden, illustrate San Francisco's close ties to Asia. The California Academy of Sciences maintains a planetarium and exhibits of North American birds and mammals. The Steinhart Aquarium delights all with eye-level views of dolphins and exotic fish. The tide-pool display offers an opportunity for close-up inspection of intertidal life like that found below the Cliff House.

You can better understand the diversity of California's plant life in the Strybing Arboretum. Wander among cacti from a Sonoran desert, observe understory plants in a coast redwood forest, and see specimens of nearly every conifer (cone-bearing tree) that grows in California. A sand-dune exhibit shows the original landscape upon which the park was built. A sensory walk focuses on plants that can be identified by their smell, taste, or feel.

After the museum complex, Kennedy Drive passes the McLaren Memorial Rhododendron Dell. John McLaren was a creator of the park and its superintendent for fifty-three years. During May and June a profusion of red, magenta, and pink blooms on these tree-size shrubs remind one of the scientific name (*rhodo*=red, *dendron*=tree). At the stop sign following the McLaren Dell, tall tree ferns give the semblance of a tropical rain forest.

Seasonal plantings of flowers splash across the hillside below the Conservatory. This Victorian glass house was transported around Cape Horn by James Lick and assembled here in 1879. It is filled with exotic floral displays as well as banana trees, orchids, and coffee and vanilla plants.

The one-way exit from the park, Oak Street, passes a narrow, tree-lined lawn called the Panhandle, which was saved from becoming a freeway by a valiant botanist, Elizabeth McClintock. She wrote a little book called *The Trees of the Panhandle* that rallied support for preservation of this former carriage entrance to the park.

To visit our **Favorite Diversion** to Mission Dolores, San Francisco's oldest building, turn right on Divisadero two blocks after the end of the Panhandle. Otherwise, continue on Oak Street, which leads directly to the Laguna Street ramp to Interstate 80 and the Bay Bridge.

MISSION DOLORES

Take Divisadero to 16th Street and turn left. The mission is on the corner of 16th and Dolores streets. To reach Interstate 80 and the San Francisco-Oakland Bay Bridge, retrace your route to Oak Street and turn right.

The mission and its cemetery reflect the earliest days of San Francisco. Original Indian designs still decorate the ceiling of the chapel, and some of the city's founders are buried in the graveyard.

The site for the Mission San Francisco de Assis was chosen because of its relatively flat terrain and its proximity to a small freshwater pond and stream. The stream was called Arroyo de Nuestra Señora de los Dolores because it was discovered on the day of Our Lady of Sorrows. The name *Dolores* was used to identify the mission and avoid confusion with the Bay and Presidio, which were also named after San Francisco de Assis. Mission Dolores was the sixth of the twenty-one established by the Spanish Church between 1769 and 1820. Mass was said here for the first time in June of 1776. The official possession of the mission took place on October 4, the feast day of San Francisco de Assis. Father Francisco Palou, the first mission priest, described the ceremony in his journal.

A solemn Mass was sung by the ministers, and when it was concluded the gentlemen performed the ceremony of taking formal possession. This finished, all entered the chapel and sang the *Te Deum Laudamus*, accompanied by peals of bells and repeated salvos of cannon, muskets, and guns, the bark responding with its swivel-guns, whose roar and the sound of the bells doubtless terrified the heathen, for they did not allow themselves to be seen for many days.

The mission building was completed in 1791. Its four-foot-thick adobe walls withstood the 1906 earthquake. When you enter the chapel, look up at the ceiling paintings. These original Indian designs were painted on the ceiling with vegetable dyes. Everything in the mission church is basically as it has been since its founding. The statues in the niches were sent from Mexico. To preserve the old chapel it is now a museum, and services are held in the church next door. An old classroom is used to display artifacts from the mission's past. The baptismal registry of 28,000 entries goes back to 1776.

Spend some time wandering around the adjacent cemetery. Gravestones of early settlers usually proclaim the country or state of their birth. The number of different former homelands indicates the diversity of San Francisco's early population. In the center of the cemetery is a large, man-made rock monument. It marks the common grave for all unidentified bodies that were moved to the present site when the original graveyard was consolidated.

Gardeners will enjoy old-fashioned varieties of flowers in the well-tended garden. While admiring the old roses near the grave of Don Luis Antonio Arguello, first governor of Alta California under Mexican rule, consider the melancholy love story of his dearest daughter, Concepcion.

In April of 1806 a dashing Russian officer, Nikolai Petrovich Rezanov, arrived in San Francisco on business for the czar. He wanted to purchase food and other necessities from the California missions to supply the Russian outposts in Alaska and northern California. During interminable negotiations, Rezanov was often a guest of the Arguellos. He fell in love with the governor's beautiful daughter. He described her thus:

> I could not fail to perceive her active, venturesome disposition and character, her unlimited and overweening desire for rank and honors, which, with her age of fifteen years, made her, alone among her family, dissatisfied with the land of her birth. She always referred to it jokingly; thus, as "a beautiful country, a warm climate, an abundance of grain and cattle,—and nothing else."

Rezanov wooed the beautiful señorita, who obviously wished to leave California for the possibility of an exciting life in the court of the czar. Don Luis Antonio was not disposed to favor the union, particularly because of Rezanov's Eastern Orthodox faith. He demanded that the Russian suitor obtain official permission from the pope in Rome. Concepcion reluctantly watched her betrothed sail away with his shipment of grain and the precious letter to the pope, fully expecting his return within a year. She vowed to await his return. Year after year went by, but Rezanov did not return. Finally, Concepcion entered a convent. Thirty-six years later a Hudson Bay Company official reported the tragic death of her fiancé on his way to deliver the letter to the pope.

THE HISTORIC WATERFRONT

Parking structures are located along North Point Street and other streets parallel to the waterfront. It is much easier to park away from the waterfront.

The dotted line on the above map suggests a walking tour that begins at Aquatic Park and the National Maritime Museum. Ships of several eras are on display at Hyde Street Pier. Tourist attractions abound at Fisherman's Wharf, Ghirardelli Square, the Cannery, and Pier 39. Round-the-Bay boat trips and ferries to Angel Island and Alcatraz leave from the Red and White Fleet dock near the Balclutha.

One could say that modern San Francisco was born from the holds of ships. In the early days of Spanish settlement, Russians and Englishmen anchored here to buy grain and hides and sell silks, silver, and household goods to Spanish dons and their families. Boston whalers and Far East trading vessels entered San Francisco Bay to make repairs. Sailors seeking opportunity often jumped ship and disappeared inland to find a piece of land. With the advent of the gold rush in 1848, ships arrived from every corner of the globe, disgorging passengers and crew alike and leaving rotting hulls in the harbor to form a base for San Francisco's first landfill.

Walk out onto the Aquatic Park breakwater and look south and east to the modern waterfront. Today's busy tourist activities bear little resemblance to the scene during gold rush days. Hyde Street Pier, Fisherman's Wharf, and the other docks in sight did not exist. Ships were anchored in a cove southeast of where you are standing. A pier called Long Wharf jutted out into the Bay from the end of Montgomery Street below Telegraph Hill, where Coit Tower stands today. This view of life along Long Wharf was written in 1854 by Alonzo Delano.

> Here, on both sides, are ships, barks, schooners, steamboats, and propellers, just off for Gold Bluff, Panama, Sacramento, Marysville, or Stockton, as you please; in fact, one may go to China, or eternity, for about the same price. For the one take a ship; for the other a steamboat, and in due time the port of destination will be reached. Take out papers for the one from the Customs House for the other at the monte [gambling] table.

In those days the arrival of any ship, particularly the mail steamer, was an event of major importance. Semaphore signals from Telegraph Hill announced arriving ships. The coded signals identified the kind of incoming cargo. Young boys would watch all day, waiting to run to street

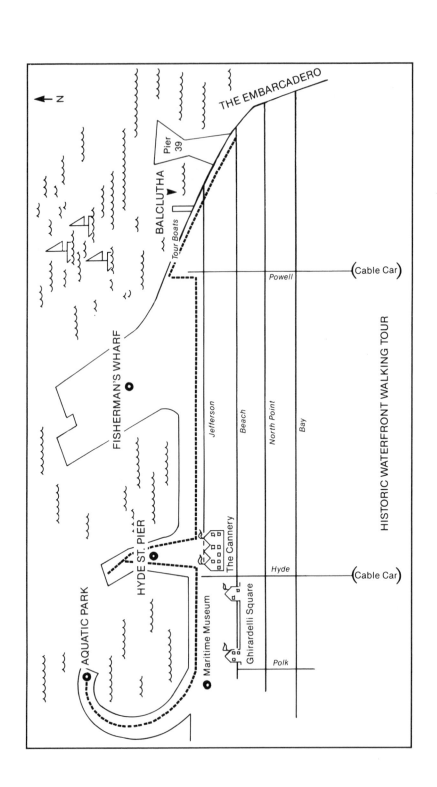

N

THE EMBARCADERO

Pier 39

BALCLUTHA

Tour Boats

Powell

(Cable Car)

FISHERMAN'S WHARF

Jefferson

Beach

North Point

Bay

HYDE ST. PIER

The Cannery

Hyde

(Cable Car)

AQUATIC PARK

Maritime Museum

Ghirardelli Square

Polk

HISTORIC WATERFRONT WALKING TOUR

San Francisco in 1847 before the gold rush. Sandy hills came down to the water's edge at Montgomery Street. (*California Historical Society, San Francisco*)

corners and like newsboys spread the news of arriving passenger steamers or mailboats. As soon as the word was out, wagons, businessmen, workers, and hotel runners rushed shoreside, most of them to the mail line for those long-hoped-for communications from loved ones left behind. Any passenger lucky or smart enough to have brought copies of an eastern newspaper could make a fast profit. One such early arrival sold three-cent copies of the *New York Tribune* for twelve dollars on his first afternoon in town. Little did it matter that the news was three months old.

When leaving the breakwater, you may wish to visit the National Maritime Museum to see ship models, old photographs, and nautical artifacts. At Hyde Street Pier several nineteenth- and early twentieth-century sailing vessels are on display. The lumber schooner *C.A. Thayer* plied the waters of the Bering Sea until 1950, in its latter years the only commercial sailing vessel on the Pacific Coast. The double-ended ferry *Eureka* carried passengers between Oakland and San Francisco from 1890 to 1957. Other vessels are typical of the hundreds of ships that transported people and goods between west coast ports and to inland cities along the Sacramento River.

While below deck on these sailing ships, you may lose any longings you once had for a life at sea. Cramped living quarters and the constant stench of codfish or salmon being salted made this the last place a sailor would want to be, regardless of the weather topside. You might test whether you could stretch out in any of the bunks provided for sailors of those days. While standing on the bow, feeling the gentle roll of ocean waves, the romance of the sea returns.

Fisherman's Wharf is east of Hyde Street Pier. Bubbling cauldrons along the sidewalk issue forth tantalizing smells of cooking shrimp and crab. The *Balclutha*, berthed nearby, is typical of the square-rigged merchant ships that for fifty years carried wine, whiskey, wool, window glass, and other necessities to a burgeoning San Francisco population.

Trips to Alcatraz, that rocky island prison, and Angel Island depart from the pier next to the *Balclutha*. Pack a picnic and spend a day on Angel Island, or learn the story of Alcatraz with the National Park Service rangers. Both trips offer an opportunity to cruise on the water and enjoy views of San Francisco from an unusual perspective. Bay cruises also leave from this wharf.

NORTH OF THE GOLDEN GATE

Drive across the Golden Gate Bridge on Highway 101. The complete trip takes a day, although Muir Woods can be visited in a half day. Few restaurants or accommodations are located on the Pacific Ocean side of Mt. Tamalpais.

Alexander Avenue off Highway 101 leads to the Marin Headlands and to Sausalito. Take Highway 1/Stinson Beach exit to reach Muir Woods and Mt. Tamalpais. This loop returns to Highway 101 via Sir Francis Drake Boulevard, which continues east to the San Rafael-Richmond Bridge and Interstate 80.

The trip takes you to relatively uninhabited areas protected by federal, state, regional, and local governments. The parks are roped together with scenic roads that lead up to mountaintops and along steep ocean cliffs.

As you drive across the Golden Gate Bridge be alert for the vista point pullout on the right. What a vista! Anglers and cormorants below; sailboats on the Bay; and the San Francisco skyline.

The Marin Headlands

The first exit north of the bridge is Alexander Avenue. A half-mile downhill on Alexander is the turnoff to the Marin Headlands, a northerly

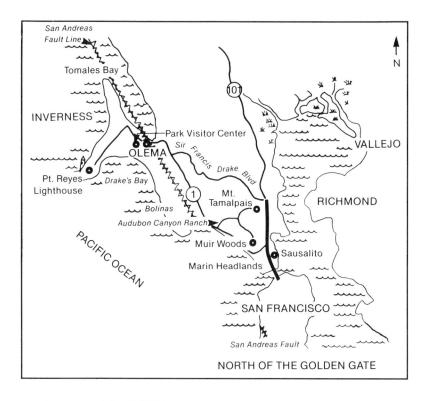

continuation of the GGNRA. Interconnecting roads lead to an American Youth Hostel, the Marine Mammal Center, a protected beach, and a spectacular drive along the cliffs. A few operating military facilities remain on this windswept bluff, but the headlands recreation area is the result of creative trades within the federal government. Without the efforts of concerned citizens and legislators, many of the steep hillsides would be covered with houses.

Sausalito and the Bay Delta Model

Take Alexander Avenue downhill, where red chert cliffs line the road. Sausalito is a bayside town catering to tourists and pleasure boats. Alexander becomes Bridgeway, and in the northern part of town Dunphy Park is a good picnic site.

A giant warehouse at 2400 Bridgeway contains the Bay Delta Model built by the U.S. Army Corps of Engineers. It is open to the public Tuesday through Saturday and offers tours. Visitors here have a bird's-eye view of an exact replica of the Bay and its landforms laid out on an acre and a half. When experiments are being conducted, water flows in and out so that scientists can study the effects of tidal action on the bay and delta. The successful Save the Bay campaign of the 1960s used information gathered here to show adverse effects of bay fill on fish, wildlife, and Bay Area climate.

Bridgeway leads to Highway 101. Take the next exit, Highway 1 to Stinson Beach. At the stoplight, turn left onto Shoreline Highway. After several curving miles turn right on Panoramic Way and follow signs to Muir Woods.

Muir Woods

Visitors feel immersed in a primeval setting in the grandeur of this forest of towering redwood trees. When William Kent dedicated the park to conservationist John Muir, Muir was heard to say, "This is the best tree-lover's monument that could be found in all of the forests of the world."

Most of the remaining redwood forests are found north of Marin County to the Oregon border. They hug the coast where summer fog and winter rain provide the plentiful moisture they require. Muir Woods is in a protected canyon where these conditions prevail. On the mile-long interpretive trail, pick out an individual tree. Feel the fire-resistant, fibrous bark. The bumpy growths near the base of the tree are called *burls,* from which new sprouts emerge. The child in each of us responds to the "fairy rings," the encircling stands of trees around the space where a mother tree once grew.

At your feet the duff on the forest floor is deep and acidic. Few flowers grow in the duff and deep shade. Groundcover plants propagate by runners, and the moist, sunless habitat is a welcome place for ferns and mosses. There are few mammals or birds in this forest, so seed dispersal is accomplished by ants or by special adaptations of the plants, which enables them to shoot their seeds out at the proper time.

Redwood Creek is a funnel catching the water that drains from one-quarter of the slopes of Mt. Tamalpais. The creek reaches the Pacific Ocean at Muir Beach after it passes through a flat valley, where it drops its sediment. Silver salmon and steelhead still use the waterway as spawning grounds.

Mt. Tamalpais

Leaving Muir Woods, turn left and climb Panoramic Way.

It is quite a contrast to go from the dark and shady glen of redwoods into the elfin forest of the *chaparral* community on the sun-baked upper slopes of the mountain. Here woody shrubs with small, leathery leaves thrive. This widespread California plant community draws its name from the Spanish *chaparras*, meaning brush through which you cannot ride a horse. Spanish and Mexican cowboys wore chaps to protect themselves from these scratchy shrubs. The most common species of this community are fine-needled chamise, blue-flowered ceanothus, manzanita, and chaparral pea. Many trails that cross the chaparral leave the Mountain Home Parking Lot. At Pan Toll Ranger Station continue upward on Ridgecrest. The steep drive to the summit passes Douglas firs and dwarfed redwoods alternating with grasslands waving in the breeze.

At the top of Mt. Tamalpais you have reached 2600 feet above sea level. It is time for a stretch, so try the Verna Dunshee Trail, a short walk that circumnavigates the peak. Proceed counterclockwise through the chaparral and enjoy views of San Francisco, the Bay, and Mt. Diablo on the eastern horizon. On the cooler north side, Mt. St. Helena near Napa will come into view. On this side the vegetation changes to the *canyon forest* community, or mixed evergreen forest. Here the conifer Douglas fir is mixed with broadleaf evergreens such as live oak, red-barked madrone, and the pungent-smelling bay laurel. At one point along the trail an unusual conifer, the California nutmeg, can be detected by its spiny needles, sharp enough for sewing. Its cone is not the nutmeg used as a spice. In fact, the tree has quite an unpleasant odor and is sometimes called stinking yew.

When you drive back down the mountain look for pitted snags used by the acorn woodpeckers, whose Woody Woodpecker squawk and rakish antics make them the clowns of the canyon forest. Their wealth is measured in acorns, which are stuffed into holes in dead trees in order to protect them from robbers like scrub jays and gray squirrels.

At Pan Toll Station, turn right toward Stinson Beach. With binoculars on a clear day you may be able to pick out the Farallon Islands, and in winter and spring you may see migrating whales. The Bolinas Lagoon is a favorite feeding area for herons and egrets, which nest in the tops of redwood trees at Audubon Canyon Ranch. The ranch is open from

March 1 to July 15 on Saturdays, Sundays, and holidays from 10 A.M. until 4 P.M. A trail and overlook allows inspection of the heron nests.

Like an arrow, the lagoon points to a narrow valley that terminates in Tomales Bay. All three features mark the line of the San Andreas fault zone. The epicenter of the 1906 earthquake was near here in Olema, where the earth was jolted sixteen feet in a northwesterly direction.

As you drive along, note the differences in vegetation. The Point Reyes peninsula has been conveyed from Mexico on the Pacific Plate and has brought granite rocks where Mexican bishop pines thrive.

Point Reyes National Seashore

Drive past Olema and its historic inn and watch for the left turn into the park service visitor center, which features extensive interpretive displays. Friendly rangers will direct you to the Morgan Horse Farm, the Miwok Indian Village, an earthquake interpretive walk, or to the trail down Bear Valley to the ocean.

To many, the main attraction of this park is the windy point itself with its lighthouse and beach and spectacular show of wildflowers. The turnoff is just north of the village of Inverness, and the road is slow and very crowded on nice days. The energetic are encouraged to climb down the 300 steps to the lighthouse, which is open throughout the year, weather permitting. The first telegraph in the West flashed signals from here to the Marin Headlands and hence to San Francisco announcing ship arrivals.

Returning inland from the lighthouse turn right to Drake's Beach and the Patrick Visitor Center. Here you can learn of the controversy of just where Sir Francis Drake, the English explorer, landed in 1579. Was it here, inside San Francisco Bay, or near Santa Barbara?

Even though the north end of the peninsula has secret coves to explore, elk to see, and swimming at Heart's Desire Beach, some things must be left for the next trip. To reach Interstate 80, take Sir Francis Drake Boulevard east to Highway 101 or on to the San Rafael-Richmond Bridge.

Yesterday's Voices

EARTHQUAKE ALMANAC

By Mark Twain

America's most famous humorist sometimes hits below the emotional belt. His view of the reactions of San Franciscans to an earthquake in 1862 parodies their many attempts at explanations. Over a century later, our predictions are not much more scientific.

At the instance of several friends who feel a boding anxiety to know beforehand what sort of phenomena we may expect the elements to exhibit during the next month or two, and who have lost all confidence in the various patent medicine almanacs, because of the unaccountable reticence of those works concerning the extraordinary event of the 8th inst., I have compiled the following almanac expressly for this latitude:

Oct. 17.—Weather hazy, atmosphere murky and dense. An expression of profound melancholy will be observable upon most countenances.

Oct. 18.—Slight earthquake. Countenances grow more melancholy.

Oct. 19.—Look out for rain. It will be absurd to look in for it. The general depression of spirits increased.

Oct. 20.—More weather.

Oct. 21.—Same.

Oct. 22.—Light winds, perhaps. If they blow, it will be from the "east'ard, or the nor'ard, or the west'ard, or the suth'ard," or from some general direction approximating more or less to these points of the compass or otherwise. Winds are uncertain—more especially when they blow from whence they cometh and whither they listeth. N.B.—Such is the nature of winds.

Oct. 23.—Mild, balmy earthquakes.

Oct. 24.—Shaky.

Oct. 25.—Occasional shakes, followed by light showers of bricks and plastering. N.B.—Stand from under.

Oct. 26.—Considerable phenomenal atmospheric foolishness. About this time expect more earthquakes, but do not look out for them, on account of the bricks.

Oct. 27.—Universal despondency, indicative of approaching disaster. Abstain from smiling, or indulgence in humorous conversation, or exasperating jokes.

Oct. 28.—Misery, dismal forebodings and despair. Beware of all discourse—a joke uttered at this time would produce a popular outbreak.

Oct. 29.—Beware!

Oct. 30.—Keep dark!

Oct. 31.—Go slow!

Nov. 1.—Terrific earthquake. This is the great earthquake month. More stars fall and more worlds are slathered around carelessly and destroyed in November than in any other month of the twelve.

Nov. 2.—Spasmodic but exhilarating earthquakes, accompanied by occasional showers of rain, and churches and things.

Nov. 3.—Make your will.

Nov. 4.—Select your "last words." Those of John Quincy Adams will do, with the addition of a syllable, thus; "This is the last of earthquakes."

Nov. 6.—Prepare to shed this mortal coil.

Nov. 7.—Shed.

Nov. 8.—The sun will rise as usual, perhaps; but if he does he will doubtless be staggered some to find nothing but a large round hole eight thousand miles in diameter in the place where he saw this world serenely spinning the day before.

From *Golden Era* (as reprinted from the San Francisco *Dramatic Chronicle*), October 22, 1865. *Mark Twain's San Francisco*, by Bernard Taper (New York: McGraw-Hill, 1963).

THE MIGHTY TASK IS DONE

By Joseph Strauss

Upon completion of the Golden Gate Bridge in 1937, its designer wrote this poem to commemorate the achievement. He exemplified the idea that to design with nature is the essence of art.

At last the mighty task is done;
Resplendent in the western sun
The Bridge looms mountain high;
Its titan piers grip ocean floor,
Its great steel arms link shore with shore,
Its towers pierce the sky.

On its broad decks in rightful pride,
The world in swift parade shall ride,
Throughout all time to be;
Beneath, fleet ships from every port,

Vast landlocked bay, historic fort,
And dwarfing all—the sea.

To north, the Redwood Empire's gates;
To south, a happy playground waits,
in Rapturous appeal;
Here nature, free since time began,
Yields to the restless moods of man,
Accepts his bonds of steel.

Launched midst a thousand hopes and fears,
Damned by a thousand hostile sneers,
Yet ne'er its course was stayed,
But ask of those who met the foe
Who stood alone when faith was low,
Ask them the price they paid.

Ask of the steel, each strut and wire,
Ask of the searching, purging fire,
That marked their natal hour;
Ask of the mind, the hand, the heart,
Ask of each single, stalwart part,
What gave it force and power.

An Honored cause and nobly fought
And that which they so bravely wrought,
Now glorifies their deed,
No selffish urge shall stain its life,
Nor envy, greed, intrigue, nor strife,
Nor false, ignoble creed.

High overhead its lights shall gleam,
Far, far below life's restless stream,
Unceasingly shall flow;
For this was spun its lithe fine form,
To fear not war, nor time, nor storm,
For Fate had meant it so.

From brochure of Golden Gate Highway and Transportation District, 1937.

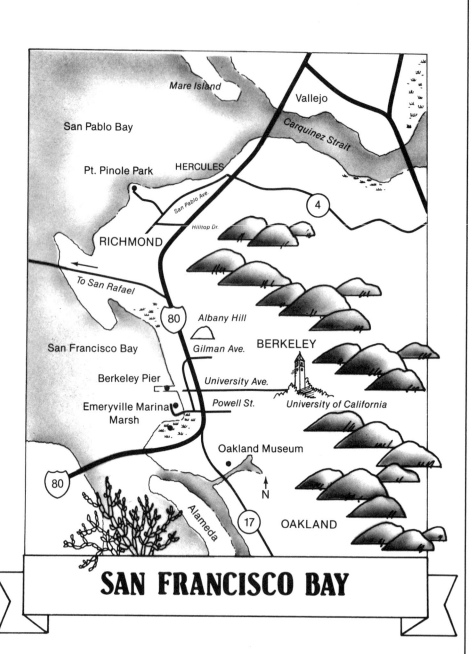

SAN FRANCISCO BAY

2

SAN FRANCISCO BAY
The S.F.-Oakland Bay Bridge to Hercules

Trip Planner

EXPLORING

This eighteen-mile drive along the East Bay
shoreline includes three bayside stops offering views
across the water to San Francisco and closeups of
marshlands. After you leave the Bay Bridge you may
take a frontage road along the water's edge.

The **Emeryville marina** is one of the newer
park developments along the Bay and has a fine
panorama of the San Francisco cityscape.

The **Emeryville marsh overlook** is a short walk to
a bird-viewing platform constructed over the marshlands.

The **Berkeley pier** allows a long walk out over the water.
All manner of saltwater dwellers are caught here.

FAVORITE DIVERSIONS

The **Oakland Museum** is a short detour worth the drive.
The excellent exhibits of natural history, California history,
and paintings provide a foundation for the variety and beauty
found along the Interstate 80 corridor. A pleasant stroll can be
taken around nearby **Lake Merritt.**

Point Pinole Park trails pass through shady eucalyptus
groves and across expansive grasslands, with magnificent views
of the North Bay. A shuttle bus serves a well-maintained fishing pier.

THE BAYSCAPE

The San Francisco Bay is one of the world's great estuaries. Extending
south to San Jose, north to Napa County, and east into Suisun Bay, it originally covered an area slightly less than the state of Rhode Island. For
thousands of years before the Spanish arrived, the Bay was fringed with
salt marshes crisscrossed by meandering streams called sloughs. Coast
redwood trees, some approaching twenty feet in diameter, once fronted
the surrounding hills.

The Bay is encircled by mountains of the Outer and Inner Coast
Ranges. These hills are broken in two places, to the west at the Golden
Gate and to the east through the Carquinez Strait. This inner barrier
effectively contains the summer flow of fog, except at Carquinez, where
consistent winds carry fingers of fog toward the hot interior valleys.

Before the Ice Ages, the Bay was an elongated coastal valley through
which an ancient Sacramento River flowed to the sea. Several small,
rocky mountains protruded from the valley's sandy floor. When the last
glaciers melted, the ocean level rose and broke through the Golden Gate
to drown the valley. The resulting bay was a twin-armed, shallow body of
water. The tops of the mountains became Alcatraz, Angel, and Yerba
Buena islands. The Sierra rivers filled with debris and flowed into the
Bay, dropping sediment to provide soil for the marshlands.

Today the Bay is a magnificent example of an estuary, a place where salt and fresh waters meet. Such environments are among the most productive in the world. Both plants and animals of an estuary must adapt to daily and seasonal fluctuations in salinity as well as rising and falling tidelines. Rising tides extend the ocean's salty influence up the Sacramento River. As the tide ebbs, fresh river water follows the retreating sea. In the spring, torrents of melting snow bring additional fresh water and dilute the Bay's salty water even more. As summer approaches, snow melt ceases and mountain dams and canals divert part of the fresh water, changing the Bay water composition. Plants and animals must adapt to a saltier environment.

The principal plants of the salt marsh are cordgrass and a curious succulent called pickleweed. Both are halophytes, able to grow and reproduce in or near salt water. These halophytes are arranged in layers within the tidal zones, based upon the time spent in or out of brackish water. At the lowest level—sometimes completely covered at high tide—is cordgrass, whose survival mechanism is to exude salt as crystals on its leaves. Its three-foot, bamboo-shaped stems support golden, wheatlike sprays of flowers. Cordgrass is one of the most productive plants on earth, producing more food energy for marsh birds and animals than a similar amount of midwestern corn or wheat produces for its consumers.

Pickleweed thrives closer to the dry shoreline above the cordgrass. This halophyte stores salt inside its stems, which resemble a series of pickles and taste salty. Entwined in the pickleweed are mats of orange threads, a parasite called dodder with roots deep in the pickleweed stems.

Along the dry banks above the high tideline, yellow daisy blooms of grindelia burst forth from buds capped with a white, gummy juice, giving rise to the common name of sticky gum plant. Head-high shrubs of coyote brush also line some banks, providing nesting sites for herons, raptors (birds of prey), and songbirds. In fall the shrubs' small, fragrant flowers support butterflies and other insects.

During this century, scientists have begun to understand the role of marshes in the Bay's ecosystem. They are the indispensable lungs of the Bay as well as a nursery for its diverse fish and bird populations. The often unsightly and sometimes smelly mud captures oxygen from the air while the tide is out and releases it into the water when the tide is in. These oxygenated tidal flats host a variety of small crustaceans, tiny shrimp, worms, and clams, all part of a vital food chain. These mud dwellers are fed upon by fingerlings of salmon, sturgeon, and the introduced sea bass as well as many other fish species. Airborne travelers feast in the mudflats during their annual migrations to and from Alaska or Chile and points in between. Sandpipers, terns, and grebes are frequent visitors, and predictable residents are black-necked stilts, avocets, and willets.

The murky waters hide an array of marine life, each variety of which occupies a particular niche. Dark-colored bottom feeders lie on the mud awaiting unsuspecting prey. Schools of shy, silver-sided fish dart above. Harbor seals will sometimes surface to check out the world along the shore.

Large-scale gold mining in the late 1800s added new and larger loads of sediment to the Bay. Hydraulic mines using huge water cannons washed hillsides into Sierra rivers. This mountain debris containing traces of mercury from gold processing flowed into the Sacramento River and finally settled out along the shallower shores of the Bay. In this century growing cities have dumped their garbage and unwanted detritus atop the marshes that people considered smelly, useless, and unsightly. This process, called bay fill, eventually converted two-thirds of the marshes into building sites.

In the 1960s concerned citizens banded together to stop the filling of the Bay. A law was passed in 1969 to empower the Bay Conservation and Development Commission to review all proposed filling of the marshlands. Permits are now required for any bayside development project. If the commission does allow a project to proceed, the developer is sometimes required to purchase other marshland that will be permanently protected as a park or open space. In addition, public access to the Bay must be an integral part of any development plan.

NATIVE TRIBES OF THE BAY

People began migrating into California perhaps as early as 15,000 years ago. They settled in many separate valleys, along myriad rivers, in coastal areas and around San Francisco Bay. By the time the Spanish arrived, it is estimated that forty different native communities were scattered around the Bay and south along the coast to Big Sur. These small tribelets were all part of the Ohlone group (which the Spanish call Costanoans), and they spoke eight different languages. In all of California there were 500 tribal groups speaking about 120 different languages.

These people were hunters and gatherers whose customs were influenced by the habitats in which they lived. A common cultural thread was woven into the complex design of California native life. The tribes made a gruel or cake from acorns, pine nuts, or mesquite beans. All used knives and speartips carved from animal bones or horns, and arrows were usually tipped with obsidian obtained through trade with tribes to the north or across the Sierra. Trade did not seem to be hampered by the variety of languages. Tribes lived in apparent peace with each other for thousands of years. Excavation of village sites in the Bay Area has shown that some were in continuous use for up to 5000 years, with little evidence of catastrophic events such as fire or war. All tribal groups created explanations for the appearance of the earth they understood so well. **Yesterday's Voices** relates a legend about the mountains from a California tribe.

Zipping by factories and highrise office buildings on I-80, it is hard to imagine the homeland of these native groups that greeted the first Spanish explorers of the East Bay. The interstate is built upon former marshland once laced with meandering sloughs and freshwater creeks that drained the grassy, oak-studded hills to the east. The Bay and its hillsides supported an unimaginable variety of wildlife and edible plants.

These native people lived easily off the land. They understood the nutritional and medicinal value of the plants available to them. Bulbs and seeds were often roasted. The staple, however, was a gruel or cake made from ground acorns. Preparation time was lengthy, for it was necessary to leach bitter tannins from ground acorn flour. Acorn cake was nutritious, and Spanish explorers treated to the bread described it as "rich and oily."

For the tribes close to the Bay, its bounty was endless. Clams and oysters were a major part of the residents' diet, evidenced by the more than twenty large mounds of shells found along the shores of Emeryville during the early 1900s. The Bay was host to millions of migrating waterfowl, and ducks and geese were lured with decoys and snared in large nets.

The Ohlone used boats made out of tule reeds. When the salmon and steelhead were running upstream to spawn, people waited with spears and nets. What could not be eaten at once was dried and stored. Salt obtained from salt grass was used to preserve food and was traded to inland tribes.

Herds of deer and elk roaming the grasslands were easy prey to a group of organized hunters. An early chronicler of San Francisco Bay wrote, "Herds of small stags were so fearless that they suffered us to ride into the midst of them." The Ohlone were also master trappers, making snares for rabbits and rodents living in the grasslands. Naturally, the skins of furred animals were prized for robes and blankets. Acorn woodpeckers and flickers were hunted for their colorful feathers, which were used to decorate ceremonial robes, headdresses, and baskets.

Basket weaving was both a necessity and an art form. Large, lightweight baskets were essential for gathering and storing food. Smaller, tightly woven baskets were lined with pitch to make them waterproof and were used as cooking pots. Acorn flour and water were mixed in such baskets and cooked into a mush by means of hot rocks attached to stirring sticks. Some baskets seemed to have been purely decorative. Woven from many different-colored roots and stems in intricate designs, they were often adorned with shells or feathers to produce particularly pleasing effects.

A typical Ohlone village contained conical huts made of tule reeds hung over a willow frame that seldom housed more than one family. Near a stream bank there was a low grass- and mud-covered building, larger than the rest and dug down into the soil. This was the sweathouse. Here the men gathered to chat, play games, and prepare for the hunt. Without horses to chase antelope and deer, these hunters relied on stealth and good planning. An important ritual for men was to cleanse the body of human odors and eat no meat before a hunt.

For thousands of years before the Spanish arrived, life along the Bay's shores existed in a pleasant round of hunting, fishing, gathering, saunas, games, and dancing. Then the Spanish came, riding horses and carrying flaming guns, a fearful sight for those first native Americans who encountered them. Even so, many tribes were known to have assisted weary, hungry Spanish explorers.

Life for the Ohlone changed dramatically with the arrival of the priests. The mission fathers were guided by a utopian vision of Christian communities to benefit the "poor, heathen Indians." The native peoples were to learn skills and labor industriously for the Church, learn Spanish, and become baptized, thereby assuring their entrance into the Kingdom of Heaven.

Early Spanish chroniclers often described the native people as beasts. They were routed from their villages, assembled in missions, and pressed unwillingly into the service of the Church. People whose life was once regulated only by the seasons and the need to provide food were forced to schedule their days by the mission bells. The cozy village was replaced by cheerless dormitories, with men separated from women and children and denied the cleansing of the sweathouse. Individual languages were lost as different tribes were crowded together on mission grounds. This new lifestyle resulted in disease and stress heretofore unknown to these people.

It is estimated that 10,000 native Americans lived between San Francisco and Monterey in 1776. By the end of the nineteenth century only a few hundred poor souls were left, and their villages had disappeared. Those who had not died of measles, tuberculosis, or venereal disease had scattered to the four winds when the missions were secularized. The game they had formerly hunted had fled before the invading armies of cattle that roamed the hills. When the American settlers poured in they brought with them fear and hatred of all Indians, whom they hunted down and killed with only the slightest provocation.

In the twentieth century anthropologists have taken a keen interest in reconstructing the life of these early inhabitants. What has been pieced together is a picture of people living in a Stone Age culture, directed only by the need to seek food from the abundant natural resources of the land they were fortunate to inhabit.

Exploring

THE S.F.-OAKLAND BAY BRIDGE TO HERCULES

Leaving Yerba Buena Island, the Bay Bridge enters Alameda County and becomes an elevated highway over the mudflats. The docks of the port of Oakland loom ahead. Huge cranes, looking like giant praying mantises, lift containers into cavernous holds of ships as long as two football fields. As you leave the bridge, follow signs for Interstate 80 to Berkeley and Sacramento. Get into the right lane as soon as you join incoming traffic. The Emeryville/Powell Street exit comes up very quickly.

EMERYVILLE MARINA

Drive toward the Bay on Powell Street to the end and turn right into the parking lots. Park opposite the flagpole. From the restrooms walk to the middle bridge of the yacht docks, then follow the trail counterclockwise around the edge of the park.

This new park features a re-created salt marsh, fishing piers, and pleasant picnic grounds with panoramic views of San Francisco and the Golden Gate Bridge.

From the bridge, the new marsh is laid out before you. The highest level of the marsh is home for the sticky gum plant. Touch the white buds and you will find that the surface is sticky. Nearer to the water look for pickleweed. Summer visitors will see orange threads of dodder festooning its stems.

When the tide is out, clams, mussels, and snails—or their air spaces—will be visible on the surface of the mud. The mud does not look very inviting to us because it is filled with decomposing plant material. Here is natural recycling at work, producing food for the mud-dwelling

A pair of western grebes motoring on the Bay. (*Photo by Ken Gardiner*)

creatures that are eaten by shorebirds and baby fish that inhabit the shallow water. Those fish are an important food source for the thousands of ducks that live here or visit during migration.

Look for a western grebe gliding over the water. This long-necked diving bird has a white bib down its neck. Try holding your breath as long as a grebe stays under water on a fishing expedition. A stately white great egret may also be nearby, waiting to nab an unsuspecting young fish as the tide comes in.

On the tree-covered hills above the Berkeley shoreline you can see the University of California campus surrounding the prominent Campanile. The university was established by two New England teachers who came west in the 1860s to bring their eastern brand of church-sponsored education to California. They opened a small college in Oakland, which later became a public university and moved to its beautiful campus on sloping hills overlooking the Bay. The football stadium, clearly visible at the top of the campus, is built directly across the Hayward fault, which lies along the bottom of the steep hills behind the campus. This fault is a parallel system to its westward neighbor, the San Andreas. Its southernmost part is actively creeping at a rate of about two inches per year.

The hills behind the campus remain undeveloped because of early interest in preserving open space. In 1934 citizens of Alameda and Contra Costa counties held an election to create the East Bay Regional

Park District and to assume a special tax. In the last fifty years the district has bought 57,000 acres of open space and parklands in the two counties.

If you follow the path around the north end of the marina peninsula you will most likely encounter the westerly winds streaming through the Golden Gate. The trail passes a fishing bridge and several excellent picnic areas. You may see barn swallows swooping over the lawns, waiting for an insect lunch to fly out of the grass.

When you reach the bayside, watch for harbor seals poking their heads above the waves. They differ from the sea lions found on Seal Rocks in that they are much smaller and have no outside ears. These harbor seals raise their young on the mudflats of the South Bay, now part of the San Francisco Bay Wildlife Refuge.

Anglers will tell you that the fishing is poor when harbor seals are around. Look among the rocks of the breakwater for castoff fish, too small to keep or not very good to eat. You may see a small, lumpy fish called a bullhead sculpin. This fish lives in the bottom level of the Bay's multilevel "apartment house" along with flattened flounders. Both fish are camouflaged to blend into the sea floor. One eye of the flounder has migrated so that both eyes are on one side, looking upward in order to watch for enemies above. Leopard sharks also live at this level. Perch and striped bass live in the middle levels, and schooling fish with silvery sides like anchovy, smelt, and Pacific herring swim near the surface. Gulls, terns, and pelicans snatch them from above.

As you return to your car, notice the poplar trees planted around the restrooms. Although not the native Fremont poplar for which the Spanish named Alameda County, they are a fitting reminder of the county whose Spanish name is translated as "grove of poplars."

EMERYVILLE MARSH OVERLOOK

The overlook is located at the corner of Powell Street and Frontage Road. Park along Frontage Road about 100 yards north of Powell. Cross Powell at the light to the signed public-access path.

From the platform built by the local Audubon Society, the Emeryville Crescent salt marsh is close at hand. Again you can identify the various plants of each level. The tall, narrow-leaved plant closest to the water is cordgrass, whose summer blooms look like wheat. A sign helps identify the numerous birds, including endangered species that nest nearby. A path next to the cyclone fence leads to a view of the mudflat art, huge driftwood fantasies created by students of local art schools. These often humorous and sometimes political sculptures greet westbound travelers entering the toll plaza of the Bay Bridge.

Take Frontage Road north to Gilman Street for a **Restful Parallel** of several miles. Because this section of Interstate 80 is often clogged with traffic, the shoreside Frontage Road provides pleasant driving. Both pavements cover former marshlands. When local cities began construction projects here in the early 1900s, numerous shell mounds of former tribal settlements were discovered. Excavation indicated that these villages had existed for thousands of years.

On summer afternoons, look across the Bay to see the fog gently caressing Alcatraz and Angel Island. The setting sun will wash the Golden Gate with a crimson brush and dab rainbow hues on the San Francisco cityscape.

BERKELEY PIER

From Interstate 80 or Frontage Road, turn toward the Bay on University Avenue. Park at the end of the road. A walk onto the pier takes you three-quarters of a mile over the water.

The pier once extended two and one-half miles into the Bay, where Berkeley commuters took ferries to San Francisco. Given today's Bay Bridge traffic jams, the 1902 ferryboat commute from Berkeley to downtown San Francisco was faster, and certainly more peaceful, with its fifteen-minute boat trip across the sparkling water.

The Berkeley Pier has recently been improved, and visitors can walk three-quarters of a mile onto the Bay to watch the everpresent anglers waiting patiently for the big one to bite. Most are very willing to share their expertise. You will see feathered fishers such as scoters, western grebes, and terns, and also scavenging gulls. South of the pier, windsurfers race across the waves at breakneck speeds and weekend yachters ply the Bay, presenting a multicolored spectacle.

After the Albany exit the highway passes by Albany hill. Spaniards who passed this way in the late 1700s gave it the name *El Cerrito*, "little hill." Now highly developed and planted with eucalyptus trees, it bears little resemblance to the grassy promontory that greeted the explorers.

For the next several miles the interstate is lined with plantings of Mediterranean imports that thrive even in close proximity to automobile exhaust. Acacia trees bloom with a profusion of yellow flowers as early as January, and broom shrubs are covered with yellow blossoms most of the summer. Interspersed are several species of eucalyptus trees imported from Australia in the 1800s. Some have gray-green, lance-shaped leaves, and others have silvery, rounded ones. Flowers vary from white to red. An entrepreneur decided that this fast-growing tree would be a money-maker because it could be harvested every thirty years. He imported thousands of seedlings only to find that the lumber was totally unsuitable for building or even for railroad ties. Farmers discovered that eucalyptus makes an excellent windbreak, and this pungent evergreen from "down under" is now found throughout California.

After MacDonald exit in Richmond look for the elevated rails of BART (Bay Area Rapid Transit). This system speeds commuters from Richmond, Concord, and suburbs south of Oakland into San Francisco via a tunnel under the Bay. It is hoped that one day this form of fast commute will connect all communities around the Bay and reduce the traffic that now brings cars to a standstill.

The exit for the **diversion** to Point Pinole Park is on Hilltop Drive. North of the town of San Pablo the interstate cuts through a series of undulating, grassy hills, the prelude to the Inner Coast Ranges. Across San Pablo Bay on a clear day you can make out the Sonoma and Napa mountains to the north.

As you pass through Pinole toward Rodeo and Hercules you will notice that suburban asphalt is sprouting on former cattle ranches and the valleys are filling with shopping centers. Where once the land served as a natural sponge for rainfall, it is now rapidly becoming impervious.

Favorite Diversions

OAKLAND MUSEUM AND LAKE MERRITT

Drive south on Highway 17 to the Jackson Street exit in Oakland. In three blocks turn left on Oak. The museum is at 10th and Oak. There is parking under the museum. Lake Merritt is a short walk from the museum. Here you can visit the Camron-Stanford Mansion or the Rotary Science Center.

The museum, mansion, and science center all have special school programs. Allow several hours for the museum tour and the walk around Lake Merritt. The permanent exhibits of the museum are free and are open Wednesday through Saturday from 10 A.M. to 3 P.M. and on Sundays from noon to 7 P.M.

A visit to this free public museum provides the foundation for an understanding of the landscapes of California and Nevada. The natural science section provides displays of the life zones of California and explanations of the idea that "things live where they do because they can." All but one of these zones is found on or near the route described in this book. Specimens of insects, birds, and amphibians are displayed among meticulously preserved vegetation. Large animals no longer encountered can be observed as they might have appeared to native Americans and pioneers. Seldom-seen nocturnal animals are also on display as well as exhibits explaining flower pollination and stages in the natural fire cycle.

Native American and gold rush artifacts highlight the museum's exhibit. In the art section the enormous oils of Thomas Hill, William Keith, and Albert Bierstadt present romanticized visions of the California known to John Muir, Ralph Waldo Emerson, and Theodore Roosevelt.

It is pleasant to stroll around nearby Lake Merritt, an artificial lake created from an original salt marsh. Tides can be seen coming and going through the southwest channel toward Alameda. Partway around the lake, four blocks from the museum, stands the former Camron-Stanford Mansion (no relation to Leland Stanford, the former governor and founder of Stanford University). The house has been restored and is open for tours Wednesdays from 11 A.M. to 4 P.M. and Sundays from 1 to 5 P.M. Near the Rotary Science Center, bay birds and raptors, usually seen only with binoculars, can be observed at close range. These are injured birds unable to live in the wild.

POINT PINOLE PARK

From Interstate 80, take Hilltop Drive west through San Pablo to the dead end at San Pablo Avenue. Jog right for one block and turn left at the light onto Atlas Road, following signs to the park.

This park is part of the East Bay Regional Park District. It encompasses four miles of shoreline around a 500-acre peninsula jutting into San Pablo Bay. The Bayview Trail starts at the end of the bridge over the railroad and climbs onto a grassy bluff overlooking the Bay and marshlands. A free shuttle bus leaves the parking lot hourly on the half hour each day of the year for the round trip to the fishing pier at the end of the peninsula.

Point Pinole Park was created from lands of former gunpowder plants. The necessity to isolate powder production far from civilization kept this beautiful corner of Contra Costa County natural. The Giant Powder

SANDPIPER

Company operated on the site from 1881 to 1960. An early advertisement for the company offered "gelatine dynamite and powder for mining, railroad, and bank blasting." Some of the old bunkers where powder was mixed have been transformed into windbreaks for picnic areas.

The shoreline you see from the Bayview Trail is a remnant of original salt marsh. Acres of cordgrass form a sparkling green necklace around the park. Mudflats stretch into the Bay beyond the cordgrass. Bird-watchers delight in winter gatherings of shorebirds poking the exposed mud with their long bills. Late-afternoon visitors discover backlit views of Mt. Tamalpais wreathed in fog or watch the setting sun paint a golden causeway across the Bay waters.

The Bayview Trail continues onto a bluff covered with grassland expanses that are filled in spring with a colorful display of yellow buttercups, orange poppies, and blue wild irises. If you are here when poppies (California's state flower) are in bloom, examine a clump of these orange flowers. You may find buds, full flowers, and seed pods on the same plant. The bud may be wearing a green cap, which will be pushed off as the bud opens. Look into the cup of the flower to see which insects may be having lunch. When the petals are gone, two-inch-long seeds are held aloft on their platter-shaped bases.

CALIFORNIA POPPY

When hot summer winds have dried the grasses golden brown, pink farewell-to-spring makes its debut. The predominant grasses today are introduced annuals, but very observant visitors may spot a clump of native bunchgrass, representative of grasses that grew here before the Spanish came.

Wandering across the meadows, imagine the landscape that greeted early inhabitants. The entire peninsula rippled with green in spring breezes. Herds of antelope, tule elk, and black-tailed deer dotted the hillsides above marshes and mudflats filled with thousands of shorebirds. Golden eagles and redtail hawks shared the sky with hovering marsh hawks (northern harriers) and kestrels. You can easily spot the soaring marsh hawk. Its straight tail has a distinctive white patch at the base. The hawks remain, but the eagle has moved on, and antelope and elk survive only on preserves.

The fishing pier at the end of the peninsula is beautifully maintained. Perhaps someone will reel in ocean perch, bass, or a huge sturgeon while you are there. In 1983 a 400-pound, monster sturgeon was caught in the Bay.

Retrace your route to Interstate 80, or drive north on San Pablo Avenue, Old Highway 40, which intersects Interstate 80 in a few miles at Highway 4.

Yesterday's Voices

WHY THE COAST RANGE IS SMALLER THAN THE SIERRA

A Yokut Indian Legend

The Yokuts lived in the southern part of the Central Valley. Like most peoples they created explanations for what they did not understand.

Once there was a time when there was nothing in the world but water. About the place where Tulare Lake is now, there was a pole standing far up out of the water, and on this pole perched a hawk and a crow. First one of them would sit on the pole a while, then the other would knock him off and sit on it himself. Thus they sat on top of the pole above the waters for many ages. At length they wearied of the lonesomeness, and they created the birds which prey on fish such as the kingfisher, eagle, pelican, and others. Among them was a very small duck, which dived down to the bottom of the water, picked its beak full of mud, came up, died, and lay floating on the water. The hawk and the crow then fell to work and gathered from the duck's beak the earth which it had brought up, and commenced making the mountains. They began at the place now known as Ta-hi'-cha-pa Pass, and the hawk made the east range, while the crow made the west one. Little by little, as they dropped in the earth, these great mountains grew athwart the face of the waters, pushing north. It was a work of many years, but finally they met together at Mount Shasta, and their labors were ended. But, behold, when they compared their mountains, it was found that the crow's was a great deal the larger. Then the hawk said to the crow, "How did this happen, you rascal? I warrant you have been stealing some of the earth from my bill, and that is why your mountains are the biggest." It was a fact, and the crow laughed in his claws. Then the hawk went and got some Indian tobacco and chewed it, and it made him exceedingly wise. So he took hold of the mountains and turned them round in a circle, putting his range in place of the crow's; and that is why the Sierra Nevada is larger than the Coast Range.

From *Tribes of California*, by Stephen Powers (Washington, 1877). Reprinted in *California Heritage*.

MEETING THE YANKEE TRADERS

From the diary of Prudencia Higuera

Prudencia wrote this memoir when she was an adult, but her child-hood remembrances are fresh and clear.

In the autumn of 1840 my father lived near what is now called Pinole Point, in Contra Costa County, California. I was then about twelve years old, and I remember the time because it was then that we saw the first American vessel that traded along the shores of San Pablo Bay. One afternoon a horseman from the Peraltas, where Oakland now stands, came to our ranch, and told my father that a great ship, a ship "with two sticks in the center," was about to sail from Yerba Buena into San Pablo and Suisun, to buy hides and tallow.

The next morning my father gave orders, and my brothers, with the peons, went on horseback into the mountains and smaller valleys to round up all the best cattle. They drove them to the beach, killed them there, and salted the hides. They tried out the tallow in some iron kettles that my father had bought from one of the Vallejos. . . . The captain soon came to our landing with a small boat and two sailors, one of whom was a Frenchman who knew Spanish very well, and who acted as interpreter. The captain looked over the hides, and then asked my father to get into the boat and go to the vessel. Mother was much afraid to let him go, as we all thought the Americans were not to be trusted unless we knew them well. We feared they would carry my father off and keep him a prisoner. Father said, however, that it was all right: he went and put on his best clothes, gay with silver braid, and we all cried, and kissed him good-by, while mother clung about his neck and said we might never see him again. Then the captain told her: "If you are afraid, I will have the sailors take him to the vessel, while I stay here until he comes back. He ought to see all the goods I have, or he will not know what to buy." After a little my mother let him go with the captain, and we stood on the beach to see them off. Mother then came back, and had us all kneel down and pray for father's safe return. Then we felt safe.

He came back the next day, bringing four boat-loads of cloth, axes, shoes, fish-lines, and many new things. There were two grindstones, and some cheap jewelry. My brother had traded some deerskins for a gun and four tooth-brushes, the first ones I had ever seen. I remember that we children rubbed them on our teeth till the blood came, and then con-cluded that after all we liked best the bits of pounded willow root that we had used for brushes before. After the captain had carried all the hides and tallow to his ship he came back, very much pleased with his bargain, and gave my father, as a present, a little keg of what he called Boston rum. We put it away for sick people.

After the ship sailed my mother and sisters began to cut out new dresses, which the Indian women sewed. On one of mine mother put some big brass buttons about an inch across, with eagles on them. How proud I was! I used to rub them hard every day to make them shine, using the tooth-brush and some of the pounded egg-shell that my sisters and all the Spanish ladies kept in a box to put on their faces on great occasions. Then our neighbors, who were ten or fifteen miles away, came to see all the things we had bought. One of the Moragas heard that we had the grindstones, and sent and bought them with two fine horses.

Soon after this I went to school, in an adobe, near where the town of San Pablo now stands. A Spanish gentleman was the teacher, and he told us many new things, for which we remember him with great respect. But when he said the earth was round we all laughed out loud, and were much ashamed. That was the first day, and when he wrote down my name he told me that I was certainly "La Cantinera, the daughter of the regiment." Afterward I found out it was because of my brass buttons. One girl offered me a beautiful black colt she owned for six of the buttons, but I continued for a long time to think more of those buttons than anything else I possessed.

From *Century*, XLI, 1890. Reprinted in *California Heritage.*

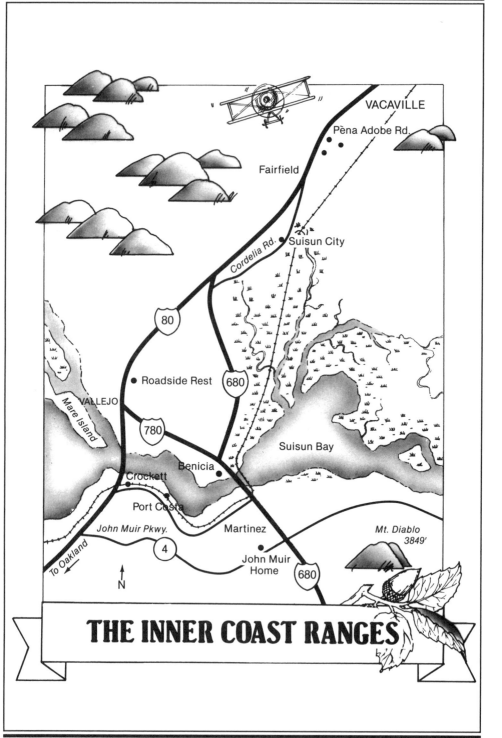

THE INNER COAST RANGES

3

THE INNER COAST RANGES
Hercules to Vacaville

Trip Planner
EXPLORING

The first part of this thirty-mile drive is through fast-growing suburbia. The last stretch follows a gentle swath through the Inner Coast Range hills past productive farms.

Carquinez Strait overlook offers vistas of the mouth of the Sacramento River.

Crockett is a factory town, until now bypassed by the latest trends.

Port Costa is tucked away at the edge of the water and was a bustling shipping port a century ago.

Hunter Hill roadside rest is a pullout for trucks. Here is an opportunity to see and feel serpentine, California's state rock, and to learn about landslides.

Peña Adobe and Lagoon Valley offer a smorgasbord of activities: a
historic adobe home and local museum, a jogging path,
a commercial water slide and gran prix course, a small
fishing and sailing lake, and a gliderport.

ALTERNATE LOOP—ALONG SUISUN MARSH

This variation adds twelve miles and crosses the strait upriver at
Benicia. Part of the way is on Interstate 680, which follows along salt
marshes and rejoins Interstate 80 at Cordelia. Or you may continue on
Cordelia Road to Fairfield, which passes through Suisun City, a former
shipping port at the end of Suisun Slough.

John Muir's home is a mecca for environmentalists. With its period
furniture and the study where he wrote, a visit is to slip back to the
time when California was a verdant wilderness and to learn of the
man whose name is synonymous with conservation.

Benicia is a little-publicized town offering interesting historical stops,
including a refurbished early state capitol and a well-preserved,
turn-of-the-century home and garden.

FAVORITE DIVERSION

Mt. Diablo is an hour's drive south of Martinez. It is an amazing
mountain of botanical and geologic diversity.

THE WINDY HILLS

From satellite altitudes, California's Inner Coast Ranges look like a gigantic rumpled carpet next to the smooth floor of the Central Valley. Travelers through this region encounter a series of north-south-trending mountain ranges enclosing valleys and lakes, vineyards and orchards, expanses of oak and grassland, slopes of gray-green chaparral, extinct volcanoes, geyser plumes and hot springs, and even a petrified redwood forest.

The Inner Coast Ranges are seventy miles wide in the north and taper to half that in the south. They form the wedge-shaped west wall of the Central Valley. In the northern Yolla Bolly Wilderness, some peaks reach up to 8000 feet. The only major break in this mountainous barrier is at Carquinez Strait, where the Sacramento River drains into the Bay. The most prominent mountain in the range is Mt. Diablo, a twin-peaked, dark mass rising 3849 feet. This landmark is visible on clear days from many spots around the Bay and punctuates the southern horizon along the Interstate 80 corridor between Cordelia and Sacramento.

The origins of these mountains go back at least twenty-five million years, when volcanic activity was related to the northward movement of the San Andreas fault. Volcanoes erupted from Pinnacles National Monument near Monterey to Mt. Saint Helena at the head of Napa Valley. The more recent eruptions produced volcanic rocks visible as immense palisades overlooking the upper Napa Valley wineries. Volcanic ash buried redwoods, creating Calistoga's petrified forest, and molten lava cooled to form entire glass mountains of obsidian. Native Americans chipped pieces of this shiny black rock into arrowheads. Remnants of this volcanic activity today include geysers and geothermal power plants as well as the soils that support the wine industry.

The forces that pushed the Inner Ranges upward also elevated quantities of gray-green serpentine, California's state rock, along fault zones. Fossil-bearing sedimentary rocks formed on the margins of interior seas were folded and tilted during the uplift.

The Inner Ranges produce strangely localized climates. Pacific storms that drench the western slopes are often exhausted by the time they cross the hills. Areas in the rain shadow east of the peaks often receive less than ten inches of rainfall per year. What rain does fall east of the crest of the hills drains into the Central Valley watershed. The Inner Ranges are a battleground for coastal and interior climates. In the Central Valley summer temperatures can climb to 110 degrees. As the heat rises, cooler bay air rushes inland. Fierce coastal winds funnel through wind gaps, especially along the interstate corridor, cooling the edges of the baking valley.

In winter, the Central Valley produces its own chilling tule fogs, which pour westward through these same gaps to cool the more moderate Bay Area. Winter brings snow every year to the top of Mt. Diablo and to the high peaks of the northern ranges. Occasional frost in the Coast Range valleys is a problem for agriculture.

Between Vallejo and Vacaville is a region of undulating green and golden hills. On slopes below 1000 feet, oaks living in the *foothill woodland* are scattered along the edges of the valley *grassland* community. If antelope still roamed, seasoned travelers would be reminded of some places in Africa. The sun-tolerant chaparral community thrives on rocky, south-facing exposures above 1000 feet. Its counterpart, the shady canyon forest community, is found mainly on north-facing exposures. Across the Central Valley this landscape is mirrored along the lower western slope of the Sierra Nevada.

California's Inner Ranges offer dazzling displays of spring wildflowers that paint the hills with a mosaic of orange, yellow, blue, and purple. Certain valleys dazzle the eye with five solid miles of color. Over 100 rare flowers and shrubs are found only within these Inner Ranges, some isolated on ecological islands atop a few mountains. As suburbia reaches out into these protected valleys and up the hillsides, less and less color remains.

RANCHOS AND SETTLERS

Spanish exploration of the land east of the San Francisco Bay began in 1772 when Pedro Fages led a small band of soldiers on a mapping expedition north from the San Jose Mission. He sought a land route around the Bay to its northern coast but was stopped by the fast-moving water of the Carquinez Strait.

Although Spanish land grants had been made throughout the late 1700s in southern California, it was not until after Mexican independence from Spain in 1821 that northern California land was parceled out. Most of what is now Alameda County was given to one family, the Peraltas of San Jose. They did not occupy their ranch, known as Rancho San Antonio, preferring to live nearer civilization.

In 1823 Don Francisco Castro was the first settler in the area. He built a modest adobe on his isolated Rancho San Pablo and spent his remaining years there raising cattle, holding fiestas in his courtyard, and watching his sons expertly ride their beautiful stallions. Castro's only neighbors were Indians. When he died in 1831, Ignacio Martinez had just been granted the Rancho el Pinole bordering the Carquinez Strait. In a few years Joaquin Moraga, Juan Bernal, and others brought their families to the region. They built homes, planted gardens, and sunned in their walled patios surrounded by children and grandchildren.

These grandees of the last days of Alta California lived a quiet rural life. Their only wagon was a primitive conveyance with solid wooden wheels drawn by oxen. Useless on muddy winter roads, it limited transportation to summer months. Horses were the pride and joy of every rancho. The size and quality of a man's stable indicated his wealth, and every member of the family had several horses to ride.

The ranch owners' income was derived from cattle that roamed free, feeding upon the natural grasses. They were slaughtered for tallow and hides, products shipped at first to Mexico and Spain and later to New England. This trade provided the Californios with luxuries from all over the world. Stories abound of young men dressed in silk and velvet imported from Spain and boots imported from Boston, riding on Mexican saddles trimmed with silver, galloping across the hills to serenade a pretty señorita whose wardrobe had been imported from Europe.

The daily routine of ranch life was broken by social visits, roundups, and fiestas, forerunners of today's rodeo. These warm, hospitable people welcomed all who came to their doorsteps, opening their houses and stables with equal generosity. It was well known that travelers could ride from one end of the state to the other and stay as long as they wished at each rancho, feasting on their host's food and continuing their journey on prize horses picked from their host's stable.

The time of gracious Spanish living was destined to be brief. Barely twenty years after those Mexican grandees had set up housekeeping on their vast acres, American pioneers were beginning to cross the Sierra and former trappers were settling in the Napa Valley. By the 1850s gold miners were bringing their families west to settle. The ranchos most affected by this American invasion were those in the Inner Coast Ranges, for their lands were along the routes between San Francisco and the gold fields. Mexican landowners unable or unwilling to fight for title to their lands in the American courts sold out to early arrivals and departed to southern California, where Spanish traditions remained unaffected by the tide of the gold rush.

Former New Englanders settled along the waterways of Carquinez Strait and Suisun Bay as well as in the Napa Valley. They brought their knowledge of shipping and farming, soon recreating towns like those they left behind. Spires of Protestant churches loomed over village squares, and solid stone granaries rose beside wheat fields. Abundant harvests of wheat and fruit soon filled the holds of sailing ships captained by former Boston mariners. The main evidence of Mexican California left in the region is in the names of towns and streets and the one or two restored adobe buildings.

The pastoral life continued until World War II brought millions to California in a second population explosion. Now fruit ranches are being replaced by homes and light industry, and some towns are struggling to retain their identity. Where it ends will depend upon the citizens and their planning commissions.

Exploring

HERCULES TO VACAVILLE

The **Alternate Loop** exits on Route 4 at Hercules. This loop connects with Interstate 680 at Martinez. The route joins Interstate 80 either at Cordelia or Fairfield. Stops include the John Muir home and Benicia. The **Favorite Diversion** to Mt. Diablo is reached by taking Interstate 680 south from Martinez.

Approaching Carquinez Strait the hills on either side of the freeway are rounded. Their soils are mostly of clay, which when wet expand and flow slowly downhill like glaciers. One wonders about the stability of the streets and homes now climbing the hills.

In early spring the open hillsides are covered with mustard blooms. This yellow, four-petaled flower came here with the Spaniards. A story is told that when Spanish priests first explored California, they dropped mustard seed along the way. Like Hansel and Gretel, they hoped for a golden path the next spring. Their wish came true the first year. Later, however, this native plant of Europe found the climate and soil of California so like home that it thrived and multiplied so that the path became a carpet.

Between Hercules and the Carquinez Strait, tanks of oil refineries painted in pastel shades utilize the proximity to San Pablo Bay. Long pipes laid into the Bay connect the refineries to oil tankers far out in the deeper water.

CARQUINEZ STRAIT OVERLOOK

Take the Crockett exit just south of the Carquinez Bridge. Turn under the bridge, then stop at the park-and-ride lot. From the bank across from the parking lot you get an excellent view of the strait.

The water flowing below you comes from rivers draining the Sierra Nevada. The Sacramento River originates north of Mt. Shasta, and during its southward journey it is joined by the Feather, Yuba, and American rivers. A few miles east of Carquinez Strait the Sacramento comes together with the San Joaquin River, carrying the snow melt from Yosemite Valley and the central Sierra. Oceangoing ships can be seen on their way up the river. Most are bound for Sacramento about fifty miles upstream via the deep-water ship channel. **Yesterday's Voices** recounts Jack London's vivid description of his drunken journey floating with the boiling current.

The southbound span of the Carquinez Bridge, closest to you, was opened in 1926 when the Northern Lincoln Highway became U.S. Route 40. The completion of the bridge brought an end to ferry service here. The northbound bridge was built more than three decades later as part of the construction of Interstate 80. The completion of that span signalled the demise of U.S. 40.

Across the strait, the former ferry terminus is now the docking site for the *Golden Bear*, chief training vessel of the California Maritime Academy. This state-supported college trains officers for the maritime industry. To the northwest of the academy is Mare Island, the first naval shipyard established on the west coast. Now nuclear submarines are built and repaired at this facility. On the south shore below you are the twin tracks of the Southern Pacific Railroad. The railroad crosses the strait upstream at Martinez. Before construction of a railroad bridge in the 1930s, train cars were rolled onto barges with tracks and were ferried across the water to Benicia.

The Strait seemed an impassable barrier to Pedro Fages in 1772. While searching for a route around the north end of San Francisco Bay his group straggled to this point. They were dispirited by the difficult hiking all the way from San Jose across hills and through thickets lining every stream. To their dismay, further progress was blocked by this mile-wide section of the Sacramento River. Short on food, they came upon an Indian village and were treated to an acorn mush. They mistakenly thought it was ground pine nuts and called it "pinole." From that time on the Spanish referred to the point of land along the strait as Point Pinole, and Ignacio Martinez called his rancho nearby Rancho El Pinole. Carquinez Strait was named after one of the local tribes that was called Karkin.

CROCKETT

The road to Crockett twists down under the bridge. Take Ceres and Pomona streets and turn left past a city park to the parking lot in front of the sugar factory.

The Carquinez Bridge may provide an ugly backrop to Crockett, but it has helped preserve the town's quaint look and winding streets. The town is dominated by the red-brick California and Hawaii (C and H) Sugar Factory, converted from a flour mill in 1906. It is said to be the largest sugar mill in the world, and this site was chosen because the huge ships bringing partly processed raw sugar from Hawaii could dock directly beside the mill. Once refined, the sugar is distributed throughout the country on the Southern Pacific Railroad, whose tracks are contiguous to the factory.

Crockett, Port Costa, and other towns along the southern shore of the river were carved from the Mexican ranchos by early American settlers moving out of the gold fields. The towns prospered during the last century as shipping depots for Central Valley wheat. They were also on the first transcontinental rail line. In this century the first paved transcontinental road passed nearby.

In the parking lot in front of the C and H Sugar Company, look for the town museum, which used to be the train depot. An old homestead is nearby. It was built by Thomas Edwards, Sr., on land purchased from Judge Joseph B. Crockett. His home, many of whose timbers were shipped around Cape Horn, became the nucleus of the town. The museum is open Wednesday and Saturday afternoons, and the homestead is now used by a local women's club. Both are owned and maintained by the C and H Sugar Company. The factory is not open to tours.

PORT COSTA

To enrich your trip into California's past, take the road out of Crockett to Port Costa. A fifteen-minute drive on a former Indian track and wagon road hugs the contours of the hills, winding to a dead end at Port Costa, once the largest wheat port in the world.

As early as 1854, wheat was being shipped from this town to Oregon, China, Mexico, Chile, and Europe. One of the "kings of wheat," as the early ranchers were called, built the grain-storage building that still stands opposite the railroad tracks at the end of the road. By 1859, fifty million bushels of California wheat were being shipped each year from here. **Yesterday's Voices** recites a horror story of man against wheat.

It is hard to imagine the hustle and bustle of those days, for today's town is a nearly forgotten village. Recently, however, Port Costa has experienced a modest revival as an artists' colony and tourist attraction. Some renovation of the old grain warehouse is creating shops and restaurants. One old-time attraction is the doll museum located a block up the road from the warehouse. Singed eucalyptus trees nearby record the 1983 fire that miraculously jumped the canyon above the town, leaving most of its homes unscathed. Return to Interstate 80 via Crockett or take McEwen Road to Route 4 and the **Alternate Loop.**

On the interstate halfway across the Carquinez bridge you leave Contra Costa County and enter Solano County. The interstate slices through the town of Vallejo, named after General Mariano G. Vallejo, a prominent Mexican grandee. In 1850 he made a magnanimous gift to the fledgling California legislature, granting land from his vast holdings and promising to erect buildings for a state capitol. Although Vallejo had suggested the name *Eureka* ("I have found it"), the legislature named the town in his honor. A frame capitol was built for the first meeting of the legislature in 1852, but lodgings and other amenities were not forthcoming, and the dissatisfied lawmakers moved to Sacramento one week later. Not long after that a devastating flood forced the legislature to adjourn. On January 3, 1853, those disgruntled legislators found themselves temporarily in Vallejo once more. A few months later Benicia built a beautiful brick statehouse, and the lawmakers settled upstream. Even the town of Benicia could not please the legislators, who eventually decided to make Sacramento the capital.

The naming of Mare Island is also connected with the general. In the early 1800s a bargeload of prize horses capsized during a squall in Carquinez Strait. One white mare, a favorite of the general's wife, swam to an island nearby. When Vallejo rescued the horse, he was so pleased that he bestowed the name *Mare Island.*

In 1851 the U.S. Congress, wishing to establish both naval installations and dry docks on the west coast, bought Mare Island from Vallejo. The first commandant was young Commander David G. Farragut, later the hero of the Civil War battles of Vicksburg and Mobile. Commander Farragut was instrumental in establishing the first public elementary school in the town of Vallejo.

A few miles north of Vallejo, summer and fall travelers may see horses training at the Solano County Fairgrounds. The interstate crosses a low point in a series of hills of the Inner Coast Range. Here south-facing slopes are virtually without trees, because they are subjected to high evaporation from sun and wind. Rock outcroppings on the hills to the east are part of Sulphur Springs Mountain.

Not far from the fairgrounds Route 37 exits to Napa Valley. Just off the interstate Marine World/Africa USA is planning to open its park in 1986. All manner of land and water mammals will be on display.

HUNTER HILL ROADSIDE REST

The truckstop exit is at the top of the hill after the Highway 37 exit to Napa County. Pull off the road and park at the far end of the strip.

Serpentine rock is easily distinguished by its dark, greenish-gray color and smooth texture. Most of this rock is fractured and split, but at the end of the parking lot nearest the exit to the freeway, rounded pillows of serpentine "knockers" will feel smooth to the touch, especially if wetted. This heavy rock is common along fault zones and has been squeezed up from deep in the earth's crust, producing grooves called slickensides or "squeeze marks." Serpentine is often processed for asbestos fibers. With its unusual chemical composition of magnesium silicate, only certain wildflowers and grasses have adapted to live on its soil. These serpentine wildflowers produce spectacular spring displays of gold, pink, and blue. The floral exhibitions are so special that conservationists are working hard to protect the most important remaining serpentine outcrops. One of these is on Ring Mountain Preserve of the Nature Conservancy and is located north of San Francisco in Tiburon.

Climb the serpentine to the pavement of old U.S. 40. The cattle ranch across the field is protected by eucalyptus windbreak plantings dating from the last century. Native coast live oaks and buckeye trees hug the sometimes moist depressions. The latter bloom in June, producing long white spikes.

Close to the far side of the ranch fence you can see remnants of the native, perennial grasses that dominated this landscape well into the last century. These grasses grow in clumps and have roots deep in the soil. The variety seen here is called needlegrass because of its long seed spines. These coil during the first autumn wet spell, forming a natural drill to penetrate the freshly dampened soil.

Typical of European weeds that have taken over cleared and compacted soils, dense thickets of fennel crowd the roadside. Fennel is a tall, fern-leafed relative of celery. It puts out flat clusters of tiny yellow blossoms that turn to dill-like seeds on umbrella heads in autumn. They smell and taste like licorice.

Walk uphill on the roadbed. How quickly the earth is reclaiming the road. At the sheared end of the pavement you look across a recent landslide. Here gravity has taken its toll on a soil of old marine shale that

An interstate maintenance problem! (*Photo by Nils J. Nilsson*)

became too heavy with excess water to stay put on this steep hillside. To inspect the purple and red rocks across the slide, take the narrow path. The brightly colored rocks contain iron oxides released from the hot springs that gave Sulphur Spring Mountain its name. On the way back to your car look across the freeway and down the canyon toward the salt ponds of the Napa Marsh.

Take I-80 to the American Canyon Road exit for a short **Restful Parallel** on McGary Road. Rejoin the freeway at Red Top Road. Released from the hypnotic pace of the interstate, you will be able to enjoy the landscape along an intermittent stream lined with willows.

An old windmill is visible to the south of the American Canyon Road exit. In the days before electric pumps and twentieth-century cheap energy, windmills dotted the Inner Coast Range. A single, contemporary, airplane-propeller windmill is visible above Sunnyside Farms just after Red Top Road. It merrily turns in every breeze, producing renewable energy.

Note the small terraced trails that contour each hill, evidence of the presence of cattle. Washed often with summer fog, these hills remain green longer than those on the hotter eastward slopes and are prized for cattle grazing. Notice curved headwalls of recent landslides, whose bulging toes produce a dimpled and puckered terrain.

In autumn the multicolored willows and maples prepare to drop their leaves. Among the occasional red trunks of madrone, buckeye catches the eye with its bare branches and brown, tennis-ball-size seeds. Near the Fairfield City Limit sign, the coast live oak has reached its eastern limits. Beyond this point summer heat is too much for this variety of oak.

Just before the Red Top Road exit the Central Valley opens up before you. At times the Sierra Nevada is visible, 100 miles away. On the north side of the freeway the Vaca Range, with its dark chaparral plant cover, reaches down toward the headwaters of Suisun Slough. The Suisun Valley and marsh is spread before you to the southeast. Who would suspect that the San Francisco Bay marshlands would extend so far inland? Eighty-five thousand acres of this slough and marsh are visited yearly by tens of thousands of migrating ducks and geese.

At the intersection with I-680 you can join a portion of the **Alternate Loop** by taking Green Valley Road south. After passing through Cordelia you can travel a 1920s farm road among spring-blossoming fruit trees. In summer you may buy fresh produce from one of the Yolano Farm Trails ranches. The loop ends in Suisun City, once a port for shipping the valley's produce and quarried rock to San Francisco.

North of the I-680 intersection toward Rockville is a volcanic ridge where the first drought-resistant deciduous oaks ring the Central Valley. Here eastward travelers will encounter the first summer heat of the Valley.

Four linear valleys occur in quick succession along the I-80 corridor between Cordelia and Vacaville. Cordelia, Suisun, Green, and Lagoon valleys are blessed with thirty to forty feet of topsoil left from eons of erosion from surrounding mountains. The first settlers noticed the rich soil and started planting fruit trees. On both sides of the road, pear trees can be seen stretching their branches upward. Heavily laden limbs of peaches are propped up by sticks in June and July. Cherries are the favored crop in Lagoon and Green valleys.

The next few miles present a drastic change in scenery. The once-bucolic county seat for agricultural Solano County is now the site of a military base and its support community, a large retirement center, and new industrial parks. This kind of development may be the destiny of most of the agricultural lands you have passed. It is estimated that in twenty years this entire stretch of I-80 will be continuous suburbia. An organization called People for Open Space has been working with citizens in local counties to find ways to keep the precious resource, prime agricultural land, in production.

The military calls Travis Air Force Base outside of Fairfield the "gateway to the Pacific." Giant C5A Galaxies and C141 Starlifters fly soldiers and supplies westward. The base was the site of some poignant

A valley oak outstanding in its field. These stately trees may soon be only memories because of the grazing animals that eat oak seedlings. (*Photo by Nils J. Nilsson*)

scenes during the Vietnam War. Returning POWs and the first Vietnamese refugees touched down here at Travis.

In east Fairfield the orange roof of Howard Johnson's signals the North Texas Street exit and an opportunity for a pleasant **Restful Parallel** on Nelson Road to Peña Adobe Road, our next stop.

Immediately after passing North Texas Street, scan the hillside a mile to the south of the freeway for a castle. Fantasies notwithstanding, it turns out to be an abandoned quarry tower for a cement factory near what was once the town of Cement, population 4000.

As the road climbs the hill, you can see the first valley oaks outstanding in their field. From the crest of the hill look for row upon row of flower beds, part of the Hines Wholesale Nursery.

As you drop into Lagoon Valley take yourself back to the 1840s. Near the lake sparkling in the distance, large shade trees proclaimed the presence of the Rancho Los Putos, home of the Peña family. With their friends the Vacas they ran thousands of cattle across the almost 50,000 acres granted to them by the governor of Alta California. Their presence provided a needed buffer between the coastal settlements and the growing colony of John Sutter along the banks of the Sacramento River to the east.

Perhaps what has changed least since that time is the lake, formed from subsidence along an active earthquake fault. In winter, occasional flocks of Canada geese and whistling swans or white pelicans may be seen taking off in V formation.

PEÑA ADOBE AND LAGOON VALLEY

The Peña Adobe Road exit leads immediately to five possible stops. Turn onto Peña Adobe Road at the Blue Lagoon Water Slide and Gran Prix. The entrance to the Peña Adobe is straight ahead. The park is open Wednesday through Sunday.

Peña Adobe Museum Park

Nestled among old almond and walnut trees, the home of the Peña family was restored to its original condition in the 1960s. The small structure was built of native adobe bricks (dried clay and straw). The adobe was covered by siding during this century. When the wood was removed, the adobe bricks appeared as new. It is furnished in simple, utilitarian style, presenting a valid picture of the life of landed Mexican gentry.

The Peñas' Rancho Los Putos stretched from the shores of Suisun Bay to the south, to the Napa Mountains to the west, and to the Sacramento River to the east. The boundaries were described on the deed as informally as that. Like many other Spanish land grants, boundaries were indistinct, a fact that led the Peñas and other Mexican landholders into difficulties with the U.S. Government.

The Peñas' good life of cattle roundups, fiestas, and horse racing was destined to last barely ten years. By 1850 the ranch was being overrun by settlers, and the Peñas were fighting for their land in the U.S. courts. Yet even as the valley was filling up with Americans, the Peña hospitality was extended to all who passed their home. A story is told of a pioneer family whose wagon became mired on the road near Señor Peña's adobe. He helped the family, offering them food and shelter, and even built them a small house on his land. Without payment to the Peñas these ungrateful squatters later filed for ownership of the land around the small house.

The little museum next to the adobe contains artifacts found on the land during restoration. Indian arrowheads and other tools were used by the tribes that resided in this valley when the Peñas came. Of particular interest is a penciled map of the San Francisco Bay drawn by General Vallejo in the early 1800s.

The park grounds offer opportunities to inspect antique farm equipment, succulent plants introduced by the Peñas, a duckpond, and a

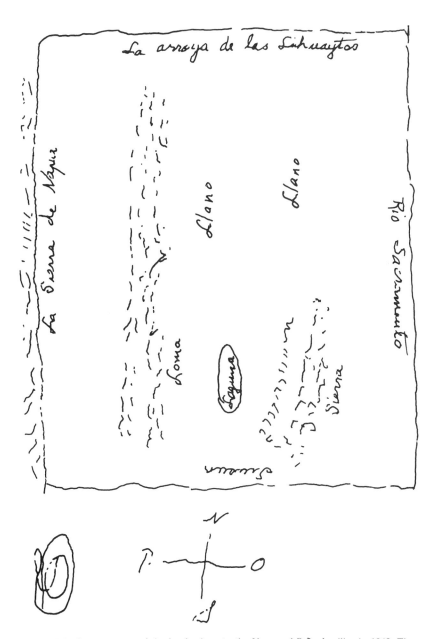

The original, vague map of the lands given to the Vaca and Peña families in 1843. The rancho was nearly seventy square miles and extended from the Napa Mountains to the Sacramento River. (From *Vaca-Peña Los Putos Rancho and the Peña Adobe* by Wood Young)

garden of native plants dedicated to the father of California botany, Willis Linn Jepson. Plants here include madrone, box elder, spice bush, and native black walnut.

East of the adobe two kinds of deciduous oaks grow. The blue oak has wavy, blue-green leaves. It grows up the dry hillside, preferring well-drained soil. Lower down on the flats, huge valley oaks present their deeply incised leaves.

Parcourse and Bike Trail

This paved trail is both a parcourse for local joggers and a bike trail. The entrance is next door to the Peña Adobe. A brief walk along this trail will reward you with a close look at both native and nonnative plants. Swallows nest under the nearby bridge, and tules, willow, and teasels are visible. Teasels were imported from Europe to do the job they have done for centuries: their dried seed heads were used to comb or "tease" wool for spinning. In April poppies, lupines, and a myriad of other flowers are visible among the nonnative yellow mustards, wild oats, rye, and red brome grass. This trail also leads to a pioneer gravesite nestled among native blue oaks atop the Peña hill.

Blue Lagoon Water Slide and Gran Prix

This private enterprise offers a welcome change of temperature on a hot day. The water slide and miniature raceway are great child pleasers. There is an admission charge.

Lagoon Valley County Park

This park circles the lake and is not yet completely developed. It is a pleasant place to picnic. Opportunities exist for bass fishing, swimming, sailing, windsurfing, and paddling your own canoe. There is an admission charge.

Vac Aero Gliderport

The Vac Aero Gliderport is located one mile west of the Peña Adobe on Rivera Road. (Notice the play on words in the name: in Spanish *vacquero* means cowboy.) Here you can arrange to take a ride among the circling hawks. Two-seater gliders are drawn aloft by propeller planes to begin a flight circling the updrafts in this valley. On clear days vistas include the lakes of the Inner Ranges as well as the San Francisco Bay and its ring of Outer Coast Range mountains. To the east the Sierra Nevada rises majestically above the Central Valley. The cost is about forty-eight dollars per ride for one person or fifty-five dollars for two.

After your visits, return to the interstate at Peña Adobe Road. As the interstate leaves Lagoon Valley it cuts through the last ridge of the Inner Ranges and enters the Central Valley. Grass fires occur on these slopes every few years, but the oak trees survive.

As you approach Vacaville, the Remark Inn is located on the south side of the freeway. It can be reached from the Merchant Street-Alamo Drive exit. The inn features a delightful shaded terrace near a grove of native trees including valley oaks, black walnuts, willows, buckeye, and planted coast redwoods.

Alternate Loop

ALONG SUISUN MARSH

To begin this loop, exit the interstate at Hercules. Go east on Highway 4 toward Martinez and Stockton. The highway is called the John Muir Parkway to honor the conservationist credited with creating many national parks.

Suburban and industrial development are encroaching on the former pastoral landscape of the 100,000-acre Rancho El Pinole of Ignacio Martinez. The Santa Fe Railroad tracks parallel the highway. The hills here have equal periods of green or golden brown coloring, bearing witness to Muir's description of the California climate: " . . . only two seasons—wet and dry." The long, rainless summers make sun-drenched, south-facing slopes treeless deserts. North-facing slopes are dotted with coast live oaks, bay laurel, and occasionally elderberry shrubs.

An alternative round trip to Port Costa leaves Highway 4 at Franklin Canyon Road. Follow signs to the town, turning left under the highway. The winding country road requires slow driving but is like a trip back in time, making it possible to enjoy a horse-and-buggy pace through the rolling hills.

JOHN MUIR HOME

*In Martinez take the Alhambra Road exit and turn left. The National
Park Historic Site Visitor Center is on the left in one block.*

The visitor center highlights John Muir's importance, sells his books,
and shows an excellent film explaining his life and his motivations to
become one of America's most revered conservationists. You can tour his
four-story, Victorian-style home where he wrote to his compatriots to "go
to the mountains and get their glad tidings." His ten books and many
articles awakened the public and the lawmakers, especially President
Theodore Roosevelt, to the need to protect special places as national
parks.

Muir's youth was spent working long hours on his father's farm in Wisconsin, where he often awoke at four in the morning to don icy boots and
work until evening. Schooling was forbidden by his stern father, but this
did not deter his inquisitive mind. He invented machines in a basement
after midnight, even making a contraption to spill him from bed so that
he could awaken early enough to read before his chores.

After studying at the University of Wisconsin, Muir found employment
in a broom factory, where his inventiveness was put to good use. Later,
while employed in a carriage factory, a frightening accident blinded him
for a time. Swathed in bandages, he swore that if he ever saw again he
would "give up the inventions of man, and study only the inventions of
God." His sight returned miraculously, whereupon he began twelve years
of exploring the Appalachians, Yosemite, and Alaska. By the 1880s his
travels had infused him with a burning desire to protect the beauty he
had come to love.

Despite months of solo adventures, Muir was a gregarious soul. His
need for human warmth periodically brought him to the Bay Area,
where he met and married Louie Strentzel. The couple settled here on
her father's land, and Muir began to assist with management of the 2600-
acre fruit ranch. When Dr. Strentzel died, Muir and his wife and two
daughters moved into the main house.

The business prospered under Muir's management. A spur of the
Santa Fe Railroad was brought into the ranch so that packed fruit could
be loaded directly into the cars for shipment. Before the railroad connec-
tion, the fruit was shipped by boat from the Martinez docks on Carquinez
Strait.

John Muir in his beloved Sierra. (*Lithograph courtesy of Andrea Hendrick*)

The ranch made Muir independently wealthy. He returned to his travels and began writing and fighting for protection of his beloved wild places. In 1892 he founded the Sierra Club and was elected its first president, a post he held until he died.

Muir felt that his greatest accomplishment was the creation of Yosemite National Park in 1906. His most disappointing defeat was the defacement of another spectacular valley in Yosemite when the Hetch Hetchy Dam was approved in 1913. He died one year later, disconsolate over the loss.

Here at his home, exhibits give visitors a glimpse into his life. Be sure to look into the second-floor writing room. It looks as if Muir has just stepped out to take a slight rest from the long hours spent here. He penned his beautiful and persuasive prose with exasperating slowness, calling the painful process "like a glacier, one long grind."

California state historians have selected Muir as "the most famous Californian." One historian wrote of him, "If you define a great American as one who helps change the direction of this country toward more socially desirable goals, then John Muir was a greater American than all but a handful of U.S. presidents." He continued, "When John Muir began his conservation career in the late 1880s, America was committed to a totally devastating attack on the environment. When Muir died in 1914, the nation was committed in spirit, if not always in fact, to the wise use of its natural resources."

Walk along the Orchard Trail, where in summer fruit is free for visitors' picking. The self-guiding trail also illustrates Muir's selection of ornamental trees, giant sequoia and incense cedar from the Sierra, and deodar cedar from the Himalayas. The Orchard Trail leads visitors back into another time, to the original Martinez adobe, built in 1849. The adobe had been purchased by Dr. Strentzel and used as a foreman's cottage, and later Muir's daughter Wanda moved in with her own family. The adobe is in remarkable condition and is open to visitors. Hanging on the wall is a map that details the original Spanish and Mexican land grants in the Bay Area.

After you leave the Muir home take Highway 4 to the intersection with Interstate 680. Take the interstate north to Benicia and toward Sacramento. Those wishing to visit Mt. Diablo should drive south on Interstate 680 to Danville.

Interstate 680 crosses the Benicia Bridge not far west of the confluence of the Sacramento and San Joaquin rivers. The railroad bridge is below on the right. It was constructed in 1930 to replace the ferry service that had transported entire trains between Benicia and Martinez since 1879.

Upstream from the bridge row upon row of old naval vessels are tied together off shore. These are the National Defense Reserve Fleet of the Department of Transportation Maritime Administration. Ninety ships are currently preserved in this "mothball fleet." A few are kept ready to be put into service in from five to twenty days. The remainder would require up to two months' preparation before they could sail. These ships have been in and out of service since World War II, most recently to haul supplies during the Vietnam War.

BENICIA

Exit left after the bridge onto Interstate 780 toward Vallejo. Exit to central Benicia and drive south to Military Street. Turn right onto Military and left onto First Street. The old town is along First and Second streets.

Benicia is a town of many California firsts. It was the first of two cities to be incorporated in 1850, was the site of the first Protestant church built in the state, had the first railroad ferry west of the Mississippi River, and housed the state's first military hospital; the list goes on and on.

Benicia was established in 1847 by Robert Semple, Thomas O. Larkin, and General Mariano Guadaloupe Vallejo, who owned the land upon which Benicia was built. The founders named it after the general's beautiful wife. The town began modestly with twenty homes. Semple used a scow to provide much-needed ferry service to the Contra Costa shore. During the gold rush the town served mainly as a stopping point for those on their way to the diggings. This did not stop the city fathers from aspiring to greater things. When the city of Vallejo failed to satisfy California legislators as a capital, and when Sacramento was under water in the great flood of 1852, Benicians quickly erected a beautiful, brick hall and invited the legislature to their town. Despite the handsome building with its polished wood interior, the fickle legislators stayed but thirteen months before deciding to return to Sacramento.

Today the former capitol building is preserved as Benicia Capitol State Park. It has been restored and can be toured daily for a small fee. Next to the capitol is a fascinating surprise, the original garden of Joseph Fischer. One-hundred-year-old blooming cacti with trunks one foot in diameter; a six-foot-high jade plant; and fragrant, old-fashioned roses are spread out along brick walks under gnarled pepper trees. The carriage house has lovingly been reconstructed by the park rangers so that even the manure pile is correctly placed in the horse stalls!

If you happen to be here on a weekend, volunteer docents will take you through the Fischer-Hanlon house, a replica of a New England federal-style home. When you enter, you are transported back into the life of an early California family at the turn of the century. The three granddaughters of Mr. Fischer, the never-married Hanlon sisters, simply packed their bags one day in 1960 and left the house as is to the state. The furnishings, pictures, even the hats on the coat rack belonged to the sisters, whose knitting needles and wool sit by their favorite chairs on the sun porch overlooking the garden. Be sure to go into the kitchen. These three women used their grandfather's wood-burning stove for all their cooking. We are fortunate that such generous people have allowed us an opportunity to walk into their past.

Benicia has other original homes and churches. A walking guide to the town is available at the chamber of commerce and in some restaurants. The Episcopal church and rectory were built in 1852 and are still in use. On First Street, the Union Hotel offers repasts in an authentic nineteenth-century decor. At the end of First Street the yellow Central Pacific train station stands alone in a field and reminds us of Benicia's heyday. The railroad ferry dock is now a fishing pier. Jack London spent time here as a fisherman and sometime oyster pirate. His story in **Yesterday's Voices** had its beginning right here.

As you return to Interstate 680, notice the white gazebo in the park. One can imagine the Hanlon sisters sitting nearby dressed in their Sunday best, parasols protecting them from the sun, listening to a band concert.

On the way to Cordelia the freeway hugs the volcanic upland over-looking the Suisun Marsh. For an excellent view of this remarkable 85,000-acre marsh, take the exit for the vista point and park above the highway. From here sloughs, ponds, marshes, and the expanse of Suisun Bay are laid out before you. The Montezuma Hills outline the eastern edge of the bay.

During the 1800s the marsh before you was diked off to create farm-land. In this century, Sierra dams began to hold back much of the fresh-water flow into the strait, and brackish water invaded. The low-lying land became too saline and the farms were abandoned. Now the marsh is managed by the California Department of Fish and Game as a wildlife refuge and as a hunting and fishing recreation area. Much of the acreage is in private hands. Each spring the diked ponds are flushed with fresh water. Ponds are then drained, disked, and planted with grasses that attract waterfowl during their winter migration along the Pacific Flyway.

Continue your marshside drive on Lopes Road until it intersects with I-680. You may be able to pick out two sizes of white egrets standing in the marsh. If you pass by during spring or fall migration you may want to stop. Binoculars will help to identify some of the twenty-one species of waterfowl visiting the area yearly. Not visible so close to the road will be river otters, beavers, muskrats, and other mammals that inhabit the islands and waterways of Suisun Marsh.

You will understand the meaning of Suisun, "west wind," when you experience the area's high and consistent winds. On the left, shortly before Cordelia, Pacific Gas and Electric Company has installed the world's largest demonstration wind generator—the Boeing 25–60. The propeller is the length of a football field and attached to a 200-foot tower.

Egrets provided Victorian ladies with beautiful plumes for their hats. The Audubon Society was formed to protect these and other endangered birds. (*Photo by Ken Gardiner*)

It was engineered to move in the slightest wind. When the winds reach 40 miles per hour, a frequent occurrence here, the tips of the propeller travel over 200 miles per hour. In early stages of operation frequent delays for repairs have kept this twentieth-century behemoth idle. Wind farms using smaller versions of this machine have been installed in a similar windy tunnel through the hills at Altamont Pass forty-five miles southwest of here.

Just before the I-80 intersection, those wishing to continue the **Alternate Loop** may exit onto Green Valley Road to Cordelia. The loop will return to Interstate 80 on West Texas Street in Fairfield.

Cordelia is one of the oldest towns in Solano County and retains its turn-of-the-century character. Located on the lower end of Green Valley on the route between Benicia and Sacramento, it became a stage stop. Stone quarried from nearby volcanic deposits was shipped down Cordelia Slough to San Francisco and was used for buildings and to pave streets. Cordelia's growth continued when the Central Pacific was routed through the town. Its demise came when U.S. 40 and Interstate 80 bypassed the town and the railroad ceased to stop here.

East on Cordelia Road you curve around Olson's Hill, one of the state's oldest quarry sites. Some of its volcanic rocks arrived on glowing clouds issued forth during the eruptions near Napa several million years ago. Rocks were quarried from the top of the hill and provided cobblestones for San Francisco streets.

The Green and Suisun valleys were centers of the earliest California fruit-growing industry. This route passes several ranches that welcome the public. Signs at the entrance will proclaim what is currently being picked, offering an opportunity to load up on fresh cherries (for which the region is famous), pears, peaches, or apples. You can also buy the usual field crops of tomatoes and corn.

Upon entering Suisun City—hardly a city—turn left on Main Street to find the town center. Its plaza was laid out in front of a large, white-colonnaded house that looks like it had been transported directly from the New England coast. Complete with a widow's walk, the Lawler house has stood at its present location since 1862.

Across the street is Josiah Wing's Restaurant, named after one of the town's founders. Wing was born in Barnstable, Massachussetts, and sailed his brig the *Diantha* around the horn in 1849. He was not looking for gold; rather, he docked his ship at San Francisco and turned it into a store. After sailing home in 1850, he returned in 1851 and sailed up the Suisun Bay, where he found the island of Suisun sitting nicely above the high tideline. He bought some land, built his warehouse, and proceeded to transport the products of the burgeoning valley agriculture. The restaurant is in the renovated warehouse and contains many old photos of Suisun City and its founders as well as a beautiful original oak bar upstairs.

Suisun City was incorporated in 1854 and thrived as a port town for several decades. During the 1800s the island town was separated from its neighbor to the north, Fairfield, by a long plank walk. Today the marsh under the walk has been filled in, and one can drive directly to Fairfield.

Continue north on Main Street until it dead-ends at the county courthouse in Fairfield. On the left, just before West Texas Street, a statue of Chief Solano stands on the lawn of the county library. This exceptionally able native leader was baptized as Chief Solano by the mission fathers. He became a close friend of General Vallejo, who honored the chief by naming the new county after him. Turn left on West Texas Street to return to Interstate 80.

Favorite Diversion

MT. DIABLO

Drive south thirteen miles on Interstate 680 from Martinez to Danville. Follow signs to the mountain park, which looms out of the valley to the east. Allow a minimum of four hours for a round trip.

This state park offers hiking trails, picnic sites, camping, and a visitor center. From the observation tower you can enjoy spectacular views over much of central California. Mountaintop trails pass by unusual plants.

On a clear day the views are not quite forever from the top of this 3849-foot mountain, but like Kilimanjaro in Africa, it rises alone out of the plain. When the weather is right more of California can be seen from the top of this mountain than from any other point in the state. Two 14,000-foot landmarks, Mt. Shasta in the north and Mt. Whitney in the southern Sierra Nevada were visible during past decades when the air was less hazy. Mt. Hamilton is directly south, and the Bay Area spreads out below to the west. On a particularly clear, windy day you may be lucky and see the Farallon Islands on the horizon.

The observation tower on the top of the mountain has been constructed out of sedimentary rocks containing ancient fossilized shells. These rocks, brought from the mountain's foothills, are remnants of a time ten to twenty million years ago when the mountain did not exist and the land lay beneath a sea. Mt. Diablo is an anomaly in the Inner Coast Ranges. Arthur D. Howard in his *Geologic History of Middle California* wrote of its formation.

> . . . a pimplelike protuberance began to appear on the crest of one of the growing folds. The welt continued to grow until it measured about 5 miles (8 kilometers) across, at which time it ruptured. Out of the rupture rose a mass of ancient Franciscan rocks, including a body of dark intrusive igneous rock since altered to serpentine. So was Mount Diablo born.

Mt. Diablo, the devil mountain, was supposedly named for a dramatic event when Spanish soldiers were treated to a diabolical dance by an Indian medicine man. The name *devil* is often attributed to dark-looking objects, and the name could as well be derived from the dark appearance of this massive, singular mountain.

The plants on Mt. Diablo intrigue botanists, for they exist as if isolated on an island. Localized species of Mt. Diablo manzanita and the yellow Diablo fairy lantern inhabit this high ecological island. The hot, dry, south-facing slopes provide the habitat for California desert junipers, even though the mountain is located less than ten air miles from the moisture-loving coast redwoods.

Visitors can take an easy quarter-mile trail to overlook Coulter pines with their large, heavy cones. On the way stop to smell bay laurel leaves. Does the aroma remind you of spaghetti sauce? The bay laurel trees and the adjacent madrones and canyon oaks were Indian food plants of the canyon forest community.

Yesterday's Voices

THE POWER OF WHEAT

By Frank Norris

Here is the dramatic conclusion of a novel about California's farmers pitting themselves against the new, powerful railroad. S. Behrman is the railroad's representative. In his death we see that neither faction won but that wheat, with the promise of feeding the hungry of the world, overcame both.

Upon descending from his train at Port Costa, S. Behrman asked to be directed at once to where the bark *Swanhilda* was taking on grain. Though he had bought and greatly enlarged his new elevator at this port, he had never seen it. The work had been carried on through agents, S. Behrman having far too many and more pressing occupations to demand his presence and attention. Now, however, he was to see the concrete evidence of his success for the first time.

He picked his way across the railroad tracks to the line of warehouses that bordered the docks, numbered with enormous Roman numerals and full of grain in bags. . . .

S. Behrman stood watching, his ears deafened with the roar of the hard grains against the metallic lining of the chute. He put his hand once into the rushing tide, and the contact rasped the flesh of his fingers and like an undertow drew his hand after it in its impetuous dash. . . .

As his eyes became used to the shadows of the cavern below him, he began to distinguish the gray mass of the wheat, a great expanse, almost liquid in its texture, which, as the cataract from above plunged into it, moved and shifted in long, slow eddies. As he stood there, this cataract on a sudden increased in volume. He turned about, casting his eyes upward toward the elevator to discover the cause. His foot caught in a coil of rope, and he fell headforemost into the hold.

The fall was a long one, and he struck the surface of the wheat with the sodden impact of a bundle of damp clothes. For the moment he was stunned. All the breath was driven from his body. He could neither move nor cry out. But, by degrees, his wits steadied themselves and his breath returned to him. . . .

Then began that terrible dance of death; the man dodging, doubling, squirming, hunted from one corner to another, the wheat slowly, inexorably flowing, rising, spreading to every angle, to every nook and cranny. It reached his middle. Furious, and with bleeding hands and broken nails, he dug his way out to fall backward, all but exhausted, gasping for breath in the dust-thickened air. Roused again by the slow advance of the tide, he leaped up and stumbled away, blinded with the agony in his eyes, only to crash against the metal hull of the vessel. He turned about, the blood streaming from his face, and paused to collect his senses, and with a rush, another wave swirled about his ankles and knees. Exhaustion grew upon him. To stand still meant to sink; to lie or sit meant to be buried the quicker; and all this in the dark, all this in an air that could scarcely be breathed, all this while he fought an enemy that could not be gripped, toiling in a sea that could not be stayed. . . .

Reason fled. Deafened with the roar of the grain, blinded and made dumb with its chaff, he threw himself forward with clutching fingers, rolling upon his back, and lay there, moving feebly, the head rolling from side to side. The wheat, leaping continuously from the chute, poured around him. It filled the pockets of the coat; it covered the great, protuberant stomach; it ran at last in rivulets into the distended, gasping mouth. It covered the face. . . .

From *The Octopus*, 1901. (New York: The New American Library, 1981.)

FLOATING IN THE STRAITS

By Jack London

Well known for The Call of the Wild, *London was pursued by John Barleycorn, the demon alcohol.*

I now made the old town of Benicia, on the Carquinez Straits, my headquarters. In a cluster of fishermen's arks, moored in the tules on the water-front, dwelt a congenial crowd of drinkers and vagabonds, and I joined them. I had longer spells ashore, between fooling with salmon fishing and making raids up and down bay and rivers as a deputy fish patrolman, and I drank more and learned more about drinking. . . .

At one o'clock in the morning, after a prodigious drunk, I was tottering aboard a sloop at the end of the wharf, intending to go to sleep. The tides sweep through Carquinez Straits as in a mill-race, and the full ebb was on when I stumbled overboard. There was nobody on the wharf, nobody on the sloop. I was borne away by the current. I was not startled. I thought the misadventure delightful. I was a good swimmer, and in my inflamed condition the contact of the water with my skin soothed me like cool linen.

And then John Barleycorn played me his maniacal trick. Some maundering fancy of going out with the tide suddenly obsessed me. I had never been morbid. Thoughts of suicide had never entered my head. And now that they entered, I thought it fine, a splendid culmination, a perfect rounding off of my short but exciting career. . . .

Below the town of Benicia, where the *Solano* wharf projects, the straits widen out into what bay-farers call the "Bight of Turner's Ship-yard." I was in the shore-tide that swept under the *Solano* wharf and on into the bight. I knew of old the power of the suck which developed when the tide swung around the end of Dead Man's Island and drove straight for the wharf. I didn't want to go through those piles. It wouldn't be nice, and I might lose an hour in the bight on my way out with the tide. . . .

I was elated, for I had succeeded in avoiding the suck. I started to raise my death-chant again—a purely extemporized farrago of a drug-crazed youth. "Don't sing . . . yet," whispered John Barleycorn. "The *Solano* runs all night. There are railroad men on the wharf. They will hear you, and come out in a boat and rescue you, and you don't want to be rescued." I certainly didn't. What? Be robbed of my hero's death? Never. And I lay on my back in the starlight, watching the familiar wharf-lights go by, red and green and white, and bidding sad, sentimental farewell to them, each and all. . . .

Next I discovered that I was very weary and very cold, and quite sober, and that I didn't in the least want to be drowned. I could make out the Selby Smelter on the Contra Costa shore and the Mare Island lighthouse. I started to swim for the Solano shore, but was too weak and chilled, and made so little headway, and at the cost of so painful effort that I gave it up and contented myself with floating, now and then giving a stroke to keep my balance in the tide-rips which were increasing their commotion on the surface of the water. And I knew fear. I was sober, now, and I didn't want to die. I discovered scores of reasons for living. And the more reasons I discovered, the more liable it seemed that I was going to drown anyway.

Daylight, after I had been four hours in the water, found me in a parlous condition in the tide-rips off Mare Island light, where the swift ebbs from Vallejo Straits and Carquinez Straits were fighting with each other, and where, at that particular moment, they were fighting the flood tide setting up against them from San Pablo Bay. A stiff breeze had sprung up, and the crisp little waves were persistently lapping into my mouth, and I was beginning to swallow salt water. With my swimmer's knowledge, I knew the end was near. And then the boat came—a Greek fisherman running in for Vallejo; and again I had been saved from John Barleycorn by my constitution and physical vigor.

From *John Barleycorn* (New York: The Century Company, 1914).

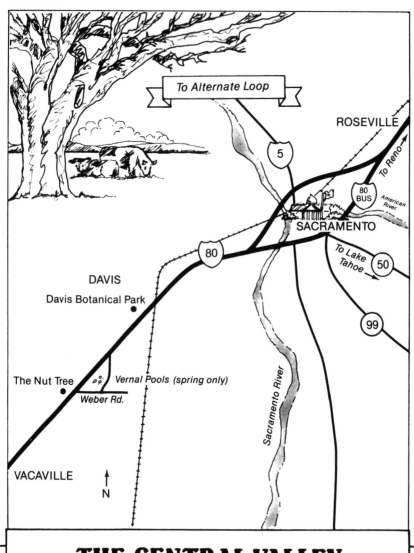

To Alternate Loop

ROSEVILLE

To Reno

5

80
BUS

American River

SACRAMENTO

80

To Lake Tahoe

50

DAVIS

Davis Botanical Park

99

The Nut Tree

Vernal Pools (spring only)

Weber Rd.

Sacramento River

VACAVILLE

N

THE CENTRAL VALLEY

4

THE CENTRAL VALLEY
Vacaville to Roseville

Trip Planner

EXPLORING

For forty-two miles the interstate cuts across the flat valley. The drive is hot in the summer and can be dangerously foggy in winter.

The Nut Tree is an oasis for well-heeled travelers with its restaurant, shops, and small airport. Its story goes back to pioneer days.

Davis Botanical Park is better known as Putah Creek Park on the Davis campus of the University of California. Marked specimens follow the edge of a small lake and the creek.

ALTERNATE LOOP—A COUNTRY DRIVE

This drive is detailed on a map. It is a relaxed forty-two mile drive through farmland to the foothills.

FAVORITE DIVERSIONS—SACRAMENTO

Sutter's Fort and State Indian Museum offer a look at California before the gold rush and at the fort, which was the destination for many of the earliest wagon trains.

The **Old Governor's Mansion** offers guided tours through the mansion used by governors until the 1960s.

The **capitol** has been handsomely refurbished and is surrounded by a park, cool under a canopy of large trees.

The **California State Railroad Museum** displays shiny machines that made transportation history. **Old Town** looks like a stage set from the 1860s.

Discovery Park is on the north side of the city, at the confluence of the American and Sacramento rivers and offers picnicking and fishing.

THE GREAT VALLEY FLOOR

California's Central or Great Valley is a vast plain, impressive in its size and flatness. From aloft in summer and fall, the pattern of cultivated fields resembles an elongated green and golden checkerboard. Geometrical lines of freeways and canals cut across the leaf-vein pattern of the natural drainage system. In wintertime all can be obscured by a billowing fog that gives the Valley the semblance of a giant's bathtub. From end to end it is 400 miles long and approximately 50 miles wide. The states of Rhode Island, New Jersey, Connecticut, and Massachusetts could be contained within it.

The Valley is the state's principal watershed, collecting nearly half of California's water. The Sacramento River flows south from an area around Mt. Shasta, and the San Joaquin River and its tributaries drain the central Sierra. The two rivers become one in the labyrinthian delta region southwest of Sacramento. From there the combined flow exits to the Pacific Ocean via Carquinez Strait, through the Bay, and out the Golden Gate.

A deep trough formed when the Pacific Ocean floor was being subducted under the North American Plate. For millions of years this trench was covered by oceans that lapped against the slopes of ancient hills where the Sierra stands today. Snakelike heads of swimming dinosaurs could have been spotted in the water. Remains from marine plants and animals of this period drifted to the bottom of the trench to become oil and gas fields that now lie deep underground.

When the Sierra was uplifted and became steeper, the rate of erosion increased, bringing layers of sediment to the Valley floor. Finally, melting glaciers sent granitic and volcanic debris downhill in Sierra rivers. When the water reached the Valley floor it fanned out and deposited its cargo. Heavier rocks were left along the eastern edge of the Valley, and the finer silt flowed on further to cover the land with rich alluvial deposits. Sparkles of gold of negligible value joined the sediments of sand, silt, and clay. Mixed with organic remains of living things, these sediments became rich soil, the true gold of the Valley.

The climate of the Valley is almost ideal—for most agricultural plants, that is. Nature's growing season begins in midwinter and continues during the warm spring. Irrigation has lengthened the season through the hot, rainless summer. In summer, coastal fog can creep into the delta and bring a modest cooling, appreciated by crops and people alike.

Dense, low-lying fog blankets the Valley between the infrequent winter storms. On clear nights after rains—when cool air lies close to the ground—the earth radiates its heat, causing the moisture to condense into fog. This is the infamous tule fog, named for the tules or bulrushes that grew extensively throughout the marshy delta. Tule fog may protect crops from freezing temperatures, but it depresses humans by obscuring the sun for days and even weeks on end.

Along with the midwestern plains and the Palouse Valley in Washington, California's Central Valley ranks as a major prairie region. A century ago, before plows disturbed the land, John Muir walked across the Valley to the Sierra, calling it "the greatest of flower gardens." Carpets of wildflowers shared the earth with perennial bunch grasses that stayed green much of the year. Today these hardy grasses have been replaced by immigrant annuals that turn brown by June. Only tiny remnants of the original grasslands remain, some of which contain miniature and colorful fairy rings of wildflowers called vernal pools.

Today's travelers would not guess that much of the Valley was covered by marshes and sloughs until a century ago. Only a quarter of this wetland area is left to attract millions of migrating birds each winter after thousands of acres have been diked to create farmland.

Tangled jungles of deciduous trees, shrubs, and vines once lined the banks of rivers. A few of these *riparian forests* are found all along our corridor. Where they are seen, one can be sure that water is nearby. These plants are similar to eastern varieties but have adapted to the hot, dry climate by keeping their roots wet the year round. In fall the riparian trees become winding threads of gold on the baked, brown plain. In winter their bare, silvered branches stand ghostly in the tule fog.

In the driest and more southerly portions of the Valley, residual salts lie on the land. Here spiny shrubs from Mexico's Sonoran desert and pickleweed of the salt marsh eek out an existence.

Over the last century the Valley's grasslands have been replaced by farmland. Settlers and ranchers were quick to notice that the rich soils and long, hot growing season were ideal for agriculture, especially after year-round water was assured. And how right they were. Today's Central Valley farms are among the world's top producers.

FROM FORT TO CAPITAL CITY

In 1839 two sailing ships and an open launch anchored at the confluence of two rivers near present-day Sacramento. An ebullient Swiss gentleman began barking orders to unload the ships. A German, a Belgian, an Irishman, an Indian, and ten Sandwich Islanders (Hawaiians) began hauling two brass cannons and a mountain of supplies onto the riverbank. The ships departed to the sound of a nine-gun salute, causing local Indians to run for cover and flocks of geese to take to the sky. John Augustus Sutter had chosen the spot to fulfill his dream of a rich settlement in the New World.

Sutter had arrived at a propitious time. The Mexican government of California was concerned about increasing incursions into the Central Valley by American mountain men and trappers from the Pacific Northwest. California's governor was happy to let Sutter settle in the Sacramento Valley, granting the Swiss immigrant Mexican citizenship and 50,000 acres of land.

The volley of shots frightened the local tribes, but within days they were working for Sutter, stomping grass into wet clay to make adobe bricks and clearing the land for crops. Within a year Sutter's outpost of civilization included a large house containing a blacksmith shop, kitchen, and a room for himself. Outbuildings with grass roofs were built by Sutter's Hawaiian crew. Two years later the adobe was surrounded by walls 3 feet thick enclosing a courtyard 500 feet long and 150 feet wide. Sutter's dream of a miniature empire was coming true. He named it New Helvetia after his homeland. He even created a coin of the realm, a tin round with a cut-out star in the middle, which was handed out to Indians for each day of work.

Stories of the rapid growth of Sutter's colony were soon being published in American newspapers east of the Mississippi River. By 1841 the first American pioneers struggled over the Sierra and on to the fort. Then other Americans arrived, some crossing the Sierra, some sailing up the river from San Francisco, and a few coming south from Oregon. Always in need of skilled workers, Sutter hired any and all who wished to stay in New Helvetia. The American population of his empire mushroomed.

Among those who came to Sutter's Fort was a sometime carpenter and handyman named James Marshall. Sutter hired him to supervise a group of Mormons to build a lumber mill on the American River about thirty-five miles east of the fort. Before the mill was completed Marshall was dashing to New Helvetia to confirm his suspicions that the shiny nuggets discovered in the millrace were gold. Sutter's own description of Marshall's fateful disclosure is quoted in this chapter's **Yesterday's Voices.**

News of gold in Sutter's mill soon spread to every corner of the globe. In Paris and Singapore, Boston and New Orleans, piles of baggage lined the docks imprinted with three words: "Sutter's Fort, California." Sutter's dream of a rich, world-famous colony came true.

Nuggets and flakes of gold poured out of the hills in pouches, in saddlebags, and into almost everyone's pocket but Sutter's. Incapable of saying no, he helped anyone who asked a favor. Some took advantage of his philanthropy and stole his stock or failed to repay loans. Sutter's workers left to toil in the gold fields instead of the wheat fields. Wheat rotted before it could be threshed; the lumber mill stood idle, and Sutter lost control of his colony. He sold much of his Sacramento Valley land to pay off his debts, and city lots were laid out on his property near the river. The town-to-be was called Sacramento City, after the river that Spanish explorers had christened Rio del Sacramento, "River of the Sacrament." Overwhelmed by events he could not control, Sutter left his fort and retired to his land on the Feather River near Marysville.

The city that soon surrounded Sutter's crumbling fort became the way station between the coast and the gold fields. Everything and everyone bound for the "diggins" was loaded onto a boat in San Francisco and unloaded at the Sacramento riverbank known as the Embarcadero. Competition was so fierce between the growing number of shipping companies that the price of a San Francisco-to-Sacramento ticket dropped to one dollar. Dock space was so limited that it took more time to unload goods at Sacramento than it did to make the day's journey.

In the first decade of the gold rush, New Helvetia's population of 300 swelled to 14,000. Private postal services, wagon companies, hardware stores, and the inevitable gambling tents quickly filled the town to meet the needs of miners. City lot prices skyrocketed from $200 to $5000. By 1854 Sacramento had grown in influence to the point that it could elect itself capital of the new state.

By 1860 the gold fever had subsided. The easy pickings had disappeared, prompting shrewd miners to turn to former skills. Many began to mine the rich dirt of the Sacramento Valley. Miners-turned-farmers diked off islands in the delta region south and west of the city. There they planted fruit trees and vegetables and made fortunes from produce transported to Sacramento in rowboats and sold on the streets. Other disenchanted miners bought large tracts of land and planted fields of winter wheat. The Valley's wet spring followed by hot, rainless summer produced a hardy grain that did not rot during its journey to market.

While the Central Valley was being transformed into an agricultural cornucopia, its transportation system remained tied to the river and wagon tracks. Dusty summer roads turned to impassable muck as soon as winter rains began, and storms often upset shipping schedules. The need for railroads was acute.

The Valley's first railroad was completed in 1856 and ran twenty-two miles from Sacramento to Folsom. The man who engineered this line, Theodore Judah, dreamed of bigger things, a transcontinental line that could carry California's harvests to the rest of the United States. He convinced four Sacramento merchants that a railroad could be built over the Sierra Nevada, a railroad to link east and west. Together they formed the Central Pacific Railroad Company and began to lobby the U.S. Congress to provide federal construction loans of millions of dollars.

It was no small feat these men accomplished. When Theodore Judah approached Collis Huntington, Mark Hopkins, Charles Crocker, and Leland Stanford to tell them of his plans for a railroad route over Donner Pass, they pledged their own money plus that of a few outside subscribers to finance an accurate survey. Judah finished his survey, and Huntington traveled east to Washington to lobby Congress for a Pacific Railroad Act. That was 1860. By 1862 the legislation authorizing government loans to construct the line was a reality; however, no money would be forthcoming until forty miles of railroad had been built. Frantically the Central Pacific owners tried to sell stock in California and Nevada, but most people thought the whole idea too risky. San Franciscans scoffed at the foolish scheme, deeming it unfeasible. Finally, Huntington began to sell stock in New York, but there was not enough money to insure the

Chinese laborers in the 1870s filling the Secret Town trestle to create an embankment. *(Photo courtesy of the California State Railroad Museum, Sacramento)*

construction of those all-important first miles. Again these merchants put up their own money to employ 800 men to work on the road for one year.

Theodore Judah, who conceived the bold plan and helped lobby for passage of the Pacific Railroad Act of 1862, never saw his dream accomplished. He died of yellow fever in 1863 while traveling to Washington. Only one change was made in his original survey of the Sierra crossing: the line was put through Auburn instead of passing north of the town.

For six and one-half years railroad construction was directed from the hardware store belonging to two of the company's owners. Thousands of Chinese workers were hired to do the back-breaking labor of grading the roadbed and hacking tunnels through the mountains. The Sacramento Embarcadero bustled with activity as whole engines and thousands of iron rails arrived on ships from the east.

In the spring of 1869, twenty years after Sutter's Fort was overrun by gold miners, the Union Pacific and Central Pacific were joined at Promontory Point, Utah. It was obvious to the Central Pacific owners that feeder lines were needed. No sooner had the celebrations ended than track was being laid across the Sacramento Valley to Benicia and south

Twenty-two mules were needed to pull the thresher through waving golden grain in the Valley. (*Nancy Albertson Fremsted collection*)

along the Bay's east shore to Oakland. The Central Pacific owners were also buying up connections to southern California and building lines north to Oregon. At this time the firm changed its name to the Southern Pacific Railroad.

By 1874 the dome of a grandiose new capitol building graced the city skyline not far from Sutter's abandoned fort. The government had scarcely moved in before the building was threatened by floods. Silt from hydraulic mining operations in the foothills was filling the Sacramento River channel. In heavy rainfall years, the river overflowed its banks, flooding farmlands and the state capital. Finally in 1884 legislation was adopted to forbid hydraulic mining companies from dumping their debris into Sierra rivers. Each spring the Sierra runoff contained less silt. The Sacramento River was dredged, and the mud was used to build higher levees to protect the capital and surrounding farmland from possible flooding during runoff after wet winters.

From 1870 to 1890 wheat was king of valley crops. Teams of twenty-two horses were needed to draw the huge threshers harvesting the bountiful crops. Large companies bought out small landowners so that by 1889 more than fifty million bushels of wheat were grown by fewer than thirty ranchers. That year countless river barges bulging with wheat made their way to Port Costa and Crockett along the Carquinez Strait. The grain was loaded onto ships bound for Liverpool and Boston. By the end of the nineteenth century, however, monoculture took its toll and wheat crops diminished in size. The smart farmers understood and began to diversify. Soon fields of wheat gave way to vines, fruit trees, and row crops.

While the rest of America went through cycles of boom and bust, the Valley remained a paradise of opportunity for any willing to work the earth. Dams were built high in the mountains to impound the runoff from melting Sierra snows and to regulate flooding. Irrigation canals embroidered the Valley floor, carrying the river to fertile acres. Even during the worst of the Depression in the 1930s, there was room in the Valley for dust-bowl refugees to find a place in the sun.

In the 1980s the Valley's flat, agricultural land is being eyed by a new brand of entrepreneurs. Former orchards face the chainsaw to make room for warehouses, high-technology computer companies, shopping centers, housing tracts, and parking lots. The residents of the Central Valley are pondering the issue of how much of the world's richest soil will be covered with cement.

Exploring

VACAVILLE TO ROSEVILLE

After Peña Adobe Road, the freeway descends from the last hills of the Inner Coast Ranges. Imagine standing on one of these hills before setting out to cross the Central Valley before you. One day in 1868 John Muir stood on just such a knoll and wrote of his first view of the Valley:

> . . . as far as I could see lay a vast level flower garden, smooth and level like a lake of gold. . . . From the eastern margin of the golden plain arose the whole Sierra. At the base ran a belt of gently sloping purplish foothills lightly dotted with oaks, above that a broad dark zone of coniferous forests, and above this st zone arose the lofty mountain peaks, clad in snow.

Others saw the Valley in a different light. John Bidwell struggled over the Sierra with the first wagon train to enter California. Crossing the Valley in 1841, he wrote:

> Winter had come in earnest, and winter in California then, as now, meant rain. . . . It was wet when we started, and much of the time we traveled through a pouring rain. Streams were out of their banks; gulches were swimming; plains were inundated; indeed, most of the country was overflowed. There were no roads, merely paths, trodden only by Indians and wild game. We were compelled to follow the paths, even when they were under water, for the moment our animals stepped to one side down they went into the mire.

Today you may be lucky enough to cross the Valley on a shimmering day in spring with the Sierra Nevada filling the low horizon to the east. In winter, however, you may grope across in a misty never-never land, all signs of the landscape obliterated.

The interstate enters the Valley at Vacaville, one of the area's oldest towns, which was laid out on land purchased from Don Manuel Vaca and named to honor him. Tall palms reach toward the sky on both sides of the freeway. Perhaps these palms formed the avenue to Señor Vaca's adobe home.

The earliest American settlers here cut wild oats to sell for hay. Later the deep, fertile soils near Vacaville supported thousands of pear and cherry trees, and in springtime the remaining orchards fill with clouds of pink and white blossoms. Your nose will tell you which bulb crop has just been harvested.

THE NUT TREE

Exit on Nut Tree Road. The restaurant complex is located on the north side of the freeway.

The Nut Tree restaurant is a grandiose modern version of the original 1920s fruit stand that served hot and weary travelers crossing the Valley in their newfangled automobiles. Food, train rides, and children's amusements fill the shaded grounds of this historic ranch.

The Nut Tree's owner is a descendant of the pioneer fruit rancher Josiah Allison, who came to California in 1851. Allison didn't find much gold, but he soon realized a fortune could be made from the combination of California climate and soil. He was so entranced by the Valley that he traveled back to Iowa, loaded his family into a wagon, and made the return trip in 1855. He bought some Vaca Valley land and began to farm.

Life was good and Allison encouraged his sister and her daughter to join him. On the trip west his niece, Sally Fox, picked up some nuts near the bank of the Gila River in Arizona. When she arrived in California, she planted the nuts on her uncle's ranch. One tree that sprang from the fertile loam was a black walnut. It grew to magnificent proportions and shaded the original fruit stand as well as later visitors to the larger restaurant and park. After the tree died in 1955, a new one was planted in the same spot by Josiah's daughter and his great-great granddaughter.

On Independence Day in 1921, Josiah's granddaughter constructed a fruit stand under Sally's tree. Nearby was a rocking chair, an American flag, and a sign reading "The Nut Tree." That fruit stand grew into the

Opening Day at the Nut Tree in 1921. What's a summer celebration without watermelon? (*Photo courtesy of the Nut Tree*)

Valley's most famous eatery. It is known for its California cuisine and the small loaves of freshly baked bread served with every meal.

The dirt road that passed Josiah Allison's ranch in 1860 grew into the two lanes of the Northern Lincoln Highway, then the four lanes of U.S. 40, and finally the multilane Interstate 80. An airport was added, and the restaurant became a fly-in lunch stop. During one month in 1983, 2000 people flew in to dine. The Nut Tree Railroad chugs between the airport and the restaurant, providing fun for children of all ages and a shuttle for air travelers.

After satisfying hunger and thirst you may want to wander along the tree-shaded lanes and look at the Harbison House, built by Josiah Allison's daughter in 1906. Faithfully maintained as an example of Valley architecture and containing family heirlooms, it is open to the public only by appointment. A Lincoln Highway marker brought here from Vacaville to commemorate the establishment of this first transcontinental route is on the walk in front of the house.

For many miles the center strip of the interstate is planted with oleanders, whose brilliant red, pink, and white blooms form a colorful garland for highways around California. Oleanders have poisonous leaves, but

FREEWAY WILDLIFE

their long blooming season and complete resistance to smog have made this Mediterranean import a perfect freeway plant.

As you drive along the freeway after Vacaville look for examples of freeway wildlife. Some animals adapt well to the presence of the machine age. Highway rights of way are filled with disturbed soils well watered by runoff from the roadway. Lacy fennel is an instant invader, and cattails appear in the wettest places. Freeway builders install fences that California ground squirrels often choose for their personal lookouts. Male red-winged blackbirds can be heard and seen perched on top of fennel or cattails, ruffling their red epaulets to proclaim their availability to the nearest female. High overhead you may see a white, hawklike bird hovering over the grassland, preparing to dive on an unsuspecting mouse or squirrel. And of course no lowland California roadside is without a meadowlark sitting atop a fence or pole, black-trimmed vest thrust to the sun while singing his cheery song. You may even spot a modern "gas hawk" flying by on its way to Travis Air Force Base.

Just prior to Meridian Road, Dixon Power Station sprouts a forest of powerlines and transformers. This Pacific Gas and Electric Company transfer station funnels energy from four states into the lines heading south. The significance of the Meridian Road name can be appreciated by sighting southward down the line of power poles, which align exactly with the crest of Mt. Diablo. The prominent mountain was used as an orientation point for the federal survey of 1876.

Travelers often hurry through the Valley portion of their journey, either because it is too hot in summer or too foggy and damp in winter. However, if spring pastures are green, exit at Meridian and Weber roads for a short five-minute detour of two miles to see unusual puddles of wildflowers called vernal pools. Turn right onto Weber Road. Just after the intersection of Byrne Road, begin looking on the left.

Vernal pools are small, shallow depressions in fields of natural grasses that fill with winter rain. During early April when warm spring days begin, the water evaporates slowly to reveal magic flower rings. At first white meadow foam will outline the high-water mark of the winter pool. Inside this ring goldfields bloom around a central splash of yellow and white tidytips. Occasionally you may find a centerpiece of blue downingia, or lobelia. All this transpires in a few weeks after winter rains cease and before summer heat begins. After the first onset of blazing summer bakes the grasses brown, the floor of the pool will fill with gray-green eryngium, or thistle celery. To return to the freeway, turn left on Lewis Road, which will intersect the interstate in one mile.

Several miles to the south, The Nature Conservancy maintains the Jepson Prairie Preserve, which protects spectacular vernal pool displays as well as fields of California native grasses. During the season the University of California-Davis (our next stop) offers guided trips to the preserve. Contact the Institute of Ecology at (916) 752-6580 for information.

Field crops begin to line the interstate. Winter plantings of sugar beets predominate. Later in the season wheat, oats, and barley are harvested. In late summer fields of corn, tomatoes, and peppers prosper. By September huge double-trailer trucks cruise down the freeway, filled to overflowing with tomatoes destined for catsup bottles. The orchards along the freeway are mostly almonds and walnuts.

With nearly a year-round growing season, it is no wonder that this valley is such an agricultural giant. Eight California counties are among the ten most productive counties in the United States. In 1980 California's rich loam produced agricultural products worth $13.7 billion. Note the silver siphons curling over the banks of irrigation ditches to deliver water to the fields. Those ditches are connected to a statewide system of canals and reservoirs.

White water towers and multistory buildings proclaim the University of California at Davis, one of the state's nine university campuses, whose agricultural courses and laboratories attract students from around the world. Scientists here have developed many special varieties of grain and fruit. Today Davis, as it is called by its students, is also well known for its departments of viticulture (grape growing) and viniculture (wine making).

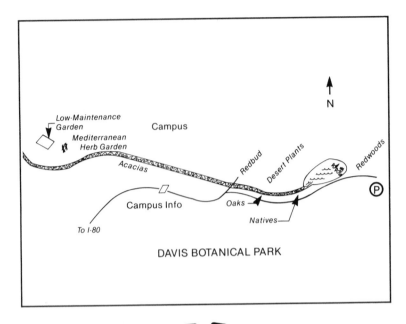

DAVIS BOTANICAL PARK

DAVIS BOTANICAL PARK

Take the U.C.-Davis exit immediately after Route 113. Cross under the freeway and after stopping at the university entrance for a map, park in Lot 5. Cross the road north of the parking lot to the grove of redwood trees. A paved walk follows the south bank of a duck pond and Putah Creek.

This public arboretum features special gardens, in which many species of native plants are identified.

Beyond the pond and across the creek almost under the water tower is an area devoted to California and northern Mexico desert plants. Farther along, at the second bridge, February and March visitors will be rewarded with spectacular displays of blooming redbud shrubs, and acacia trees sweeten the air with the scent from their multitude of yellow flowers. The arboretum includes a daffodil field and a garden of herbs and medicinal plants. A low-maintenance, low-water-consumption garden for Central Valley homes is located on the north side of the creek near the western end of the park.

The town of Davis is well known for its energy conciousness. Bicycles predominate in town and on campus. Housing developments have pioneered the use of solar energy, and the town is dotted with recreational trails. These energy-saving ideas have inspired the visits of many dignitaries, among them President and Mrs. Carter and France's President Mitterand.

Interstate 80 passes the Department of Forestry Nursery and Equipment Facility, east of the Mace Boulevard exit. Row upon row of fire trucks, bulldozers, and other fire-fighting equipment stand in readiness to be moved to hot spots around the state. If you are planning to plant a forest, seedlings are available at about a dollar apiece with a fifty-dollar minimum.

Five miles east of Davis the freeway crosses over the expanse of the Yolo Bypass, part of efforts to live with the Sacramento River during its winter rampages. In an attempt to reduce flooding, tributaries feeding the river have been dammed both to store water for summer use and to regulate runoff. Temporary storage is provided in the bypass for times when winter rains and snowmelt are particularly heavy. By allowing the water to spread out onto a plain, pressure is reduced on levees and dikes downstream in the delta. During severe winters only power poles and trees rise above the inundated land. Spring and summer dust clouds announce farmers plowing fields that have received a gift of topsoil from the floodwaters.

At the end of the elevated causeway, Interstate 80 and Business 80 separate. If you plan to visit Sacramento's **Favorite Diversions**, take Business 80.

Those not stopping should continue on Interstate 80 toward Reno. In a short distance when the freeway becomes elevated, look down on the Sacramento River, trapped between its levees. Before hydraulic mining silt choked the river channel, steamers plied this waterway to Marysville, forty miles north.

At the junction of Interstate 80 and Interstate 5 consider taking the **Alternate Loop** to Newcastle, described on the map. This pastoral, back country byway passes rice fields, vernal pools, horse farms, and valley oaks. Waterfowl greet you around each new turn on this pleasant meander into the foothills.

In Sacramento's eastern outskirts, try to determine where the highway starts to climb up a gentle slope. During the planning of the Central Pacific Railroad, conflict arose over the actual point where the Sierra Nevada commences. Department of the Interior surveyors had placed the range fifty miles east of Sacramento, but the California Supreme Court declared the Sierra edge to be at Newcastle, thirty-one miles east of Sacramento. The "Big Four," as the Central Pacific owners were called, disagreed with both interpretations. The resolution of this issue had important consequences for the railroad, which was to receive $48,000 in government loans for every mile of mountain construction and only $16,000 for each flat mile.

In order to resolve the disagreements, Charles Crocker, one of the owners, took the renowned state geologist J.D. Whitney on a little wagon ride. Crocker explained:

> I had a profile of the road [railroad] from Sacramento City to Truckee Meadows [Reno] with me. I showed it to him. I had a copy of the law and I read that to him. "Now," said I, "Professor, we want to have you decide, or give your opinion of where this spot should be located." The profile showed a perceptible rise from Arcade Creek up [seven miles from Sacramento]. It was getting up faster and faster as we went along. I did not ask him to do anything except that I wished him to decide where true justice would place the western base of the Sierra Nevadas. "Well," he says, "the true base is the Sacramento River, but," said he, "for the purpose of this bill, Arcade Creek is as fair a place as any."

When President Lincoln received Whitney's letter to this effect, he agreed. His decision put $768,000 in the coffers of the Central Pacific, dollars vitally needed to conquer the steep terrain ahead. The Greenback Lane exit marks the approximate point selected by Whitney. Could the name of that road have anything to do with President Lincoln's decision?

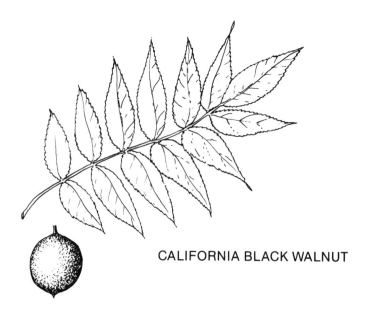

CALIFORNIA BLACK WALNUT

Alternate Loop

Your drive is on two-lane roads used by ranchers and their trucks and tractors. From first rains through spring, this is a particularly scenic byway. Travelers who have never taken a less-traveled road into the Sierra have missed a sense of the Valley as it was. This particular road presents surprises around every turn.

North of Sacramento fields of rice signify California's agribusiness. You have entered Placer County with its ranchettes, horses, and cattle as the first rolling hillocks begin. The soils here are thinner and support only grazing. Lincoln is a typical Valley farming community reminiscent of scenes in the movie *American Graffiti.* Between Lincoln and Newcastle steeper hills are wondrously diverse with handsome oaks, creekside vegetation, orchards, and granite boulders.

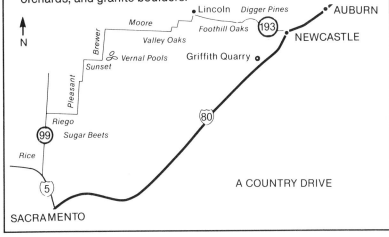

Favorite Diversions

SACRAMENTO POINTS OF INTEREST

Take Business 80 in west Sacramento. In the middle of town the freeway curves north and is marked Business 80 to Reno. Take the N Street offramp and turn left on L. There is easy parking at each stop.

Business 80 crosses the Sacramento River. To the south are the harbor, locks, and deep-water canal which were built after the natural river channel became too shallow for shipping. Ocean-going ships can be seen from the freeway and appear to sit in the middle of the fields. Large mounds are probably woodchips. Most of the ships are likely to be Japanese. Sierra lumber products are trucked here and then shipped to Japan, where they are pressed into particle boards and sold back to the United States for building materials.

SUTTER'S FORT AND STATE INDIAN MUSEUM

This state park is on L Street. Metered parking is available all around the block. There is a small admission charge at the fort.

The grounds surrounding the museum and fort include giant sequoias, sycamores, and incense cedars. Around the duck pond are native willow and cottonwood trees, grapevines, and a spice bush shrub with red blooms in late May. The leaves were used by pioneer women to provide fragrance in their cedar chests. Two venerable Fremont cottonwoods are on the northern edge of the park, one left where it fell a few years ago.

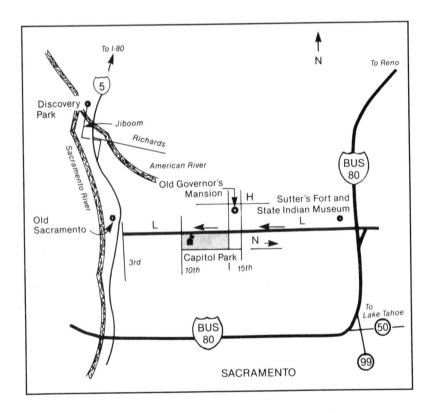

They may have beckoned Sutter to this low hill where he placed his fort above the rivers, safe from floods.

When you stand in the entrance to the fort, imagine that it is 1846. Indians dressed in blue pantaloons and white shirts and with red handkerchiefs tied around their heads stand guard by the gate. Ten similarly dressed guards are drilling in the courtyard. Others, not so proudly adorned, are being herded to the fields. The fort seethes with activity. Anvils clang in the blacksmith shop. The saws in the carpentry shop are worked by Indians, and mules drive a flour mill. The granary is bursting with wheat, and ovens are already heating to bake the day's supply of bread. Mules are being loaded with piles of sleek beaver pelts trapped along rivers to the north. While the age of fur trapping is drawing to a close, the time of pioneer wagon trains has begun. It is very obvious in this year of 1846 that there are many Americans living and working around the fort. The recently arrived are easily distinguished by their tattered, travel-worn clothing. If you are an important visitor, Sutter already knows of your coming. You are ushered immediately into his office in the adobe house before you. Dressed in frock coat and cravat, Sutter offers you a glass of his own brandy made on the premises.

John Augustus Sutter was born in 1803. He married in 1826 and moved to his wife's hometown in Switzerland hoping to become a wealthy merchant. His commercial ventures were marked by unbounded optimism mixed with financial mismanagement. There was always a new scheme to pursue that would bring him instant wealth. By 1834 Sutter had to leave his family and homeland in order to avoid incarceration in debtors' prison. Five years later he arrived in Yerba Buena on a ship from the Sandwich Islands (Hawaii). After selling his cargo he obtained permission to settle inland. He sought land far away from established ranchos and from the colonial capital at Monterey. Sutter's dream of wealth and influence did not include meddling bureaucrats to oversee his operations. He was lucky that the Mexican government wished to encourage settlement of the inland valleys of California.

Sutter named his colony New Helvetia, and for several years his enterprises prospered, allowing him to purchase other lands in California and send for his family. Sutter was generous to a fault, helping desperate pioneers who straggled over the mountains between 1841 and 1848, many of whom never paid him back. Ironically, his fortunes declined after gold was discovered in his American River mill near Coloma. He trusted both partners and employees so that fortune hunters found ways to swindle him and squatters took over much of his land.

When the Mexican deeds to Sutter's land grants mysteriously burned in the office of his lawyer, he was ruined. After years in court, only a small portion of his vast landholdings were ruled valid, and even those were contested by the new American settlers. Embittered and impoverished, Sutter moved to Washington, D.C., to seek reimburse-ment for the aid he had given to hundreds of pioneers. He died in 1871, still trying to get Congress to act.

The crumbling fort was purchased in 1890 by the Native Sons of the Golden West and donated to the state a year later. Perhaps some of the legislators who voted to remember Sutter by providing funds to restore his fort did so because their families had received Sutter's help. When reconstruction of the missing walls began, the only set of original plans was found in Germany. At one time Sutter had sent a booklet to Germany describing the fort and encouraging immigration to New Helvetia.

State Indian Museum

Living history experiences are offered by museum staff to teachers who wish to give their students this kind of experiential learning. Classes spend a night at Sutter's Fort and learn to grind acorns, make simple tools, and play native games.

The State Indian Museum offers an introduction to life in California before the Europeans came. Immediately to the left of the entrance a map outlines the regions occupied by each of the forty California Indian tribes. Imagine Interstate 80 on this map; it crosses the lands of the Ohlone (Costanoan), Wintun, Miwok, Maidu, and Washoe in California and the Washoe and Paiute in Nevada.

With the map are a few objects symbolizing the hunting-and-gathering cultures of California and Nevada Indians. These people used carved flints to kill game and baskets beautifully crafted from plant mate-rials to carry the harvest of edible plants. The stone mortar and pestle were used by all to grind nuts or acorns into flour for bread or gruel. All made some kind of garment of animal skins, which was often decorated with bird feathers.

The tour of the museum is best made proceeding in a counterclock-wise direction. Two boats are on display, one a dugout constructed from a redwood tree and the other a reed boat. Such tule boats would have been familiar to the Spaniards living around San Francisco Bay. Only two dec-ades ago Thor Hyerdahl crossed the oceans in reed boats such as these.

This museum has a valuable collection of the tightly woven baskets whose patterns were individually invented by each creator. Plant mate-rial of a contrasting color was used to make the designs. Bird feathers added decorative touches to baskets, clothes, and ceremonial robes. The orange wing feathers of the flicker, head feathers of the acorn wood-pecker, and topknot from the male California quail were highly valued. Young women were known to show off their expertise by making miniature baskets. One, the size of the head of a pin, is displayed under a magnifier for all to see. Baskets made after settlers came have repeated with beads the older designs.

A corner of the museum is devoted to Ishi, the last surviving member of a tribe in northern California. In the early 1900s he was found near Mt. Lassen, having lived alone in the wilderness for almost three years. He was brought to the University of California at Berkeley, where he was befriended by anthropologist A. L. Kroeber. For the next five years he lived at the State Indian Museum in San Francisco where he shared his skills and knowledge with both academics and visitors. From this collaboration we have a detailed record of how one tribe in California lived. By the time Ishi died he had become the most famous native Californian. His former homeland is being proposed for wilderness status.

OLD GOVERNOR'S MANSION

The former governor's mansion is located at 16th and H streets. Guided tours are available Monday through Saturday from 10 A.M. to 4 P.M. The mansion served governors until 1967, when it was turned into a museum. The furnishings and decor reflect earlier times.

CAPITOL BUILDING AND PARK

The capitol building and park are located between 10th and 15th on L Street. Metered parking is usually available on L, and there is a public parking lot at 12th and L.

A brochure identifying the trees in the park is available in the capitol. Park tours leave from the fish pond every noon, Monday through Saturday. Guided tours of the capitol begin at the tour office in the basement of the north wing. Free tickets are available thirty minutes before each hourly tour. If the legislature is in session, visitors can watch the proceedings from the galleries on the third floor.

Sunshine ten months a year and ample water have produced a flourishing park on the state capitol grounds. Spacious lawns are shaded by majestic specimens of Himilayan deodar cedars from the flanks of Mt. Everest, English elms, and magnolias from the southern United States. On the corner of N and 15th streets there is an extensive collection of trees native to California. Here you can inspect the giant sequoia, which normally grows in groves along the western flank of the Sierra Nevada.

The pond just before the east entrance to the capitol is usually filled with mature trout of every species native to California waters. The official state fish, the golden trout, has a red stripe along its side: No fishing, please!

Not far away a statue of Father Junipero Serra, founder of the California mission system, stands over a brass relief map of the state on which the location of each mission is identified. The immensity of the Central Valley is clearly shown.

To see the capitol in its classical glory, walk around to the west portal on 10th Street and climb the steps to the front entrance. The edifice was completed in 1874, a mere fifteen years after Sutter's fort was abandoned. The state's official bicentennial project restored the building to its 1906 grandeur. Replicas of the offices of that period can be found on the first floor. Volunteers are often available to answer your questions. In the secretary of state's office you will find the original, handwritten Constitution of the State of California. The flourishing signature of John A. Sutter adorns the upper-right-hand side and represents the last glorious moment in Sutter's life. Chosen as a delegate to the Constitutional Convention in 1849, he reveled in the attention paid to him as one of California's leading non-Mexican settlers; however, it was while attending the convention in Monterey that Sutter's affairs at the fort began to deteriorate.

THE CALIFORNIA STATE RAILROAD MUSEUM AND OLD TOWN

Drive west on L Street to 5th. Turn right. Turn left in two blocks, following signs to Old Sacramento. A convenient parking lot is located under the freeway at the corner of I and 2nd streets. The California State Railroad Museum and new Sacramento History Center are across 2nd Street. Both charge admission.

Before you enter the railroad museum, stroll across the railroad tracks to the cyclone fence at the river's edge. You will be standing on Sacramento's former Embarcadero, where thousands of forty-niners disembarked and headed east into the hills to seek their fortunes. Before the levee on which you are standing was built, people needed boats to navigate nearby streets during winter months. From this vantage point on January 9, 1863, you might have witnessed the celebration described by the *Sacramento Union*.

The skies smiled yesterday upon a ceremony of vast significance in Sacramento, California and the Union. With rites appropriate to the occasion, . . . ground was formally broken at noon for the commencement of the Central

Floodwaters in downtown Sacramento in 1853. Three years before, a long levee from sixteen- to thirty-feet high had been constructed, but it was unable to contain the raging river. (*California Historical Society, San Francisco*)

Pacific Railroad—the California link of the continental chain that is to unite American communities now divided by thousands of miles of trackless wilderness. . . .

The choice of scene for the ceremony was not favorable to the presence of the gentler sex, but balconies opposite—on Front Street . . .were adorned with a fair delegation. The great preponderance of pantaloons was a disagreeable necessity of the "situation." A stand was erected near the levee . . . and the ends were adorned with the national flag. A general distribution of bundles of hay gave a comparatively dry footing to the crowd. . . . The Sacramento *Union's* Brass Band was stationed on the balcony of the American Exchange Hotel. . . . Two wagons adorned with flags, drawn by horses that were also decorated with the national colors, were stationed near the rostrum, with earth ready to be shoveled out for the railroad embankment. On one of these wagons was a large banner bearing a representation of hands clasped across the continent from the Atlantic to the Pacific, with the prayer of every loyal heart, "May the Bond Be Eternal."

The idea for this great venture had begun in the hardware store once located not far away on K Street. The store has since been moved to the Railroad Museum complex and renovated. Imagine four merchants and their engineer-designer, Theodore Judah, seated around the pot-bellied stove, plotting construction of that first transcontinental railroad line.

Each of the "Big Four" made a distinctive contribution to the project. Collis Huntington, a shrewd politician and gifted persuader, spent most of the 1860s on the east coast buying iron rail and engines and arranging shipment to meet the construction schedules. Mark Hopkins,

Emigrant Train: Second-class coaches to California. (From *Harper's Weekly*, 1886)

Huntington's business partner, minded the store and the finances of the operation. His advice was sought on all aspects of the project, for all had faith in his judgment, honesty, and integrity.

Leland Stanford, who became California's first Republican governor in 1861, is said to have used his connections with President Lincoln to speed up passage of the Pacific Railroad Act. He served as the first president of the Central Pacific Railroad Company, guiding it through its most difficult years. Later he founded the university in Palo Alto that he named in memory of his son, Leland Stanford, Jr.

Charles Crocker was responsible for hiring workers and directing the construction of the railroad. A cheerful man, his enthusiasm infected all who worked for him. It was his idea to hire Chinese workers, whose daring and hard work pushed the roadbed through some of the most treacherous mountain terrain a railroad had ever crossed. Crocker was known to comment when people doubted the abilities of the Chinese to do the job, "If they could build the Chinese Wall, they could surely build a railroad." Although they were paid less than white workers, their hard work completed the railroad seven years ahead of schedule. Because they drank only tea, they did not suffer the malaise of most white workers: morning hangovers and diseases associated with bad drinking water.

The California State Railroad Museum exhibits lovingly refurbished engines and rolling stock of those early years. The *Governor Stanford*, the first engine to ride the rails, was shipped around the horn and offloaded onto the track along the Embarcadero. It chugged east to meet the eastbound Union Pacific Railroad at Promontory Point and celebrate the completion of the line. Other steam engines in shiny new paint jobs and memorabilia from nineteenth-century railroads are handsomely displayed among dioramas of the construction years.

On the Embarcadero side of Front Street you can relive 1876 days in the Central Pacific passenger station. "Be sure to wear your duster, dear, for you wouldn't believe the dust and soot which swirls around you for your week-long trip east," advises a lady in one exhibit. The admission fee for the railroad museum includes the passenger station.

The Eagle Theater, built in 1849, is also on Front Street. It now shows a humorous fifteen-minute presentation of Sacramento's past. Old Sacramento has something for everyone in the family. History buffs will want to peek into the upstairs chambers of the original California Supreme Court in the B.F. Hastings Building. Restaurants and shops along the streets sell food and collectibles to suit any taste.

The Sacramento History Center, due to open in 1985, is next to the railroad museum. Here you can learn the story of Sacramento and its valley.

DISCOVERY PARK

This riverbank park is reached from Richards Boulevard off I-5 in north Sacramento. Follow signs to Jiboom Road, then drive over the green bridge to the parking area.

The park offers a variety of activities such as picnicking, fishing, and wading. There is a boat ramp, and most of the restrooms—including those along trails—are accessible to wheelchairs. In summer a minimal fee is charged.

Discovery Park is a valuable natural resource operated by the County of Sacramento, situated at the confluence of two great California rivers. The Sacramento River begins on Mt. Shasta and drains much of the northern part of the state. Three forks of the American flow down steep canyons from the Sierra crest west of Lake Tahoe and join together in the foothills to cross the Valley's edge and meet the Sacramento at this point.

Discovery Park and its environs give a feeling of the power of spring floods. Nearly every year, usually in late spring, some part of the park is covered by water. Evidence is seen in rubbish caught on branches and flood lines six feet up on tree trunks and concrete abutments. There is no levee here, so water pours over the banks as it did in the last century. In winter the American River fills with silt, turning it a muddy brown color, but in summer it takes on the blue of a high mountain stream.

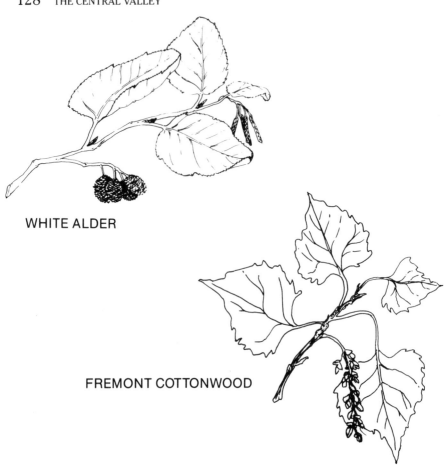

WHITE ALDER

FREMONT COTTONWOOD

What a convenient fishing spot! Here at the meeting of the two rivers a variety of fish pass by on the way to their spawning grounds. In the fall anglers look for salmon and steelhead, and at other times they can fish from the runs of striped bass and shad. Several species of catfish are often caught.

The edges of the rivers and the park's internal slough are covered with a riparian jungle. These are trees and shrubs that stand in water. The king of this jungle is the Fremont cottonwood, with its furrowed bark and cottony seeds. Dense growth of ash, walnut, elderberry, box elder, and buckeye obscure the water. The understory is comprised of buttonwillows (not a true willow), with their spherical seed heads, intertwined with thorny roses, blackberry bushes, and wild grapevines. The riparian forest was a treasure trove for native Californians. Fire drills were made from buckeye or walnut stems. Softer woods like willow and cottonwood contained the fibers that would smolder into flames. Willows provided headache relief, as they contain the same chemical as aspirin. Alder bark was used for its red dye. The water also supported families of otter, beaver, muskrats and raccoons, crawdads, freshwater clams, and many birds.

The Jedediah Smith National Recreational Trail begins near the entrance to the park. Jedediah Smith was the first American explorer to stand at the confluence of the American and Sacramento rivers and the park commemorate's this event. **Yesterday's Voices** relates in Smith's own words his encounter here with a grizzly bear. The trail begins in Old Town and follows the Sacramento River to Discovery Park. It then turns east along the banks of the American River to Folsom. Hopefully, the trail will be extended someday to Auburn and points east. Two former governors of California and Nevada, Ronald Reagan and Paul Laxalt, envisioned a capital-to-capital trail from Sacramento to Carson City.

After you leave the park, take I-5 north to the intersection with I-80 to Reno. For the **Alternate Loop** continue north on I-5.

Yesterday's Voices

THE PATHFINDER MEETS A BEAR

From the diary of Jedediah Smith

In the 1820s Smith led trapping parties across the continent. He is credited with being the first American to enter California from the east. The beaver and other pelts so eagerly sought were carried back to "civilization" to be made into coats and hats.

7th April . . . In the vicinity was considerable appearance of game and particularly bear. In the evening we shot several Bear and they ran into thickets that were convenient. Several of us followed one that was Badly wounded into a thicket. We went on foot because the thicket was too close to admit a Man on horse back.

As we advanced I saw one and shot him in the head when he immediately [tumbled] fell—Apparently dead. I went in to bring him out without loading my gun and when I arrived within 4 yards of the place where the Bear lay the man that was following me close behind spoke and said "He is alive." I told him in answer that he was certainly dead and was observing the one I had shot so intently that I did not see one that lay close by his side which was the one the man behind me had reference to. At that moment the Bear sprang towards us with open mouth and making no pleasant noise.

Fortunately the thicket was close on the bank of the creek and the second spring I plunged head foremost into the water. The Bear ran over the man next to me and made a furious rush on the third man Joseph Lapoint. But Lapoint had by good fortune a Bayonet fixed on his gun and as the Bear came in he gave him a severe wound in the neck which induced him to change his course and run into another thicket close at hand. We followed him there and found another in company with him. One of them we killed and the other went off Badly wounded.

I then went on horse Back with two men to look for another that was wounded. I rode up close to the thicket in which I supposed him to be and rode round it several times halloeing but without making any discovery. I rode up for a last look when the Bear sprang for the horse. He was so close that the horse could not be got underway before he caught him by the tail. The Horse being strong and much frightened exerted himself so powerfully that he gave the Bear no opportunity to close upon him and actually drew him 40 or 50 yards before he relinquished his hold.

The Bear did not continue the pursuit but went off and [I] was quite glad to get rid of his company on any terms and returned to camp to feast on the spoils and talk of the incidents of our eventful hunt. 16 Beaver taken. . . .

From *Jedediah Smith's Journal,* 1828. Reprinted in *California Heritage.*

GOLD!

From the diary of John Sutter

What changes would take place in California after this meeting of Sutter and his nervous employee, James Marshall!

One rainy evening in January 1848, Marshall, dripping with water, hurried excitedly into my office next to the guard house. He asked to see me alone in the "big house" where my private office and the clerk's office were located. I was utterly surprised, because the day before I had sent up everything he required, mill iron and provisions. I could not imagine what he wanted, yet I conducted him to my private rooms, which were furnished with old, clumsy laurel wood furniture made by the Russians at Fort Ross. We entered and I shut the door behind me. Marshall asked me if the door was locked. "No," I replied, "but I shall gladly lock it." I knew that he was a very strange man, and I took the whole thing as a whim of his. There was no gun in the room, but I was not in the least afraid of him. I supposed he acted so queerly because he wanted to tell me some secret which he considered important.

He first said to me: "Are we alone?"

When I replied in the affirmative, he said: "I want two bowls of water."

I rang the bell for a servant and the bowls of water were brought in.

"Now I want a stick of red wood," said Marshall, "and some twine and some sheets of copper."

"But, Marshall," I replied, "why do you need all these things?"

"I want to make some scales," he answered.

"Well," I said, "I have enough scales in the apothecary shop."

"Oh," said Marshall, "I did not think of that." I went myself and got some scales.

When I returned with them, I shut the door but did not lock it again. I considered that entirely unnecessary because the door led to my bed-room. Now Marshall pulled out of his trousers pocket a white cotton rag which contained something rolled up in it. Just as he was unfolding it to show me the contents, the door opened and the clerk, who knew nothing of our presence, passed through the room.

"There," exclaimed Marshall, quickly thrusting the cotton cloth back into his pocket, "didn't I tell you that we had listeners?"

I appeased him, ordered the clerk to retire, and locked the door. Then he brought out his mysterious secret again. Opening the cloth, he held it before me in his hand. It contained what might have been about an ounce and a half of gold dust in flakes and grains. The largest piece was not quite as large as a pea, and the smallest was hardly the size of a pin head.

"I believe this is gold," said Marshall, "but the people at the mill laughed at me and called me crazy."

I carefully examined it and said to him: "Well, it looks like gold. Let us test it."

Then I went to the apothecary shop, got *aqua fortis* and applied it. The stuff stood the test.

Marshall asked me if I had any silver. I said I had and produced a few dollar pieces. Then we placed an equal quantity in weight of gold in one scale and silver in the other. Dropping the two in the bowls of water, the gold went down and outweighed the silver under water. Finally, I brought out a volume of the Encyclopedia Americana, a copy of which happened to be on my book shelf, to see what other tests could be applied. Then I said to him: "I believe this is the finest kind of gold."

From *Diary of John Sutter,* 1848.

AMERICAN ME

By Beatrice Griffith

California's agricultural wealth is due in part to farm workers from Mexico who have been willing to do "stoop labor" in the fields. This story, written several decades ago, gives a sense of the workers' close-knit families and the fact that life cannot be all work without play.

We go every July from Los Angeles to pick the fruits. . . . We lived in tents and would get up early in the grey morning when it was cold. Then we all ate outdoors over a little fire. Everybody getting up from their tents and talking and calling to each other and cooking the beans. Then we go to work and stand on our feet from seven in the morning until six at night. Gee, man, I would get so tired. You know, in the fruits you dream, sleep, walk, breathe, and talk apricots—yellow and big and soft all around you. You pick 'em, you you dump 'em, you squash 'em, you peel 'em, you cut 'em, you count 'em. Everything is apricots. How many you pick? How many you peel? How much buckets or trays? Always it is to eat and smell apricots. Cause apricots is pennies and sometimes they are silver dollars after you pick them a long time. Now we get lots more money in the fruits cause there is a war, and now we can go to the carnival with rich money like the boss of the ranch.

This day I tell you the boss came and paid the checks. Man, it was great. To all the working people and kids he paid them. My father and mother and me and my brother gots a hundred dollars for working three weeks, would you believe it? When I saw that check I told my mother she was fooling. The boss was just playing a game. But she said it was real money, and when I heard that I jumped up crazy I guess. I told her that check was a lot of school dresses. She said that in that check was a couch that made a bed at night for my father and brother who are tired to sleep on the little iron bed by the washing machine. And it was clothes for my brother and my father, and in it was a car. Would you believe it? A little broken car was in that check? And sure it was. Oh I tell you all was happy that night for getting money and lots clothes and food and stuff in that check.

CALIFORNIA POPPY

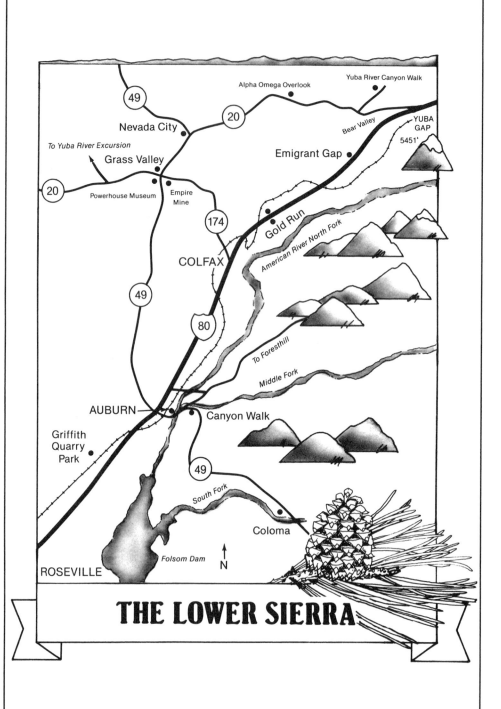

THE LOWER SIERRA

5

THE LOWER SIERRA
Roseville to Yuba Gap

Trip Planner

EXPLORING

For sixty miles the interstate ascends the gentle western
slope of the Sierra from 160 feet to 5360 feet above sea
level. Snow can fall as low as Auburn. Settlements are
located along the way, offering travel facilities.

Griffith Quarry Park is built around an old quarry pit. It
offers nice picnic spots and an introduction to foothill pines
and oaks on quiet trails around the quarry.

Old Auburn is a typical foothill town, part historic and
part with commerce of today. An old firehouse stands near
structures from gold rush days. The fine county museum
displays mining artifacts along with memorabilia from the
last century.

Gold Run Roadside Rest. The stop for travelers heading
east has restrooms and a picnic area in a grove of
closed-cone pines. The stop westward has a newly
renovated interpretive display of hydraulic mining.

Emigrant Gap vista point can only be reached going west. It is situated above the cliffs down which the pioneers lowered their wagons.

ALTERNATE LOOP—AMERICAN RIVER CANYON

The route descends on Route 49 to the **American River Canyon** at the confluence of two forks of the American River and up through an outstanding display of chaparral vegetation. The loop is nine miles and returns to the freeway at the Foresthill exit.

ALTERNATE LOOP—GOLD MINES AND GOLD TOWNS

This loop is a long one to gold rush towns in the northern section of the Mother Lode.

Empire Mine State Park in Grass Valley was one of the richest mines in California. It is preserved as a state park where docents dress in period costumes and reenact the days when the mine's owner entertained his guests from around the world.

Nearby the **Northstar Mine Powerhouse Museum** displays mining history and machinery among old photographs of the mine's heyday.

The **Lola Montez House** is now the home of the Grass Valley Chamber of Commerce. Here you can learn more about this famous dancer and entertainer.

The **Yuba River Gold Diggins Excursion** takes back roads up hills and down canyons past the world's longest covered bridge and to a unique trail built for everyone, including disabled persons.

Nevada City is a charming historic town for a walk. Gaslit streets add to your stroll back in time.

The **Alpha and Omega overlook** views a scene of devastation from hydraulic mining.

The **Yuba River Canyon Walk** offers glimpses of the wooden flumes built by the Chinese on cliffsides a thousand feet above the river.

FAVORITE DIVERSION

Coloma Gold Discovery Site is twenty miles south of Auburn on the main highway through the Mother Lode. The state park there commemorates James Marshall's gold discovery in 1848 and features the reconstructed sawmill.

HILLS AND CANYONS OF GOLD

The western slope of the Sierra rises gradually from the Central Valley, presenting a deeply wrinkled foothill terrain. River canyons separated by flat-topped ridges ascend in a complicated pattern toward the summit. The foothills form a belt of gold between the floor of the Valley and the snow-capped peaks. Golden grasses hide the gold that once lay below in a rich zone stretching from Mariposa to north of Grass Valley. The mile-wide master vein south of Auburn is called the Mother Lode.

One must go back 150 million years to begin the story of California's gold. When the mountains were lower and while molten granite was cooling and solidifying within the earth, super-heated water flowed upward into cracks and joints between the granite and the range's older rocks. These hot solutions carried minerals of gold and quartz, which precipitated when the granite cooled. The result was veins of gold-bearing quartz.

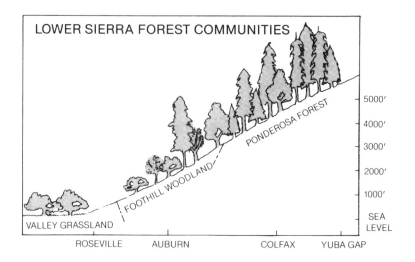

LOWER SIERRA FOREST COMMUNITIES

PONDEROSA FOREST

FOOTHILL WOODLAND

VALLEY GRASSLAND

5000'
4000'
3000'
2000'
1000'
SEA LEVEL

ROSEVILLE   AUBURN   COLFAX   YUBA GAP

About fifty million years ago ancient rivers ran north-south across a gentler Sierra slope, eroding the hills and plucking gold from the quartz veins. Nuggets as big as a fist and tiny golden flakes became mixed with streambed gravels and were deposited in broad valleys. Then the mountains along the crest erupted, spewing ash and rock over the golden riverbeds. An ooze of volcanic mud thousands of feet thick covered everything and came to rest only at the edge of the Central Valley. The "great gold coverup" was complete.

In the last few million years, the Sierra began to tremble and rise upward, lifting the mountains to their present heights. Then, in several episodes, the glaciers covered all but the highest peaks. Just yesterday by geologic standards, melting glaciers released torrents of water that flowed westward, scouring canyons through the ancient volcanic debris. Some of the golden treasure was uncovered and carried into crevices along the riverbeds. The stage was set for the foothills gold drama of 1848.

Lying between the Central Valley and the snowy High Sierra, the Lower Sierra borrows climate from both neighbors. On summer days hot valley air rises to bake the hills and snuff out the short lives of flowers and grasses. At night cool mountain air descends. Fall air becomes frosty, sparking leaves to color and giving local apples a distinctive crunch. Winter tule fogs seldom reach beyond the lower hills, and snow falls infrequently. Spring is short. Warmth moves up the slope to liberate the deep snowpack at the higher elevations into frothy cascades filling every streambed.

Innumerable physical conditions exist on the Sierra's western slope, such as differing soil types, exposures, precipitations, and temperatures. Soils can be derived from volcanic, granitic, serpentine, or sedimentary rocks. Granite soils are relatively poor, and volcanic soils host an array of wildflowers. Rivers have sliced deep canyons westward down the slope, resulting in sunny canyonsides facing shady ones. Rainfall might be fifteen inches on the lower slopes and up to sixty inches at the crest of the range. The gain in elevation provides changeable winter conditions as the temperature lowers about five degrees for each 1000 feet of rise; thus, rain at Auburn may become snow near the summit.

Called by some the green wall, the lower slopes are banded with five different forest communities. Unfortunately for the observer, the demarcations are not clearly defined; however, the *foothill woodland* and *ponderosa forest* communities are most widespread.

At the edge of the Valley, grasslands blend into foothill woodlands. Rounded hills are covered with wild oats and dotted with drought-resistant trees. The reflective colors of the blue oaks and of the grayish digger pines are believed to play a part in the ability of these trees to minimize water loss. A characteristic tree, the buckeye, has reacted to the water problem in another manner: it drops its leaves during the hot, rainless summer.

Where the foothill woodland community and ponderosa forest overlap is a localized phenomenon; chaparral plants of chamise, manzanita, and toyon survive on the hotter, sunny slopes. Across the canyon in the shade the canyon forest community thrives, with evergreen oaks and Douglas fir reaching skyward among the red trunks of shiny-leafed

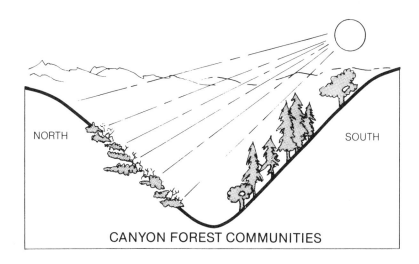

NORTH

SOUTH

CANYON FOREST COMMUNITIES

madrone. Certain plants of both communities have adapted to fires by being dependent upon the extreme heat for germination of their seeds. Others sprout from the burned root crowns.

The ponderosa forest begins where the climate is somewhat cooler and moister than at lower elevations; it is a living museum of trees that have needles rather than leaves. Its predominant plant is, naturally, the ponderosa pine, known throughout the West as yellow pine and a favorite of the lumber industry. Its branches, encircled by long, dark-green needles, resemble large bottle brushes. Above the conical ponderosas rise the sugar pines, which hold sparsely needled branches straight out. Sometimes two-foot-long cones dangle from the tips of the topmost limbs.

Scattered in this forest are Douglas fir and white fir as well as incense cedar, whose scales look as if they have been pressed flat with an iron. All of these trees are better able to reproduce in forest shade than the ponderosa, so unless fire or lumbering opens an area to sunlight, these conifers will eventually take over. For variety, one deciduous tree, the Kellogg oak, can be spotted.

THE DIGGINS

On January 28, 1848, just four days before Mexico deeded its California province to the United States, James Marshall was rushing to confirm with his boss that he had indeed found gold in Sutter's American River mill. When spring wildflowers splashed blue and gold across the fields, the mad dash to find gold was on. California's few coastal towns emptied as the first miners headed for the hills by foot, on mules or horses, or in wagons. All were amateurs whose tools were frying pans, bowls, picks, and shovels. One man is reported to have arrived with nothing but a penknife to poke among the river rocks.

The first efforts extracted gold from surface deposits by placer mining. A miner could make a fortune by digging up some gravel or dirt from a streambed and putting it in an oversized pan with water, which he swirled and tilted often to let the dirty water flow out. With time and patience the silt and sand were washed away, leaving heavy flakes of gold—or an occasional nugget—shining from the bottom of the pan.

By the end of the first season of mining, several millions of dollars worth of gold had been washed from foothill riverbeds or dry diggings by 10,000 lucky miners. Remarkably, crime was unknown during this first year. No claims were jumped, and bags of gold could be left undisturbed in a tent; it was almost easier to gather gold than to steal it.

In 1849 rumors of gold were declared a fact by none other than President James Polk, and California gold fever became an international epidemic. That year 100,000 newcomers, mostly men between the ages of eighteen and thirty, rushed to the Sierra foothills, bringing with them a vibrant mix of languages and cultures. Germans panned beside Welshmen, Peruvians dug next to Frenchmen, and Bostonians worked near Englishmen whose grandfathers had shot at Americans in the Revolutionary War. California's first census reflected a cultural diversity heretofore unknown in the world. Forty percent of the inhabitants were from foreign lands.

Settlements sprang up like mushrooms after rain. The names of these towns were as colorful as miners' talk: Rich Dry Diggins, You Bet, Drunkard's Bar, and Rough and Ready. Most of these new towns were temporary mining camps. When the nearby diggings were exhausted or when rumors spread of a rich strike upstream or over the next hill, the tents came down only to sprout up again with a new name. Near the richest foothill diggings, canvas camps were replaced by wooden towns. These towns had the trappings of civilization—a hotel, theater, newspaper, doctor, stores, an abundance of saloons, and even regular mail service. Miraculously, letters from faroff loved ones reached miners with as little address as "Diggins along the American." Mail sent home to New York, St. Louis, and Charleston lured even more people to make the overland journey to the gold fields, and families soon were traveling the now wellworn routes over the Sierra; the foothill population quickly swelled to 200,000. A new kind of miner also came to town in the 1850s, one who found it easier to rob a stage or take gamblers' gold at gaming tables than poke around in cold rivers.

For the first several years men mined with shovel and pan until the placer deposits were exhausted. New methods were needed to get at gold buried in the volcanic ridges. In 1852 Anthony Chabot gravity-fed a stream of water into a canvas hose to wash the golden gravel in his sluice box. A year later Edward E. Matteson attached a nozzle to a canvas hose to concentrate water flowing downhill. The increased pressure produced a stream of water powerful enough to demolish a hillside in minutes instead of days. His device, called a *monitor,* was nicknamed "Little Giant." Water-rights claims became almost as valuable as gold claims and just as hard to find. By 1853 hydraulic mining was born; it was to continue for thirty years.

Companies were formed to take part in the lucrative new business. The need to transport water from high in the Sierra became paramount. Chinese laborers found work hanging wooden channels called flumes from cliffs and digging ditches across the forest floor to bring water downslope to the gold. During one season it is estimated that 425 hydraulic mining companies were using seventy-two million gallons of water a day, enough to supply the needs of a modern city of half a million people. By this time mining was big business, and service industries for mining flourished. The foothills rang with the sound of ax and saw as lumbermen toiled to provide wood for flumes. Hauling companies were formed to bring machinery from Sacramento on private toll roads built over former wagon tracks and Indian trails.

For nearly thirty years the water cannons devastated hillsides in an area 120 miles long and 30 miles wide. The land still bears the scars of these operations, but some of the flumes that fed the "Little Giants" now bring water to foothill farms and towns.

At the same time that hydraulic mining companies were reshaping the landscape, gold-bearing quartz veins were discovered deep in the earth. Corporations brought capital and engineering knowledge together to exploit these new deposits. Miners who had worked for themselves were now employed by huge mining companies for three dollars a day. The deep, hard-rock mines brought unbelievable prosperity to towns like Grass Valley, where more than $900 million would be chipped from the earth's bowels before the mines closed.

Perhaps the sorriest pieces of foothill history were the systematic exclusion of Indian and Spanish-speaking miners from employment and the organized campaign in the 1870s to run the Chinese out of certain towns. The Chinese were such hard workers that whites feared for their jobs in mines and lumber mills. Unable to find jobs, the Chinese inaugurated a new episode of placer mining. They laboriously worked old tailings, finding enough flakes for meager incomes.

As the economic importance of gold mining declined in this century, the prosperity of foothill towns suffered. By the time the last mines were closed during World War II, some gold-country towns had been all but abandoned. Those that survived remained in a backwater. Their populations shrank as their young people moved elsewhere to find work. Historic buildings were left to fall into ruin.

In the 1970s gold-country towns began to flourish again as a new wave of immigrants seeking a slower pace gravitated to the foothills. Some newcomers renovated old buildings into quaint bed-and-breakfast inns. Others opened shops to sell collectibles to a generation of homeowners who had suddenly discovered Victoriana. Still others turned carpentry, weaving, and potting skills into profits by selling "handmades" to tourists. Historical societies have supported museums and have reopened mines to visitors.

The deregulation of gold prices in the early 1970s followed by an enormous rise in the value of gold brought a new wave of prospectors to the foothills. These modern gold seekers use scuba gear and suction pumps to search for gold in river bottoms. Just a few flakes a day can bring in several hundred dollars a month. A handful of hard rock mines have also recommenced limited operations.

Exploring

ROSEVILLE TO YUBA GAP

Interstate 80 climbs the gentle western slope on the Sierra Nevada on a ridge between the north fork of the American River and the Yuba and Bear rivers. This ridge is one of many similar volcanic plateaus separating northern Sierra rivers. The highway rises from 160 feet at Roseville to 5360 feet at Yuba Gap. Starting in the grasslands of the valley floor you will pass through the foothill woodland and ponderosa forests of the Lower Sierra. Sunny, south-facing roadcuts will contain chaparral species, and shaded, north-facing road cuts will sprout young Douglas firs, an indicator species of the canyon forest community.

It is important to be attuned to weather in winter. When storms sweep in off the Pacific on arctic air from Alaska, you can encounter snow as far downslope as Auburn. You may travel this route in the midst of a warm storm from Hawaii, however, and find rain all the way across the summit.

The foothills rise before you as the road leaves Roseville on its ascent to Penryn. On clear days from November to May the snowy Sierra crest fills the distant horizon. Roadcuts near the Douglas Boulevard exit provide evidence of the lava mudflows that poured down the flanks of the ancient Sierra during an era of violent volcanic activity, when a muddy slurry oozed downhill to this point almost eighty miles from the crest. To see better examples of the mudflow and lovely vernal pools in spring, take the Douglas exit east to Sierra College Boulevard and back to the interstate.

Immediately after the Atlantic Street exit on the south side of the highway you can see the rumpled terrain left by hydraulic mining operations. East of Rocklin Road and near the Penryn exit look for light-gray, rounded, weathered rocks rising out of the meadows like free-form sculptures. These are granite boulders, the first indication of the Sierra Nevada batholith.

The Penryn exit leads to a quarry established by a perceptive Welsh immigrant who exploited the local outcroppings. His quarry provided some of the finest granite in the state and was used in the construction of such buildings as the state capitol, the San Francisco Mint, and Ft. Point. Griffith named the town nearby Penryn after his Welsh birthplace and the site of a slate quarry where he and his father had worked.

GRIFFITH QUARRY PARK

Take the Penryn exit and follow the signs. Drive one mile north on Penryn Road and turn right onto Taylor Road for another mile. A picnic lunch and walk will take approximately one hour.

This Placer County park is open during daylight hours. You can stroll among native trees, walk around the abandoned quarry, or on weekends visit a tiny museum built from the granite carved here.

When Griffith arrived in California in 1853, he tried his luck at gold mining in Coloma. Like many other pioneer gold seekers, he soon decided that he could make more money using professional skills he had learned at home. His first quarry was in Folsom, but it closed when that rail line shut down. Griffith chose this spot for a second quarry for both its good quality granite and its proximity to the Central Pacific Railroad.

A quarter-mile trail starts at the wooden sign describing the quarry and soon reaches the edge of a cavernous pit. The trail around the quarry hole is safe and has railings where needed. Picnic tables are nestled among digger pines of the foothill woodland. The tree's common name is thought to come from the pioneer description of local Indians

DIGGER PINE

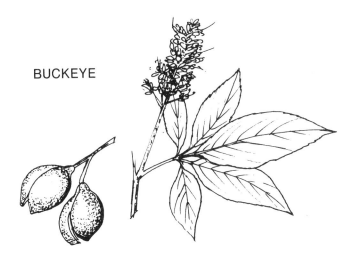

BUCKEYE

who dug bulbs with sharpened sticks. A digger pine does not provide much shade, but the sparse gray foliage reflects some of the intense summer sunlight.

In May and June white flower clusters of buckeye look like candles. Myriad insects visit this cylindrical lunch counter, but only one flower in a group is pollinated. The resulting large, brown nut falls to the ground in autumn when its soft covering opens. The buckeye nut contains a substance that tranquilizes fish. Indians crushed the nuts, which they then threw into a pond. Stunned fish rose to the surface and were easily netted.

Springtime visitors are rewarded with sweet-smelling, white flower clusters of wild lilac. Its common name is buck brush because of its value as deer forage. Wildflowers such as blue brodiaea and lupines, red paintbrush, and orange poppies embroider the trail's edge.

The willows lining the ponds are part of the freshwater marsh community. These ponds are covered by green duckweed plants, whose flowers are the smallest in the world. The name refers to the fact that the plants are carried from pond to pond on ducks' webbed feet. Often you can hear bullfrogs *harrumph* before they plop into the water. Good frog spotters may see a bullfrog's eyes raised like periscopes above the light-green duckweed scum. Scaly lizards frequent fractured granite cliffs above the quarry ponds.

To return to the freeway, take Taylor Road east until it intersects I-80 at Newcastle.

As you drive toward Auburn in springtime, roadcuts burst into bloom and shimmer blue with flowers of lupine and a wild relative of the garden sweet pea. As late as June, when the grasslands are already baked brown and pink farewell to spring makes its debut, white elderberry blossoms may be spotted. Easterners are familiar with the blue berries, which make excellent jam and wine.

After miles of straight highway the road begins a series of curves and the first elevation marker appears at Newcastle. Winter drivers can sigh with relief as they emerge from dreary miles of tule fog. The first ponderosa pines appear here, dark green and dense above the digger pines. The roadcuts change from granite at Newcastle to vertical beds of brown metamorphic rocks, indicating the beginning of Mother Lode geology.

OLD AUBURN

Exit to Auburn on Maple Street. Parking is available along the street or in a nearby public parking lot.

The statue at the exit commemorates Claude Chana's discovery of gold at Auburn on May 16, 1848, a few month's after Marshall found gold in the millrace at Coloma. Chana, a Frenchman and friend of Marshall, lived some miles northeast of present-day Auburn. When news of the gold discovery reached him, he set out to join in the hunt. The second night out he pitched his tent in a place known now as Auburn Ravine, a dry gulch that transects the present town. He tested the gravel for gold, and the first pan glittered with three sizeable nuggets. He and his companions started tapping the placers that were later dubbed Wood's Dry Diggins.

Auburn Ravine yielded fortunes to the earliest arrivals. One miner was reported to have taken $16,000 from five carts of dirt. With such a reward for a day's work, no wonder Wood's Dry Diggins developed so quickly. Isaac Annis wrote to his daughter in New York in April of 1850, "You have no idea what a rush there is for gold. All this region is full of people. It appears to me there is more men here than there is in the State of New York. You may dig anywhere, and you find some gold but some places is richer than others. If it holds on ten years they will dig up all upper California."

By 1850 there were 1500 miners digging in the ravine and up the hillside above the original strike. Wood's Dry Diggins became North Fork

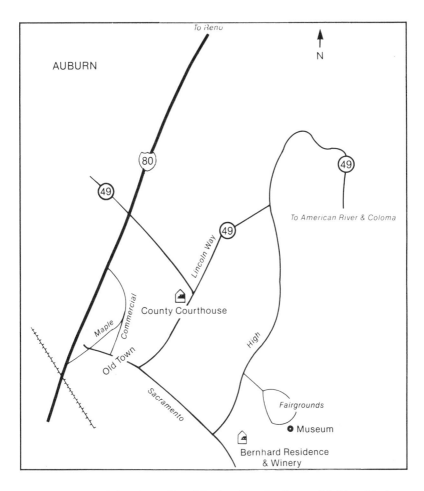

Dry Diggins and then Rich Dry Diggins. Finally, homesick New Yorkers named the town Auburn after their hometown. The name stuck.

A little red firehouse stands near the Maple Street exit. Inside is the first motorized fire engine of the state's oldest volunteer fire department, established in 1852. Gold miners' instant wooden towns were particularly subject to fire, many of them burning to the ground as often as once a year. As soon as town governments existed, volunteer fire departments were organized to provide both protection for citizens and a social club for fire fighters. Posted on the firehouse is a sign for the Northern Lincoln Highway, which passed through Auburn. Next to the fire station is a miniature outdoor museum featuring a rock mortar and pestle used by Indians to grind acorn meal and a large millstone.

Along Commercial Street you can see many of the more permanent structures of brick and stone erected after early fires. A plaque on each building gives its date of construction. One metal storefront in embossed lettering announces that this facade was fabricated by Mesher Bros. and the design patented in 1837. This storefront was probably brought around Cape Horn. Quite a team of horses must have been needed to transport that heavy iron structure from Sacramento.

These restored edifices recall a period when Auburn bustled with the activity of the new frontier. Pioneers brought traditions from their former lives into the rough-and-tumble world of gold mining. As **Yesterday's Voices** relates, Fourth-of-July celebrations were important events complete with brass bands, marching fire fighters, and political speeches. Auburn was chosen to be the seat of Placer County in 1851. In the 1890s the Courthouse was built using local materials: granite, brick, lumber, marble, and terra cotta. It is located on Lincoln Way and is being fully restored in hopes that government offices may soon return.

The Placer County Historical Museum is located on the fairgrounds off High Street, a short drive from Old Town. Its collections are among the best in the Mother Lode. Displays feature gold-mining equipment, Indian baskets, and dolls collected from the trunks and attics of local residents. Around the corner are the Bernhard residence, which dates back to 1851, and the winery. Both are open to the public seven days a week from 10 A.M. to 4 P.M. There is a small admission charge.

Above Auburn, highway plantings include native toyon shrubs with Christmas-red winter berries and redbud trees that dress for spring in red blossoms. Seventy miles of continuous ascent follow, so it is a good idea to check that your car's radiator is full. During the snow season a sign across the freeway at the Foresthill exit announces the chain control checkpoint. When chains are required, no vehicle can pass the checkpoint unless properly equipped. Hardy "chain monkeys" dressed in yellow slickers will attach your chains for about ten dollars.

The road flattens out onto a small plateau at Bowman. Looking south you can see into the chasm of the American River. Along the horizon on clear days you can see the Crystal Range of the Sierra Nevada; from November until May these distant peaks are covered with snow.

At the 2000-foot level you will see a transition from the foothill woodland with its digger pines to the ponderosa forest. The forest is more dense and the green darker. Along with the ponderosa and sugar pine, the bare winter branches of the Kellogg oak contrast with the dark-green conifers. In spring the bursting buds of this oak fill the forest with splashes of pink.

You will become well acquainted with the chaparral shrub, manzanita. Its pale-green, oval leaves contrast with its red bark. In spring, tiny pink bells adorn this bush. One mile west of the Canyon Way exit, look north of the freeway for blackened stumps of fire-ravaged manzanita shrubs and oaks that are almost hidden by new stems. This growth has occurred since a 1977 fire burned the hillside. Opposite the chaparral-covered slopes Douglas fir seedlings are beginning to grow on the shaded roadcuts.

At Applegate and eastward for several miles the roadcuts expose the oldest rocks seen on the trip. These shiny schists were formed before the age of dinosaurs, when most of California lay beneath the sea. Here shrubs radiant with yellow blossoms of Scotch and French broom are invasive members of the legume family.

The Highway 174 exit at Colfax marks the start of the **Alternate Loop** to gold mines and gold towns, where you can visit the state's richest gold mine, walk the gaslit streets of Nevada City, and study the impact of hydraulic mining. The loop returns to the interstate at Yuba Gap.

From Colfax to Donner Pass the railroad will be your companion. The ridge chosen by Theodore Judah for the railroad's gradual ascent proved an excellent choice; even twentieth-century road builders approved. Soon after Colfax a railroad trestle looms above the freeway, marking the first of many intersections between nineteenth- and twentieth-century modes of travel. On the eastern side of the bridge there is a handsome specimen of sugar pine, with cones as long as your forearm.

Take the second Magra Road exit, marked also for Secret Town Road, for a leisurely **Restful Parallel** to the next exit. The slower pace of this byway will allow close inspection of the canyon forest and ponderosa forest. You can easily distinguish Douglas fir by the light-green, new foliage on the tips of the branches in May. Among the Douglas firs are incense cedars with reddish bark reminiscent of redwood and some impressive sugar pines. You can stretch your legs at the pullout by the 3000-foot sign. Below the road you will see fine examples of canyon live oaks. Look for two kinds of leaves on the same tree, those with spiny edges and some with smooth edges. It is as if this tree could not make up its mind about which kind of leaf it prefers. The leaves with spiny edges are found near the ground on younger branches and may discourage browsing deer. As the leaves mature, the edges become smoother. Turn a leaf over and you will notice that the center vein is very straight and the parallel side veins are evenly spaced, the identifying feature of this species of oak. The underside of the leaf is often covered with yellowish hairs, as are the caps on the large acorns. This color gives rise to this tree's common name, the golden cup oak.

GOLD RUN ROADSIDE REST (GOING EAST)

The exit to the roadside rest comes just after the exit to the old town of Gold Run.

The roadside rest affords an excellent opportunity to inspect various conifers. Use the leaf and cone drawings to find examples of ponderosa, Douglas fir, and knobcone pine. If you find small, three-inch cones of Douglas fir on the ground, notice the "mouse-tail" bracts.

Ponderosa pines are the dominant trees of the middle Sierra slopes. Their cones are about four inches long and are distinguishable from cones of their higher-elevation cousins, the Jeffrey pines, by the clawlike spines on the cone scales. The saying goes, "prickly ponderosa, gentle Jeffrey."

The knobcone pine has unusual characteristics. It belongs in the chaparral community and has flimsy needles bunched in threes but slightly twisted. The knobcone's knucklelike cones remain attached to the limbs for many years, opening occasionally in summer hot spells or suddenly after a forest fire. The cone coating is like the heat shield of an astronaut's reentry vehicle. The thick skin smolders slowly during a fire, protecting the seeds until twenty minutes after the flames pass, when the seeds pop out onto the scorched earth. The singed seeds produce seedlings that compete successfully with other pioneer species.

GOLD RUN ROADSIDE REST (GOING WEST)

The exit comes after Dutch Flat. The stop features exhibits describing hydraulic mining operations and the geology of gold formation.

A "Little Giant" water cannon sits on a knoll across from the restrooms. Along the trail leading into the woods beside the geology exhibit, several plaques tell the story of the hydraulic mining process and how it changed the landscape around you. The stunted ponderosa pines throughout the area are fighting for survival in the barren cobblestones of the mining debris.

To continue your trip east, drive west to Gold Run on the frontage road, and turn left onto the bridge to return to the freeway.

A curved headwall dominates the north side of the highway as you leave Gold Run. This cliff was not blasted to make room for the highway;

DOUGLAS FIR

KNOBCONE PINE

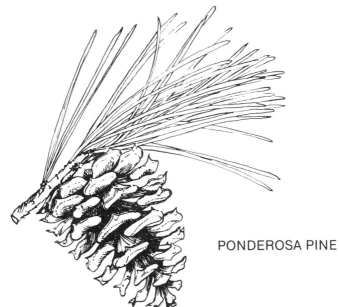

PONDEROSA PINE

its smooth contours were shaped by the water cannons. You are in the heart of one of the most prolific hydraulic mining areas. In 1865 a London firm brought its capital and miners here to exploit the vein of auriferous gravels that was two miles long and one-half mile wide. The gravels went down to a depth of 250 feet. At the height of activity the "Little Giants" were shooting millions of gallons of water a day, creating the cliffs you see nearby. Look south of the highway to see the hummocks of cobblestones left after gold had been extracted from the ore-bearing dirt. One hundred years later few trees are growing. In another hundred years the scars will still be visible.

The Dutch Flat exit leads to a sleepy former mining town and the terminus of the Dutch Flat-to-Donner Lake toll road. For two years, while rails were being laid over the summit, Dutch Flat was an important freight station. The town enjoyed prosperity due to its proximity to Gold Run's hydraulic operations. Today Dutch Flat seems to have remained in the nineteenth century, and history buffs will find interesting the old hotel and site of the drugstore where Theodore Judah first discussed his Donner route with the store's owner, Dr. Strong. A stone building constructed by the Chinese during the 1860s still stands on the road into town. The Monte Vista Inn at the exit has catered to travelers since the opening of U.S. 40. It serves hearty fare amid decor reminiscent of earlier times.

At Baxter the scenery begins to change, because this is the beginning of the zone of heavy snows. The ponderosa forest continues, but the increased precipitation allows dogwood and white fir to proliferate. The shaded slopes entering Baxter are filled with white-blooming dogwood every spring. Not far south of I-80 in Calaveras Redwoods State Park, the northernmost grove of giant sequoias is found. This species of Sierra redwood is both the rarest and most famous member of the ponderosa forest community.

The climb to Blue Canyon begins after Baxter. The name refers to the blue haze produced by hundreds of lumber mills that once operated here to supply the voracious appetites of railroad steam engines. This once-bustling community worked hard to cut down the local forests. When the forests were gone, the community, like so many in these parts, became only a stop on the railroad. When the highway took passengers away from the railroad, the town ceased to exist except for one or two former railroad employees and a few summer residents.

Driving on the ridge above Blue Canyon you enter the Tahoe National Forest. You are now at 5000 feet, and alpine vistas of pale granite peaks are your prelude to the High Sierra. In summer, winter's snow cover is replaced by expanses of granite reflecting the sun's rays to produce the glorious aura that delights photographers and prompted John Muir to call the Sierra "the Range of Light."

The *City of San Francisco* made a long and unexpected stop in the Sierra in 1952. (*Southern Pacific Railroad*)

After Nyack Road the railroad lines are visible on the left. Not far from here one of the fiercest snowstorms on record marooned the luxury train *City of San Francisco* for several days in 1952. Rescue efforts were mounted from the old Nyack Lodge. A forty-man section crew worked day and night to reach the train and its 250 passengers. State highway crews struggled with snowplows to clear the track. Meanwhile, the Donner Summit Ski Patrol skied to the train carrying coal to fire the cook stoves, and Dr. Larry Nelson of Truckee came by dogsled with much-needed medical supplies. Weary passengers wearing pillowcases over their heads to keep warm were led to the comfort of Nyack Lodge. Unfortunately the lodge has been torn down to make way for the interstate.

EMIGRANT GAP VISTA POINT

To reach this vista point while traveling east, drive to Laing Road exit and return to the overlook.

The early emigrants to California found yet another obstacle as they looked west from here. The valley to the south became a precipitous drop to the American River. At a spot not far from this vista point, most chose to make the steep descent to the Bear River Valley. Once on this trail there were advantages—the trail descended gradually and more water was available during summer and fall. The wagon road along the Bear River became the gateway to the Central Valley as well as to the gold diggings near Nevada City. As you stand by the marker, perhaps you can imagine the scene described by John Steele in his diary entry for September 19, 1850.

> . . . we wound by a curving road up a easy slope, to a brink of a precipitous descent of about four hundred yards. All but one yoke of oxen were taken from each wagon, the wheels rough locked, and a line tied to the hind axle by which three or four men held fast, to regulate the motion. The wagons were then shoved off, when one after another thundered down over rocks, through a cloud of dust, into the valley below.

Remarkably few of those wagons ended their journey in a heap at the bottom of that dusty descent. Oxen were rehitched and the wagons headed down along the Bear River. By this time, weary from five or six months on the trail, the endless series of ridges to be navigated before one reached the valley must have discouraged many.

Leaving Emigrant Gap, the interstate begins the final ascent to the summit pass. On your left the train enters the first of thirteen tunnels between here and Donner Summit. Deciduous oaks soon disappear, and forests become filled with towering conifers. At Yuba Gap you will be able to spot Lake Spaulding below on your left. Owned by the Pacific Gas and Electric Company, it is one of many reservoirs collecting runoff from the Sierra's abundant snowfall.

Alternate Loop

AMERICAN RIVER CANYON

Take Highway 49 and then Old Foresthill Road to the stop sign on the new Auburn-to-Foresthill road. Turn left to return to Interstate 80. The total distance is nine miles of country roads.

The trip offers spectacular vistas of the American River canyon. You can walk along an old railroad right-of-way, picnic by a fork of the river in which gold was first found, and inspect chaparral plants.

Highway 49 winds steeply downhill off the ridge toward the confluence of the middle and north forks of the American River. Roadcuts display the greenish, metamorphosed volcanic rocks of the region that support colorful displays of spring wildflowers. Interspersed with the digger
pines are deciduous blue oaks and evergreen interior live oaks, both also
able to tolerate the hot, dry summer.

At the canyon bottom bear right on Highway 49 to the **Favorite
Diversion** to Coloma. To take a walk, park on the Auburn side of the
bridge.

Below, in the river, the remains of an older concrete bridge lie shat-
tered, mute testimony to the power of the spring floods of 1952.
Upstream one can see the converging north and middle forks of the
American River. High above is the span of the Foresthill Bridge, built to
connect that little town to the rest of the world if the Auburn Dam is built.
If it is, this entire area will be several hundred feet below the surface of a
reservoir. The dam construction has been in a state of limbo because of
questions of earthquake hazards and concern for the natural beauty of
the canyon. There are rumors that the dam is again being considered.

The adventurous can walk across the Highway 49 bridge about 100
yards to a trail that takes off westward at a fire gate on an old railroad
right-of-way. This roadbed may someday be a connecting link in the trail
from Discovery Park to Nevada, if the Auburn Dam is not built. Spring
visitors will find blooms of brodiaea and wild onion forming a blue and
white border along the path. Some of these bulbs were used by local
Indians to add variety to their diet.

In early spring the river is full and in wet years a raging torrent. In
summer and autumn the scene changes during the day. Flow can be
reduced to a trickle, but when extra power is needed for air conditioning
in the Valley, water flows through dam generators upstream and the river
rises. Swimming and gold panning can be hazardous, but river rafters
love every minute.

To return to the interstate retrace the route to Auburn or take the
exciting loop back to I-80 on the Foresthill roads. To do this, continue on
the road where you parked the car. This is Old Foresthill Road. Drive
uphill to the stop sign. Turn left and drive over the new bridge back to the
interstate.

Along this road you drive through a true chaparral community on the
steep, south-facing Foresthill Ridge. Take time to get out and feel the heat
of the sun. The predominant plants on these slopes are chaparral manzanita, which have very small, leathery leaves. Most varieties turn their

leaves vertical to the sun, thus protecting their breathing surfaces from the hot rays. Chamise, common from here southward, is a relative of the antelope bush found in Nevada. Fire is a common visitor to these hillsides, but some plants are adapted to resprout and others to release seeds after a conflagration. Look across the canyon at the north-facing slope, where you will see Douglas fir and canyon oak thriving in their shaded habitat.

Alternate Loop

GOLD MINES AND GOLD TOWNS

Take the Highway 174 exit in Colfax; the loop returns to Interstate 80 at Yuba Gap. The route passes through Grass Valley and Nevada City with an optional excursion to the Yuba River and Bridgeport Covered Bridge. The loop may be taken as a four-hour side trip, or you can plan to stay overnight in a gold rush hotel. Westbound travelers can take Highway 20 at Yuba Gap to Nevada City and drive a reverse route. On all but a few winter days this road is passable without chains. If chains are required anywhere below Yuba Gap, Highway 20 is not recommended.

To visit the town of Colfax, stay on Business 174. The remodeled railroad freight station is now called the Fruit Exchange and contains shops and eateries. Colfax was built near the abandoned mining town of Illinoistown. It was named to honor Schuyler Colfax, speaker of the House of Representatives and vice president under President Ulysses Grant. One may assume that the honor was paid Mr. Colfax for his help in passing the Pacific Railroad Act in 1862.

Immediately beyond town, where the business route rejoins Highway 174, you can see on the right the precarious railroad embankment called Cape Horn. In the late 1800s trains stopped here to let tourists out to experience a dizzying view into the gaping chasm of the American River. This frightening vista was remembered as a highlight of the trip. You can stop for a better look at the pullout opposite Knorr Swiss Lane.

The highway begins a curving descent to the Bear River through a forest of Douglas fir and canyon live oak. The road crosses two waterways, the Yuba River encased in concrete as the South Yuba Canal, and the natural channel of the Bear River. The canal is filled with a rushing torrent flowing to lowland cities, whereas the Bear River may be a trickle, its flow reduced by nearby Rollins Lake Dam, visible on the right. To take a trail along the north bank of the Bear River, stop at the pullout after crossing the bridge over the river. The trail will take you downstream past canyon oaks and other plants of the canyon forest. It is legal to pan for gold along the river at this point.

From 1876 until 1942 a railroad trestle spanned the area now filled by the dam. It was one of the highest trestles ever built and carried the Nevada City Narrow Gauge Railroad, often called the *Never Come Never Go Railroad*. Residents of Nevada City and Grass Valley were served by eight scheduled daily arrivals and departures to Colfax and connections with the Southern Pacific main line.

The highway climbs out of the Bear River canyon to an area where springtime meadows are filled with displays of yellow buttercups. You enter the foothill orchard region at Chicago Park where, perhaps, the first settlers hailed from the Windy City. Ranches display signs offering fruit for picking and for sale. On a post in the parking lot of Happy Apple Kitchen a marker notes the 1844 route of the Emigrant Trail. A photograph of the former train trestle over the Bear River is posted just inside the door of the cafe, where delicious smells tempt you to stop for fresh apple pie and lemonade.

The road passes through a sunny ponderosa pine forest. Signs indicate recreational facilities at Rollins Lake and to the 1849 diggins camp known as You Bet. Roadcuts display the region's typical red color that is the result of iron leached from the surface soils by rain.

EMPIRE MINE STATE PARK

After Cedar Ridge follow signs to the Empire Mine. Take East Empire Street into the park, which is open all year. Ranger or docent tours of the grounds and exhibits begin at 1:30 P.M. seven days a week. From Easter to the end of November, weekend tours of the Bourn Cottage and other sights leave the visitor center in the afternoon. On summer Sundays docents in period costumes provide "living history" experiences on the grounds and in the cottage. More than 150 docents volunteer their time to assist the park ranger in interpreting the story of this unusual site.

Hard-rock mining is rumored to have started here in 1850 when Mr. McKnight's cow strayed from her pasture in Grass Valley. In his haste to retrieve the cow, McKnight stubbed his toe on an outcropping of quartz. Much to his amazement, the rock contained golden flecks. He crushed the rock and washed out several dollars worth of gold. Soon everyone was digging deep holes looking for riches.

Most early mining attempts by residents brought only frustration. Gold-bearing quartz veins were difficult to find, and once located they twisted and turned or disappeared deep into the earth. Crushing quartz and extracting its gold required knowledge and equipment beyond the means of amateur miners. Following the elusive golden veins demanded capital, engineering expertise, and skill. Cornish miners migrated to Grass Valley, bringing generations of mining experience; however, the first mine owners lacked the necessary capital to keep the early mines operating.

Finally in 1877 William Bourn, Jr., brought both capital and mining knowledge to Grass Valley. He called upon the talents of his cousin, George Starr, who organized and managed the mine. With Bourn's millions, Starr's management wizardry, and the skills of hardworking Cornish miners, the Empire Mine became the deepest and richest gold mine in California. Its shafts penetrated to a depth of one mile. By the time it closed in the 1940s, $960 million in gold had been dug out.

On a mine tour you see where hundreds of miners were loaded into the skips and dropped at a speed of 800 feet per minute down the shaft. They worked a vast network of tunnels, estimated to be 350 miles long. In this underground maze their only lights were hand-held candles. When the miners emerged at the end of the day, they were required to pass inspection to keep them from stealing chunks of ore.

Don't miss the Bourn Cottage that Billie Bourn, as he was affectionately called, used when he came to inspect his mine. The term *cottage* differentiates this residence from his other mansion in San Francisco and a country home, "Filoli," in San Mateo County. We have Mr. Bourn to thank for grand specimens of pines that shade the spacious lawns and gardens, the only old-growth ponderosa to be seen along our route.

Before you leave the park be sure to inspect the Rowe head frame, a steel tower and ore tramway located within sight of the parking lot. It is one of the last remaining elevator structures used to lower and raise men and ore to and from those deep shafts.

From the parking lot, turn left onto Empire Street to drive into Grass Valley. Cables lining the road were made from the many miles of steel used to transport men, mules, equipment, and ore up and down the inclined shafts. Over four miles of cable served the main shaft of the Empire Mine. The road passes the Bourn Cottage greenhouse, which once raised plants for Golden Gate Park's Strybing Arboretum.

NORTHSTAR MINE POWERHOUSE MUSEUM

To reach the museum, take Empire Street across Highway 49 to Mill Street. Turn right on Mill Street to the museum.

The Northstar Mine Powerhouse Museum is maintained by the Nevada County Historical Society. A fascinating facility, the museum has a large collection of local mining memorabilia including old photographs, dioramas, and the thirty-two-foot-high Pelton Wheel, which looks like a middle-sized Ferris wheel. Water was shot into cups along the wheel's rim to power the mine machinery: pumps to pull a million gallons of unwanted water out of mine shafts, skips to carry men below, and ore carts to bring the wealth to the surface. The Pelton Wheel was invented in Grass Valley and is still used in small hydro projects around the world.

Dioramas of miners at work remind us of the hard life they endured. Rising before sunrise six days a week, many walked miles to climb onto the skips that traveled on slanted rails deep into the earth. (One of these is on view outside the museum entrance.) For ten hours miners blasted, picked, and shoveled quartz into a continuous line of ore carts. It took an hour or more to reach the surface at the end of the day, and miners reached home after sunset. For this they earned three dollars, a good wage by European standards.

LOLA MONTEZ HOUSE

Take Mill Street into Grass Valley to the Lola Montez House, where the chamber of commerce maintains a small museum. The chamber provides maps for your walking tour of Grass Valley. You can also purchase an excellent map of the Lower Sierra, a help if you take the excursion to the Yuba River Gold Diggins between Grass Valley and Nevada City. The chamber is open Monday through Saturday, and helpful personnel will gladly answer your questions.

Lola Montez came to Grass Valley to retire after a career of dancing for royalty in Europe. She arrived in 1851 with a husband and a pet bear and took up residence in this little house. She stayed only two years, and when her husband disappeared after a row, Lola also left town, taking her pet bear. Her greatest contribution to the town may have been her tutelage of Lotta Crabtree, a young girl who lived down the street whose talents led to a fabled career as singer and dancer.

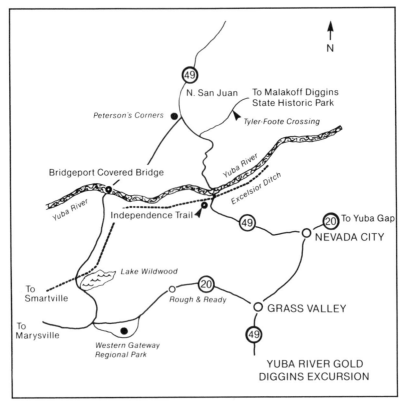

N

49
N. San Juan   To Malakoff Diggins
                   State Historic Park
Peterson's Corners
                   Tyler-Foote Crossing

Yuba River

Bridgeport Covered Bridge

Excelsior Ditch

Yuba River

Independence Trail
                        49   20 To Yuba Gap
                                  NEVADA CITY

Lake Wildwood
To
Smartville   20
              Rough & Ready
                              GRASS VALLEY
To
Marysville   49

Western Gateway
Regional Park
                   YUBA RIVER GOLD
                   DIGGINS EXCURSION

While you wander around town, why not try a Cornish "pastie" (rhymes with *nasty*), the hamburger of the mining era. Miners carried these meat-filled pastry envelopes in their three-tiered, metal lunch pails.

Grass Valley may be one of the few towns that can boast that its streets were paved with gold. In the 1880s quartz rocks from mine tailings were used to provide a hard surface for roadbeds. No one is sure how much gold remained in the road base after the townspeople were found "high-grading" rocks or gravel with a shimmer of gold.

YUBA RIVER GOLD DIGGINS EXCURSION

Take old Highway 20 west out of Grass Valley toward Marysville. The loop returns to Nevada City on Highway 49. Allow several hours for this thirty-five mile drive on winding country roads.

This meander through the Lower Sierra foothills is the home "stomping ground" of one of the authors. The descriptions of two stops are appearing in print for the first time, thanks to his and his wife's efforts to preserve and rehabilitate historic and natural sites.

On the outskirts of Grass Valley you pass the Holbrooke Hotel. At its bar Lola Montez attacked a newspaper editor with a whip for his implications about her European escapades. A few blocks farther is the turnoff for Lyman Gilmore School, named for the local aviator who claimed to have gotten off the ground before the Wright Brothers. A large mural at the school illustrates Gilmore's aeronautical adventures.

In four miles you come to what remains of Rough and Ready, a once-thriving diggings town filled with very independent souls. Stories abound of secession from the Union during the confusing early days of California statehood. Some say that mining taxes sparked the move, others that the citizens wanted to run a scoundrel out of town. Whatever the reason, Rough and Ready seceeded on April 7, 1850. When Fourth of July celebrations approached, however, the town fathers thought better of their actions and rejoined the Union in time to celebrate its founding in a proper fashion. A Secession Day celebration is still held each year the week before the Fourth.

A few miles after Rough and Ready, Penn Valley Road leads to Western Gateway Regional Park, a pleasant stop for a picnic. A modest admission fee is charged on weekends. With its giant oaks and pines, the landscape may remind midwesterners of the Ozarks.

Turn north on Pleasant Valley Road. Lake Wildwood is the midpoint of the once-famous Excelsior Mining Ditch, which brought waters from the south fork of the Yuba River twenty-seven miles down to Smartville (named for Mr. Smart, who had a hotel there). The water in the canal was used to wash eight million cubic yards of dirt from the nearby mountainside and into the Yuba River. The Excelsior Mining Company, though, was small potatoes. Upstream at the Malakoff Diggins, forty million cubic yards of San Juan Ridge were washed into the Yuba River and floated down to Marysville.

Driving this road is to take a journey into the past. On this bumpy stretch you are on the former Virginia Turnpike and Toll Road. Freight wagons rumbled up this privately owned road carrying ore from Virginia City, Nevada. Wagonmasters favored this route as it was less crowded than the Placerville Road (now Highway 50) and was the shortest way from Nevada to low-cost shipping at Marysville. By the mid-1860s, the shorter Donner Lake-to-Dutch Flat toll road connected with the new railroad, thus ending the profitability of this venture.

The Virginia Turnpike's greatest cost was the Bridgeport Covered Bridge over the Yuba River, which has stood here for over 120 years.

When an earlier bridge was washed downstream, builders decided to copy sturdy eastern designs and use expensive timbers. The decision paid off in longevity, for this is the longest single-span covered bridge in the world. Today the bridge is protected by Nevada County and Sequoya Challenge, a private, volunteer organization. They are working together to create a permanent park here that will feature family and wheelchair-accessible swimming and trails in the hope that the California State Parks Department will assume responsibility for the site.

Visitors can park and walk along the bridge, which a century ago would have cost two dollars to cross. A trail bears east on the north side of the bridge. Known as the Sierra Gateway Trail, it offers good views of the canyon and the Lower Sierra. The best swimming is just downstream from the old bridge.

After driving across the auto bridge, continue uphill. You are on San Juan Ridge, one of the richest hydraulic mining regions in California. In the small town of French Corral you may see a historical plaque hidden in the shrubbery. It commemorates the first long-distance telephone line in California. The line was built in 1878 by the Milton Mining and Water Company and other companies operating 320 miles of canals. The telephone helped the companies to regulate water flows along their many miles of flumes. The line helped to save lives when, in 1883, the English Dam upstream failed. Only seven people were killed by the fifty-foot-high wall of water, thanks to quick action by telephone operators. While people were fleeing the oncoming wave, the Oregon Creek Covered Bridge several miles north of here broke loose. It remained intact, turning around in the backwash. When it was hitched up again, workers left it wrong-way-round.

Peterson's Corners is the intersection with Highway 49. Those wishing to explore farther north may go to the old town of San Juan, now a retreat for former city folks with alternative lifestyles and for the Ananda religious organization. At the junction of Oregon Creek and the middle fork of the Yuba are Moonshine Campground and Oregon Creek Picnic Area. The wrong-way bridge is at this site.

One mile south of Peterson's Corners on Highway 49 is Tyler Foote Crossing to Malakoff Diggins State Historic Park. This twenty-seven-mile drive is a half-day adventure on dusty gravel roads to the site of the world's largest hydraulic mine. The mining operations have left bizarre landforms and leaning turrets reminiscent of the barren landscape of Bryce Canyon in Utah. A mile-long tunnel once served as the world's largest sluice box. It separated the millions of dollars worth of gold from the gravels washed off the cliffs.

After Tyler Foote Crossing, Highway 49 makes a steep descent into the canyon of the south fork of the Yuba River. The flumes of the Excelsior Ditch can be seen across the canyon.

After crossing the river, drive one-half mile and look for the sign to Independence Trail. Park on the left side of the road along a high stone wall. This most unusual trail has been constructed *in* the Excelsior flume and allows access to the wilderness to people in wheelchairs. The trail was built in the restored canal by Sequoya Challenge, the same folks who helped save Bridgeport Covered Bridge. In order to purchase the first section of land, zillions of aluminum cans were collected and sold. Along with many gifts from school classes and $4000 from a Marin High School senior class, Sequoya Challenge worked with the State of California to put together a creative scheme to buy two million dollars worth of land at one-third the price. Volunteers escaping the city for a weekend and California Conservation Corps workers have labored together to clear and restore nearly two miles of the old canal and rebuild sections of the flumes. Seven more miles are planned. The finished portions of the trail are a marvel to see. What a thrill it must be for a person in a wheelchair to gaze at small plants at eye level. Within the first mile visitors find a small waterfall and take in the vista of Yuba canyon. Plants from foothill woodland, canyon forest, chaparral, and ponderosa forest communities intermingle at this spot.

Continue on Highway 49 five miles to Nevada City. At the outskirts of town the cemetery on the left has gravestones dating back to the 1850s. Take Coyote Street right several blocks to the Nevada City Chamber of Commerce, where our walking tour begins.

NEVADA CITY

From Grass Valley take Highway 20/49 to Nevada City and exit on Broad Street. Drive over the freeway and turn right onto Coyote Street for one block. The chamber of commerce, in the building next to Ott's Assay Office, is open seven days a week. A free map gives information about historic buildings in town. In this town, curb your wheels as you park, for police love to ticket the violation.

Nevada City traces its roots back to the fall of 1849. Three men prospecting Deer Creek were joined by the Stamps family, who constructed a log cabin nearby. Soon A. B. Caldwell migrated from other diggings and set up a general store. The semiofficial name of the growing collection of cabins was Deer Creek Dry Diggins. By autumn of 1849 there were 1000 people washing the local dirt for gold. A very severe winter followed, and in March of 1850 the citizens elected Mr. Stamps to the position of *alcalde*, Spanish for mayor. They also voted to name the town *Nevada*, the Spanish word for snow covered.

Just when the easy gold diggings were beginning to play out in 1859, a wagonload of ore arrived from over the Sierra to be tested at Ott's Assay Office. To everyone's surprise, the ore contained 60 percent silver and 40 percent gold. The news spread through town like wildfire, and soon all who could were packing over the Sierra to the Comstock Lode in Virginia City. Those mines prospered beyond all expectations, encouraging the territorial settlers to apply for statehood. Imagine the consternation of the citizens of Nevada, California, when the territory surrounding Virginia City became the new state of Nevada in 1864. The citizens of Nevada in California had to make the occasional name Nevada City their permanent name. Some old-timers say that the County of Nevada is shaped like a pistol aimed at the state that stole their city's name.

The following map outlines a short walking tour of Nevada City. Begin your stroll through this historic town at the chamber of commerce office and walk up Commercial Street. Be sure to go into Firehouse Number 1, now a museum operated by the county's historical society. The town's colorful past is on display, and volunteers will be glad to tell you tales of Nevada City. Walk up the hill to the Aaron Sargent House, where a tall redwood tree towers above a grove of rhododendrons surrounding a monument to this editor of the county's first newspaper, who became a representative to the 37th Congress and author of the Pacific Railroad Act.

Turn down Broad Street and walk to the Nevada Theater, which features theater, orchestral events, and galas. Its renovation began in 1965, a century after its doors opened. Among the best-remembered events is the triumphant return of world-renowned opera star Emma Nevada in 1902. Born Emma Wixom in the nearby Alpha Diggins, she lived in Nevada City for a short time while still a girl. She made her debut singing "The Star Spangled Banner" at the tender age of three. Her family moved to Austin, Nevada—another small mining town—where she began her musical education. She went on to Mills Seminary (now Mills College in Oakland) and made her operatic debut in London at the age of twenty-one. A triumphant career took her to opera houses the world over. Emma never forgot her roots, and when she took a stage name, she used the last name of Nevada after the county of her birth and state where she grew up. When she sang "The Last Rose of Summer" from the Nevada Theater steps in 1902, there wasn't a dry eye in town.

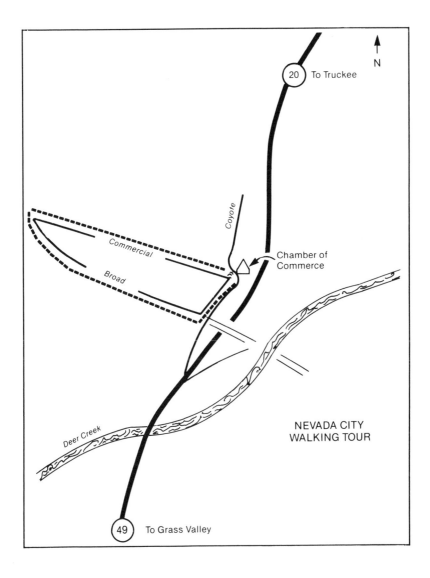

To Truckee

20

N

Coyote

Commercial

Broad

Chamber of
Commerce

NEVADA CITY
WALKING TOUR

Deer Creek

49 To Grass Valley

Explore the National Hotel, in continuous operation since 1854 despite three fires that almost burned it to the ground. It claims to be the state's oldest hostelry. The second floor reception room will take you back to days when red velvet and couches stuffed with horse hair were all the rage. Pages from an early registry are in a glass case near the stairs. You may find names you recognize, for in its prime Nevada City vied with Sonora as the third-largest city in California; many important people came to town.

Returning to your car, you can inspect a hydraulic water cannon on the corner of Broad and Union streets.

To continue, take Highway 20 East, which rejoins Interstate 80 at Yuba Gap in eighteen miles. The road ascends Harmony Ridge, where road-cuts reveal the volcanic mudflows that poured off the Sierra crest millions of years ago. The lower layer of the cut looks like chocolate-chip-cookie dough with large chips floating in dark-brown mud. The upper layer is lighter colored and represents more recent volcanic activity.

Harmony Ridge was the shortcut from Bear Valley to Nevada City for gold-hungry miners in a hurry to reach the diggings. The wagons left the main trail at Bear Valley and pulled up over this ridge, creating a road that eventually became today's highway.

A left turn at Five Mile House leads to Scotts Valley Lake, one of many local irrigation-district lakes offering camping and boating. On the right, about three miles beyond Five Mile House, a lone grave is surrounded by a white picket fence. Isolated and oft forgotten, the historical marker notes that Julius Albert Alperson—born 1855, died 1858—is buried here. The site commemorates all lone graves where loved ones were left behind on the perilous trek west.

Soon after the road enters the Tahoe National Forest, you will come to the attractive White Cloud Picnic and Day Use Area. A few miles farther up the road, stop at the turnout on the north side of the road. Across the canyon of the South Yuba River lie San Juan and Henness ridges. The distinctive, jagged Sierra Buttes are on the horizon. The curious pillar formations on the cliffs below the turnout are wind-eroded volcanic mudflows. Up the highway 200 yards a steep road curves down to Washington, one of the better-preserved Sierra gold-mining towns.

For the next several miles, Highway 20 passes through forests of ponderosa and incense cedar with occasional Douglas fir and dogwood. This area has been logged at least twice since the first emigrants arrived, and most of the current trees are under fifty years of age. When wagons pulled across these last miles to the diggings, the ponderosa pines would have been two to five feet in diameter and widely spaced in a tangled bed of what local Indians called kit-kit-dizze. The pioneers renamed this pesky shrub "mountain misery" because its long roots and runners wound around their wheels, requiring them to hack off the entangled vines, which caused long hours of delay.

THE ALPHA AND OMEGA OVERLOOK

Just beyond the 5000-foot elevation marker, turn left after the brown historic marker into the rest area.

The Alpha and Omega Diggins was one of the largest hydraulic mine operations in the Sierra. Yuba River water was diverted to the Omega Ditch and into wooden flumes hung from granite cliffs hundreds of feet above the Yuba River canyon. The Yuba River Canyon Walk a few miles up the road takes you to a view of remnants of these precarious structures.

Take a brief walk east from the restrooms past the Alpha historic marker. Here you are on the main wagon trail over Harmony Ridge, built nearly ninety years ago. You may find square nails or wagon parts under old-growth pines and white firs.

After you leave the overlook, notice the uniform size of the trees along the road. In 1959 Boy Scouts helped rangers replant this logged-over area. It will be another fifty years before the trees are ready to harvest, for growth is slow at these high elevations, where summers are nearly rainless.

The road climbs to 5400 feet before it descends to the Bear River Valley. Once again volcanic mudflows containing dark, jagged rocks can be seen in the lowest level of the roadcuts; however, there is also evidence of glaciers. A light-colored, sandy soil containing rounded boulders of granite rests on top of the mudflows. This mixture was left when a glacier scooped out the Bear River Valley below. The road flattens out across the valley, which may have been a shallow lake for a brief time after the glaciers melted.

The Placer County line is on a bridge crossing the Bear River, at this point little more than a creek. Several hundred feet above is Interstate 80 and Emigrant Gap. You are looking at the cliff down which pioneers lowered their wagons. Bear Valley was also the main site for Donner Party rescue groups in the spring of 1847. About one-half mile beyond the river, take Bowman Lake Road one mile for a short walk to view the Yuba River canyon.

What hath man wrought? The "monitors" move mountains in search of gold. (*California Historical Society, San Francisco*)

YUBA RIVER CANYON WALK

After one mile Bowman Lake Road crosses a metal flume filled with rushing water. Park just beyond the bridge over the flume. There is a good pullout on the left. Do not climb or try to walk on the flume and do not drink the water.

Walk up the reddish rocky knob and follow the white stripe in the rock. Human-sized, rounded boulders of light-gray granite lie scattered across the surface. They are different from the rock beneath your feet. When a glacier passed this way it carried the granite boulders from several miles northeast of this point. As the ice melted the boulders were left behind, stranded on this rocky promontory. You can find other evidence of glaciers in the form of deep scratches and grooves and places where the rocks have been polished smooth.

Follow the white path still farther until the canyon is before you. The South Yuba River is often quite empty, its water having been diverted in the South Yuba Canal, which you crossed on Highway 174 not far from Colfax. Looking north and west you will see rotted wooden flumes of the Omega Mining Canal that once carried water to the Alpha and Omega Diggins. In **Yesterday's Voices** you will read about the harrowing experiences of one of the Chinese who built such structures.

Returning toward Highway 20 stop at the bridge over the Bear River. You may be lucky enough to catch a glimpse of John Muir's favorite bird, the water ouzel, bobbing up and down on a rock at river's edge. This action gives rise to its other name of dipper. This gray bird with a snub tail is smaller than a robin. The ouzel has a second set of eyelids that enables it to swim and see under water when it dives into streams for the insect larvae it favors. Ouzels nest under waterfalls, raising their young in nests of moss shaped like Eskimo igloos.

At Highway 20 turn left up the hill. The road climbs through woods of big-leaf maples, dogwoods, and aspen. The maples and dogwoods will put on a pink and white display in early summer, and autumn travelers may watch yellow aspen and maple leaves cascade to earth. Corn lilies, reminiscent of eastern skunk cabbage, dot the summer meadows. The highway soon intersects Interstate 80 at Yuba Gap.

Favorite Diversion

COLOMA GOLD DISCOVERY SITE

Take Highway 49 to Coloma, twenty miles south of Auburn.

The Marshall Gold Discovery State Historic Park is an excellent place to learn about the discovery of gold and placer mining. A restored sawmill illustrates lumber milling in the nineteenth century. Try your hand at panning gold under the guidance of state park rangers, and learn the true story of California's gold discovery. There are pleasant picnic facilities at the mill.

The drive down Highway 49 takes you through a landscape little changed since the miners arrived. The highway parallels the middle fork of the American River for a short distance, then crosses a ridge to reach Coloma, which is on the south fork of the American. It is a rollercoaster ride from one volcanic ridge to the next. You are on the Gold Country road, an outgrowth of wagon roads once connecting mining settlements.

Books have been written about the actual date of James Marshall's discovery some time during late January 1848. Some have even hinted that he was not the one to find the nuggets. His crew included several Mormons whose post-facto recollections neither agree with Marshall's account nor with Sutter's diary. We do know that Marshall traveled to Sutter's Fort to show his employer what he had found and to confirm his suspicions that it was gold. There are many accounts of Sutter's desire to keep the discovery secret and even amusing tales surrounding Sutter's inspection of the site early in February. It seems that some of that Morman crew had salted the millrace so that Sutter would find a sizeable piece of gold. Sutter had a ring made from the nugget he was allowed to find, which he proudly displayed to all for many years.

No matter what the actual discovery date was, how many days it took for Sutter to be informed, or how hard Sutter may have tried to keep the fact secret, the cat was let out of the bag when Sam Brannan, a storekeeper at Sutter's Fort, traveled to San Francisco. Brannan took a little prospecting trip into the hills before leaving the fort for San Francisco, the results of which he showed to any and all who would listen in the big city. From that day forward Sam Brannan did not need to pan for gold. He stocked his store with supplies for all those other fortune hunters who rushed to the hills when the news became headlines all over the world.

Yesterday's Voices

THE FOURTH OF JULY

By J.D. Borthwick

Mining was often a lonely occupation. Holidays were a time to remember the traditions of home in combination with very western festivities. This description of the Mother Lode town of Columbia was written by an Englishman.

Early in the forenoon an immense concourse of people had assembled
to take part in the proceedings, and were employing themselves in the
mean time in drinking success to the American eagle, in the numerous
saloons and bar-rooms. The town was all stars and stripes; they fluttered
over nearly every house, and here and there hung suspended across the
street. The day was celebrated in the usual way, with a continual dis-
charge of revolvers, and a vast expenditure of powder in squibs and
crackers, together with an unlimited consumption of brandy. But this
was only the overflowing of individual enthusiasm; the regular pro-
gramme was a procession, a prayer, and an oration.

The procession was headed by about half-a-dozen ladies and a
number of children—the teachers and pupils of a school—who sang
hymns at intervals, when the brass band which accompanied them had
blown themselves out of breath. They were followed by the freemasons,
to the number of a hundred or so, in their aprons and other parapher-
nalia; and after them came a company of about the same number of
horsemen, the most irregular cavalry one could imagine. Whoever could
get a four-legged animal to carry him, joined the ranks; the horses,
mules, and jackasses were all mixed up together. Next came the Hook
and Ladder Company, dragging their hooks and ladders after them in
regular firemen fashion; and after them came three or four hundred
miners, walking two and two, and dragging, in like manner, by a long
rope, a wheelbarrow, in which were placed a pick and shovel, a frying-
pan, an old coffeepot, and a tin cup. They were marshalled by half-a-
dozen miners, with long-handled shovels over their shoulders, and all
sorts of ribbons tied round their old hats to make a show. . . .

The Declaration of Independence was read by a gentleman in a white
neckcloth, and the oration was then delivered by the "orator of the day,"
who was a pale-faced, chubby-cheeked young gentleman, with very
white and extensive shirt-collars. He indulged in a great deal of bunkum
about the Pilgrim Fathers, and Plymouth Rock, the "Blarney-stone of
America," as the Americans call it. . . .

The speech was full of American and local phraseology, but the rich-
ness of the brogue was only the more perceptible from the vain attempt
to disguise it. Many of the Americans sitting near me seemed to think
that the orator was piling up the agony a little too high, and signified
their disapprobation by shouting "Gaas, gaas!" My next neighbour, an
old Yankee, informed me that, in his opinion, "them Pilgrim Fathers were
no better than their neighbours; they left England because they could
not have everything their own way, and in America were more intolerant
of other religions than any one had been of theirs in England. I know all
about 'em," he said, "for I come from right whar they lived."

In the middle of the arena, during the ceremonies, was a cage containing a grizzly bear, who had fought and killed a bull by torchlight the night before. His cage was boarded up, so that he was deprived of the pleasure of seeing what was going on, but he could hear all that was said, and expressed his opinion from time to time by grunting and growling most savagely.

From *Three Years in California*, 1857. Reprinted in *California Heritage.*

CHINA MEN IN THE SIERRA

By Maxine Hong Kingston

Nearly all the other vignettes in this book are first-hand. But in a way this one is, too. The author is the granddaughter of the laborer who risked all to build bridges, flumes, and tunnels in the treacherous Sierra.

When cliffs, sheer drops under impossible overhangs, ended the road, the workers filled the ravines or built bridges over them. They climbed above the site for tunnel or bridge and lowered one another down in wicker baskets made stronger by the lucky words they had painted on four sides. Ah Goong got to be a basketman because he was thin and light. Some basketmen were fifteen-year-old boys. He rode the basket barefoot, so his boots, the kind to stomp snakes with, would not break through the bottom. The basket swung and twirled, and he saw the world sweep underneath him; it was fun in a way, a cold new feeling of doing what had never been done before. Suspended in the quiet sky, he thought all kinds of crazy thoughts, that if a man didn't want to live any more, he could just cut the ropes or, easier, tilt the basket, dip, and never have to worry again. He could spread his arms and the air would momentarily hold him before he fell past the buzzards, hawks, and eagles, and landed impaled on the tip of a sequoia. This high and he didn't see any gods, no Cowboy, no Spinner. He knelt in the basket though he was not bumping his head against the sky. Through the wickerwork, slivers of depths darted like needles, nothing between him and air but thin rattan. Gusts of wind spun the light basket. "Aiya," said Ah Goong. Winds came up under the basket, bouncing it. Neighboring baskets swung together and parted. He and the man next to him looked at each other's faces. They laughed. They might as well have gone to Malaysia to collect bird nests. Those who had done high work there said it had been worse; the birds screamed and scratched at them. Swinging near the cliff, Ah Goong stood up and grabbed it by a twig. He dug holes, then inserted gunpowder and fuses. He worked neither too fast nor too slow, keeping even with the others. The basketmen signaled one another to light the fuses. He struck match after match and dropped the burnt matches over the sides. At last his fuse caught; he waved, and the men above pulled hand over hand hauling him up, pulleys creaking. The scaffolds stood like a row of gibbets. Gallows trees along a ridge. "Hurry, hurry," he said. Some impatient men clambered up their ropes. Ah Goong ran up the ledge road they'd cleared and watched the explosions, which banged almost synchronously, echoes booming like war. He moved his scaffold to the next section of cliff and went down in the basket again, with bags of dirt, and set the next charge.

This time two men were blown up. One knocked out or killed by the explosion fell silently, the other screaming, his arms and legs struggling. A desire shot out of Ah Goong for an arm long enough to reach down and catch them. Much time passed as they fell like plummets. The shreds of baskets and a cowboy hat skimmed and tacked. The winds that pushed birds off course and against mountains did not carry men. Ah Goong also wished that the conscious man would fall faster and get it over with. His hands gripped the ropes, and it was difficult to let go and get on with the work. "It can't happen twice in a row," the basketmen said the next trip down. "Our chances are very good. The trip after an accident is probably the safest one." They raced to their favorite basket, checked and double-checked the four ropes, yanked the strands, tested the pulleys, oiled them, reminded the pulleymen about the signals, and entered the sky again.

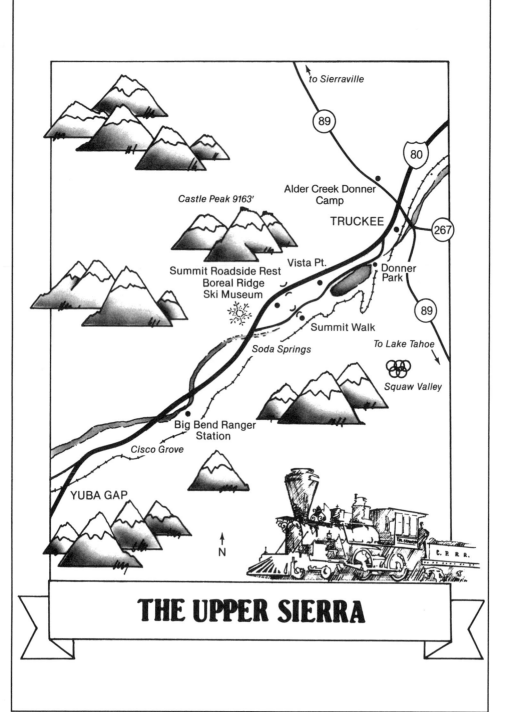

to Sierraville

89

80

Alder Creek Donner
Camp

267

Castle Peak 9163'

TRUCKEE

Vista Pt.

Donner
Park

89

Summit Roadside Rest
Boreal Ridge
Ski Museum

Summit Walk

Soda Springs

To Lake Tahoe

Squaw Valley

Big Bend Ranger
Station

Cisco Grove

YUBA GAP

N

THE UPPER SIERRA

6

THE UPPER SIERRA
Yuba Gap to Truckee

Trip Planner
EXPLORING

Up and over the Sierra summit in twenty-six miles! The interstate is bordered with pines and firs to the pass. Views open up as the highway descends steeply down the drier eastern side.

At **Big Bend** ruts from pioneer wagons can be found ground into the rock. Here is some of the most beautiful polished granite seen on the trip.

The **Boreal Ridge Skisport Museum** is open nearly all year and features stories and cumbersome skis from the American beginnings of the sport. The **summit roadside rest** a short distance east, has picnic spots in the forest.

The **vista point** above Donner Lake features a tableau naming the surrounding peaks.

ALTERNATE LOOP—OVER THE PASS ON OLD U.S. 40

Most tourists miss the quiet beauty and spectacular views of old U.S. 40. It is open only to the pass when snow covers the ground.

The **Donner Summit Walk** is a chance to stretch your legs among plants that can survive the high, windy terrain. The path leads over the rocks where the first wagon train crossed the pass.

FAVORITE DIVERSIONS—TRUCKEE

Donner Memorial Park museum highlights the tragedy and triumph of the Donner Party. The park also has camping and picnic possibilities.

Downtown is fun for window shopping and for a visit to the odd Rocking Stone.

Alder Creek Donner Camp is the last camp of the Donner family and a place to sense the tragedies encountered by the group.

THE SNOW BELT

The 400-mile "snowy range" or Sierra Nevada is one of the longest single mountain ranges in the world. For that reason it is correct to use the singular *Sierra*. The southern peaks are the highest and include Mt. Whitney at over 14,000 feet. The shining, polished granite to which John Muir gave the name the "Range of Light" is beautifully exposed around

Yosemite Park in the central Sierra. Our corridor does not cross the range at its highest pass nor does glowing granite predominate, although there are fine examples along the way. The special beauty of the Donner region is the castellated forms of ancient volcanoes and the reddish coloration of metamorphic rocks that rise from the thick carpet of forest.

The range is young, barely in its infancy according to some geologists. Its rocks tell but one-tenth of the world's history. While the oldest Sierra rocks lay beneath the sea tens of millions of years ago, the North American and Pacific plates began their geologic dance toward each other. Subducted material was heated deep inside the earth into molten rock. As it cooled it became a *batholith*, or single unit of granite, the future bedrock of the Sierra Nevada.

When the Sierra was not so high as today, another series of cataclysmic events began. Volcanoes along the crest produced flows of lava and deposits that covered the range. Starting tens of millions of years later, movement on faults uplifted the granite block on its eastern side. We see evidence of this in the steep escarpment east of the crest and in the longer, gentler slope to the west.

During the Ice Ages all but the highest peaks were buried under hundreds of feet of ice. When the last glaciers melted, the landscape we see today was uncovered. Glaciers had sculpted and polished the granite, exposed roof pendants of older sedimentary rock, and scoured out rocky bowls. Melting snow and ice filled the bowls to form lakes. Lakes also formed behind natural dams of debris, the *terminal moraines* of glaciers. Along our route glaciers left the azure jewel of Donner Lake.

The climate of the High Sierra corresponds to that found from the Canadian border north to the Arctic Circle. Plants and animals survive six-month winters. Storms with fierce winds blow across the peaks for several days at a time, dumping up to six feet of snow. In heavy winters twenty-foot drifts are not uncommon, and snow can remain on north-facing slopes well into the short summer.

West of the crest deep snows along our corridor are released in the spring to fill every river. The Yuba River rises below Donner Summit, and the headwaters of the three forks of the American River form west of Lake Tahoe. Lake Tahoe drains into the Truckee River, which ends its journey in Nevada's Pyramid Lake.

Summer temperatures are pleasantly warm and dry except for occasional thunderstorms. Winds from the west blow hot and dry, bleeding moisture from soil, leaves, and skin. Exposed ridges become alpine deserts.

The snow forest begins about 6000 feet, where the *lodgepole pine-red fir forest* community provides a continuation of the green wall. Lodgepoles are tall pines with short needles in bunches of two and cones the size of a baby's fist. The gray bark flakes off in coin-sized pieces. In and

UPPER SIERRA FOREST COMMUNITIES

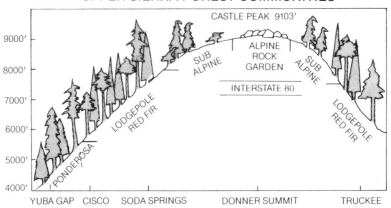

among the lodgepoles where the soil is good grow splendid red firs identified by their dark, furrowed bark and luxuriant clothing of upright single needles along each branch. The canopy of pine and fir branches keeps the forest floor cool, and few other plants live in the deep shade.

Near the summit the ponderosa pine is replaced by its cousin the Jeffrey pine, which in this part of the Sierra lives on both sides of the crest. The Jeffrey can tolerate higher, colder, and drier habitats than ponderosa and often stands proudly on rocky promontories.

Near timberline scattered, gnarled Sierra junipers stand sentinel on rocky, windswept ledges. Low-growing clumps of whitebark pine are joined by the pliant hemlock to make up the forest of the *subalpine forest* community.

Donner Pass is below the treeless mountaintop community of the *alpine rock garden*. A hike up any nearby peak brings you to the top of the world, where life is in miniature. What plants there are hug the ground, often resembling small, green pincushions.

Travelers passing over the summit in winter will find the forest dressed in snow. Should you cross on a summer day, listen to the singing pines and walk among the hemlocks; you will hear the peaceful hymn of the Sierra.

WAGON TRACKS, RAILS, AND SKI TRAILS

The Donner Pass region is filled with American pioneer history and tales of heartbreaking struggles for survival, sometimes lost but always valiant. Evidence abounds of the determination and ingenuity needed to blaze trails, build roads, and blast train tunnels through the granite wall of the Sierra Nevada.

The dominant factor of the High Sierra is snow. It covers the ground at this altitude for six months of the year. Travelers across these mountains—Indians, mountain men, trappers, families in covered wagons, railroad engineers, truckers, and vacationers—have learned, many the hard way, that Sierra snowstorms can be as fierce as any in the world. Emigrants caught in the Truckee basin during their trek west and current inhabitants alike have discovered that winter snows do not quickly melt but build up higher and higher drifts with each new storm, making travel impossible for days at a time.

The natural features of the Upper Sierra Nevada have dictated the course of its human history. For thousands of years before Spanish occupation of California, the Sierra heights were the exclusive summer hunting grounds for Nevada's native tribes, who climbed to the high country to escape the desert heat and to hunt, fish, and gather bulbs and seeds. Remnants of their camps have been found on the eastern shore of Donner Lake.

Until the 1840s the Sierra remained an impenetrable barrier to explorers. The only known route to California was by way of Santa Fe, a roundabout and difficult desert trip ending in the sparsely settled Mexican pueblo of Los Angeles. By 1840, however, Americans had established a trail to Oregon that attracted families eager to homestead the Willamette Valley. In 1841 a wagon train left the Oregon Trail at Fort Hall, Utah, to brave the unknown to California. This pioneer band successfully crossed the Sierra somewhere south of Lake Tahoe, having left their wagons behind.

The most direct route across the Sierra to Sutter's Fort was discovered by the Stevens-Murphy-Townsend Party in 1844. While still in Nevada, this group met a Paiute who directed them up the Truckee River. With the expert leadership of Elisha Stevens, they followed the river until they came to where the Truckee flows close to Donner Lake. It was November and already snowing. The lives of these pioneers were clearly in jeopardy, as none knew which route would lead over the mountains. Elisha Stevens called the group together to confer. Six young people, including two women, were sent ahead with pack animals to follow the Truckee River south. Although their journey was arduous, they made it to Sutter's Fort.

The rest of the party proceeded to Donner Lake. Here they were faced with two feet of snow, more falling, and the prospect of the difficult pass ahead. They camped while exploring the route at the western end of the lake. Six wagons were abandoned, and three young men volunteered to guard them until the owners could return. Not understanding Sierra winters, all thought that wagons would be reclaimed during a winter thaw.

Moses Schallenberger and his two friends built a small cabin at Donner Lake with pine boughs and hides for a roof. They slaughtered a few cows and proceeded to wait out the winter. When the snows continued unabated, they grew alarmed at the lack of game in the area, for they knew their supply of beef was too small to last the winter. They fashioned crude snowshoes and decided to cross the pass. Moses was too weak and sadly returned alone to his hut by the lake. As he recounts in **Yesterday's Voices**, he became obsessed with the need to find game to supplement his meager supply of beef. With very little food for his body and books as food for his soul, he survived until a rescue party found him three months later.

The main party that had gone ahead managed to find a route up the rocky cliffs below Donner Pass. They halted near Big Bend when Mrs. Murphy went into labor and gave birth to a daughter. It continued to storm so fiercely that the group decided to leave the women and children with two men. A cabin was built and the remaining cattle slaughtered. The strongest men walked on to Sutter's Fort for help. They were unable to return for several months, but all survived the ordeal. When Mrs. Murphy learned that she had spent her first California winter by a river called the Yuba, she christened her child Elizabeth Yuba Murphy.

The year of 1845 is marked by the first eastward movement over Donner Pass. An emissary for John Sutter named Caleb Greenwood traveled east to encourage settlers to come to California and to Sutter's New Helvetia in particular. Greenwood arrived in Missouri ready to guide anyone willing to pay him $2.50 per wagon; he is even credited with having urged Oregon-bound pioneers to switch and come to California by telling them that the weather was better. That same year more than fifty wagons made the journey without mishap.

But a successful crossing was not in store for the group that accompanied two Illinois brothers, George and Jacob Donner, in 1846. Lured by the thought of open land and by stories of the healthful climate, they left the main tracks to follow a shortcut described by Lansford Hastings in his book *The Emigrant's Guide to Oregon and California.*

Unfortunately for the Donners, they believed Hastings's book, possibly the most irresponsible and fraudulent guide of them all. Instead of advocating that people follow the Oregon Trail to Fort Hall and then turn south to the Humboldt River, Hastings described a route he had not used but that he declared would save several hundred miles. It left the Oregon Trail 250 miles east of Fort Hall and bore southwest to the Great Salt Lake. The Donners were educated men, and they firmly believed the written word as gospel, so they ignored the warnings of mountain men and followed Hastings's directions into a month-long detour into the canyons of the Wasatch Mountains of Utah. They emerged from this dreadful ordeal exhausted, spiritless, and weeks behind schedule. All other groups were by now ahead of them, including one led by the infamous Hastings. There was no turning back, and they had no inkling of the distance yet to travel. Lacking strong leadership, they became scattered groups of wagons forced to follow the same trail and make camp together at night.

The desert crossing made matters even worse; their oxen were failing and horses were lame. The group was forced to rest for several days along the Truckee River near what would become Reno. Some of the party worried about gathering clouds over the mountains to the west. George Donner, however, knowing that the Stevens Party had crossed successfully in snow, opted to rest his oxen for several days and take a chance on the weather. It was not yet November, and surely the snows would not come yet! A few decided to leave, but the Donners stayed another day. By the time they made the slow ascent up the Truckee River and over the two Dog Valley summits, the Donners were a day behind the rest of their group.

With a storm threatening, George Donner's wagon rolled over on a rocky slide near Alder Creek, and those traveling with him were forced to stop and make repairs. While chiseling a new axle, George sliced his hand. His wife, Tamsen, bound the gaping wound and hastily ordered all to make camp. These makeshift shelters were destined to be their last resting place. The rest of the group was six miles farther along but no better off: they had reached the shores of Donner Lake, but the storm forced them to abandon a try at the pass. Exhausted, they returned to the lakeshore, where one group used Schallenberger's cabin and others built shelters nearby. Completely unprepared for the depth of snow that would accumulate and short on provisions, almost half the party died of starvation either in camp or while attempting to escape. Each family jealously guarded its own supplies, and when food ran out, some survivors were reduced to eating human flesh. A last pathetic group walked over the pass with the remaining children in March, five months after they became snowbound.

Ironically, the pass that Elisha Stevens opened does not bear his name; instead, both pass and lake are named after the Donner Party, whose tragedy was both terrible and unusual. They were the only group to suffer such losses crossing this pass, and their story continues to fascinate as we try to understand the combination of bad luck and bad judgment that brought them so much misery.

Three years later gold-hungry emigrants bypassed the lake and the ruins of the Donner camps in their hurry to reach the diggings. By that time the favored route over the pass cut south of the lake to Coldstream Canyon. There were so many making the crossing that a road was constructed over the pass just south of Donner Peak. A few ruts of that crossing can still be found today.

The construction of the transcontinental railroad played a major role in the history of Donner Summit. Theodore Judah laid out his route close to former trails blazed by the emigrants between Emigrant Gap and the site of Reno. The Central Pacific Railroad crossed the mountains within yards of the spot where the Stevens party dragged its wagons over the summit.

Development of the region came rapidly when a toll road was constructed between Donner Lake and Dutch Flat. In the 1860s it was a main highway for stagecoach passengers and freight from Nevada's Comstock mines. A small way station was established east of Donner Lake. Before long, a jumble of shanties and bars became known as Coburn's Station. It was home for lumbermen and Chinese railroad construction workers.

For two summers and through two winters when snow fell for weeks on end, 10,000 Chinese toiled to complete a railroad engineering miracle. Thirteen tunnels were hacked through Sierran granite at a rate of seven inches per day; many workers lost their lives in treacherous avalanches.

When the first trains rolled through Coburn's Station in June of 1868, thousands cheered. Shortly afterward the shanty town burned to the ground, only to be rebuilt and christened Truckee, after the Paiute who pointed out the pass to the Stevens Party. Truckee grew as a lumbering center, supplying the railroad's insatiable appetite for wood. Sixty-five million board feet of lumber were cut from the pine and fir forests surrounding Truckee and along the river south to Lake Tahoe. As the mountains near town were denuded, lumbermen were forced to new sites. Streams and rivers were funneled into a system of wooden flumes to carry the logs to Truckee mills.

In time, narrow-gauge railroads replaced the flumes, which were then used to carry water to small ponds. When these ponds froze in winter the ice was "harvested," cut in blocks, packed in sawdust, and sent to the Comstock mines to cool miners toiling in oven-like temperatures deep in the earth. Ice was also shipped to the Central Valley to preserve California produce on its journey east. By the late 1890s, however, the Comstock mines began to play out and the hills near town were barren and stump covered. Hard times came.

All was not lost, however. Charles F. McGlashan arrived in Truckee in 1872 to become a schoolteacher. Later he edited the local newspaper and became a lawyer and a leading citizen. He decided to wed the railroad to the area's abundant snowfall and bring prosperity back. He had water sprayed over a fantastic structure in the middle of Truckee and called it an "ice palace," which housed an ice rink and concessions. He talked the railroad management into running excursion trains from San Francisco to Truckee for winter carnivals, thus introducing winter sports to the Sierra. Carnivals, sled races, and a newfangled sport called skiing continued to fill Truckee with trainloads of tourists.

The railroad had been running its own summer excursions. Leaflets extolling the beauties of the Sierra region encouraged people to take the train to Truckee. A relaxing vacation included accommodations in one of Truckee's hotels and excursions to Donner Lake. More adventurous souls were enticed to ride a narrow-gauge train to Lake Tahoe (no longer in existence). There they could take a boat trip around the lake and connect with a stagecoach over the mountains to Carson City, Nevada. A ride on the Virginia and Truckee Railroad to Reno brought them to the main line back to Truckee.

The automobile once again brought hard times to Truckee. When U.S. 40 was opened over Donner Pass, trains stopped at Truckee only twice a day. Auto traffic from the transcontinental highway clogged the town's main street, making it an undesirable vacation haven. When skiers flocked to the slopes after World War II, Truckee had become only a place you drove through on your way to the new resorts.

The 1960 Winter Olympics at Squaw Valley signaled a revival. The new Interstate 80, bypassing Donner Pass, Donner Lake, and Truckee, brought peace to downtown and to summer vacationers at the lake. Just as foothill towns are discovering new gold in their historic pasts, Truckee is working to preserve its old buildings. Skiers crowd new resorts along Lake Tahoe's shore and at Donner Summit, and second-home developments have sprung up around Truckee. The lumber mills are quiet, the ice ponds are now reservoirs for Reno's water, and Truckee remains as it began—a way station for travelers.

Exploring

YUBA GAP TO TRUCKEE

Interstate 80 uses one of the lower passes and the only year-round route over the Sierra. The freeway crosses the summit at 7239 feet through forests of lodgepole pine and red fir. Nearly 2000-feet higher, treeless peaks reveal a volcanic past, their dark buttresses rising above the range's granite base.

At Yuba Gap you have reached the High Sierra. Vistas open up, and it seems as though you are coming to the top of the world. This altitude just below 6000 feet is higher than that of most mountains in New England. Two peaks fill the horizon, Old Man Mountain to the left and Red Peak before you. Summer drivers will notice they have left the oppressive valley heat behind. Lodgepole pines and red firs have replaced the ponderosa pines and Kellogg oaks.

The interstate stays close to the Emigrant Trail from Yuba Gap to the summit. Few traces remain, but as you gaze at the rough terrain think of those weary pioneers urging oxen or mules to drag wagons over this rocky landscape. At the gap, today not more than an hour's drive from Sacramento, those tired emigrants still faced a week or more of hauling wagons over ridges and across rivers before they reached the welcome sight of Sutter's Fort.

Just after the Eagle Lakes Road exit, notice an old roadbed curving up the bank on your right. This is a remnant of the Dutch Flat-to-Donner Lake toll road, once filled with rumbling stagecoaches and wagons drawn by four teams of mules. In winter you would have seen mules wearing huge iron snowshoes plodding over the pass, bringing supplies for the construction of the railroad. One winter an engine was placed on a sled at Cisco and dragged over the summit.

Cisco Grove was formerly Cisco, a railroad town and tourist mecca. None of the town buildings remain. The hotel pictured was used by a hardy breed of early skiers from the Auburn Ski Club. The club began in 1930 when the owner of Auburn Lumber Company ordered some wooden skis from a Chicago catalog; they looked similar to the "Norwegan skates" used by Sierra lumbermen to race down local slopes. He and his friends were enchanted with the idea of skiing, and before long they formed the ski club and built a ski jump at Towle, slightly to the west of Cisco. In those days there was no winter traffic on U.S. 40, and the hardy skiers had to hand-shovel the road to their ski jump. Soon the club was promoting legislation for a gas tax to fund snow removal on major Sierra highways. Club members employed a novel approach to convince lawmakers of the necessity for the funds. Before hearings began on the bill, legislators were invited to a party at the Towle ski hill. On a bright, sunny January day a caravan of fifty-six cars transported lawmakers up the single-lane, hand-shoveled road. The highlight was an exhibition of ski jumping followed by complimentary mountain dew. Somehow a thousand other cars followed the caravan up the cleared road. By late afternoon there was a monumental traffic jam when everyone tried to turn around and drive down the single lane through the snow. The tired lawmakers went home convinced.

The Auburn Ski Club later moved its operations to Cisco, where the hotel management was happy host to skiers every winter weekend. In 1932 the club hosted the National Championships, staging the first

Little remains of this once-bustling resort at Cisco. (*From postcard collection of Carol Ryan*)

slalom and giant slalom races in California and perhaps in the United States. The 1939 World Championships were also held at Cisco.

In the 1950s, when the club found that the proposed Interstate 80 would put their land under concrete, they sold out to the state and bought acreage near Castle Peak at Donner Summit. That hill was leased to the Boreal Ridge Ski Area, and the club developed a museum of skiing in conjunction with the resort.

Soon after Cisco Grove, the South Yuba River becomes a welcome companion. Watch for riverbank groves of black cottonwood and aspen trees, their silver-green leaves dancing in any breeze. Cottonwoods usually grow closest to the water they crave, whereas aspens prefer meadows above the water's edge; other deciduous trees of this altitude are alders, which also seek moist places. The white blossoms of creek dogwood fill the shaded understory of springtime forests. Near the highway you may see beaver dams changing the course of the river. Beavers eat the bark and leaves of both aspen and cottonwood before using the clean logs for their engineering projects.

At 6000 feet you have entered the deep snow belt, where snowdrifts usually obscure roadside views. In spring, melting snow presents a water symphony to accompany freeway traffic—every turn will disclose another rivulet streaming down a rocky crevice. Vacation cabins perched on granite boulders seem perilously close to the Yuba's cascading torrents.

After the snow has melted, travelers find a different landscape. Roadsides glow with lupines and pentstemons in shades of blue and scarlet, and forest meadows are carpeted with yellow daisy blossoms of mule ears. In fall, quiet settles on the landscape. The rushing torrents have become dripping creeks or damp meadows. The Yuba flows gently over its rocky course, and grassy meadows turn golden brown to complement the yellow aspen leaves.

BIG BEND

Exit at Big Bend and turn left. The ranger headquarters appears on the left in one-quarter of a mile. The ranger station and campground are maintained by the National Forest Service and are open from May 30 (snow level permitting) until Labor Day.

Park in front of the headquarters, where there is an excellent little museum depicting pioneer life along with good examples of wildlife found in the region. Volunteers keep the office open from 10 A.M. to 12 noon and from 1–4 P.M. Fridays and Saturdays only.

A five-minute stroll takes you to the Emigrant Trail. Walk down the road to the left of the historical marker toward the campground. Just before the bridge over the Yuba River, descend a path to the right and join a trail along the riverbank. Young lodgepole pines crowd the edge of the trail. When warmed by summer sun the pines emit a sweet fragrance. Purple lupines abound during much of the summer, and anglers can be seen casting into the river.

The trail crosses shifting sands dropped here each year during spring floods. Walk to a solitary giant pine, prickly Ponderosa or gentle Jeffrey? What tales this tree could tell! How many weary people have passed by hauling and pushing their wagons over the rocky surface! Perhaps it was under this tree that Mrs. Murphy gave birth to Elizabeth Yuba in 1844. Not far away some of the Donner Party suffered a Christmas of death during a terrible snowstorm while trying to reach Sutter's Fort on foot. The granite surface by the riverbank near the pine shows unmistakable parallel indentations, the trail of thousands of wagons that had joined the Yuba several miles upstream and followed its course down to Yuba Gap.

On the granite knoll above the river isolated boulders called *glacial erratics* are strewn across the landscape like giant bowling balls. Glaciers plucked these boulders from the mountains to the east and carried them here imbedded in the ice. When the glaciers receded they left these calling cards. In the crevices rainbow-hued gardens bloom amid the glacially polished granite.

Walk or drive east a short distance to the Rainbow Tavern Lodge. Built in the late 1920s when automobile traffic began over the summit, it was first called Rainbow Tavern and Trout Farm. Diners caught trout from a

CASTLE PEAK

stocked pond near the river and brought them to the cook. During the 1940s the lodge offered guided ski tours to Donner Summit. Movie stars like Bing Crosby and Norma Shearer were said to have enjoyed these excursions.

The tavern has also seen a wild-west-style murder. In 1935, when card games were common here, a local card shark was shot and killed by a player who thought he had been cheated. The perpetrator of the crime was later sentenced to ten years in prison.

The stone-walled dining room and entry hall of Rainbow Tavern Lodge are worthy of a visit, as is the bar where the shooting took place. The tavern offers hearty meals. A loyal clientele returns each year to fish the Yuba and relax in this quiet inn among the firs and pines.

The road rejoins Interstate 80 at Hampshire Rocks Campground. For a more leisurely pace you can continue on this two-lane road with its green forested walls and rejoin the interstate at Soda Springs.

At Kingvale, Castle Peak first comes into view. Eighteen hundred feet higher than the pass, its treeless volcanic crags guard the summit. This peak was one source of the mudflow on which you drove below Yuba Gap.

The freeway climbs steadily from Soda Springs where you can exit onto the **Alternate Loop** on old U.S. 40. Notice that the lodgepole and fir trees closest to the freeway exhibit a modern deformity. Devoid of branches halfway up their trunks, they are well on their way to becoming peeled logs. These trees have been sandblasted by streams of snow and road dirt thrown out by the rotary snowplows that keep this highway open.

BOREAL RIDGE SKISPORT MUSEUM
AND SUMMIT ROADSIDE REST

Boreal Ridge Ski Area is reached from the Castle Peak exit. This resort offers winter skiing, and in summer you can ride a little sled down a chute called an alpine slide. The Skisport Museum, operated by the Auburn Ski Club, features the history of winter sports. Of special interest to Sierra history buffs are the twenty-foot skis used by Snow-shoe Thompson, a remarkable Norseman who carried the mail free of charge over the Sierra between 1856 and 1876. Old ski movies are also shown at the museum.

At the summit roadside rest, a short drive east of the ski area, you can picnic among lodgepole pines and look for the scarlet flowers of mountain pride pentstemon tucked in the cracks of granite boulders. A trail circles a glacial tarn (a small pond) where you will find Labrador tea, a shrub with a lemony smell to its leaves that lives in moist places. Here you can also see specimens of the mountain hemlock, the evergreen with drooping branches.

Just beyond the summit the interstate passes another tarn. Glaciers scoured small depressions in the granite, which filled with water from the melting ice. In the thousands of years since the ice melted, eroded material has been deposited in layers around such ponds, producing over time a ring of seedlings that grew into encircling forests. As the trees grow and more soil is deposited, the water will become shallower and shallower, and eventually the tarn will become a meadow.

The freeway begins a steep descent toward Donner Lake. The highway patrol keeps busy with accidents here, particularly in winter. Even seasoned truck drivers sometimes take the series of curves too fast. The Carson Range, a spur of the Sierra northeast of Lake Tahoe, fills the far horizon. Two miles below the summit is a vista point.

VISTA POINT

At the vista point a map describes the railroad line, old roads, and emigrant wagon routes. Without guides or maps and with precious little knowledge of what lay ahead, the pioneers dragged their wagons over these precipitous granite walls. They knew only that Sutter's Fort lay somewhere over this pass to the west.

The railroad snowsheds along Schallenberger Ridge are just a few of the thirty-seven miles of sheds that once protected the tracks from heavy snows and avalanches. The earliest snowplows mounted in front of the steam engines could not handle Sierra snowfalls. Early in the twentieth century rotary plows were developed that could clear the snow, allowing many sheds to be removed. Those that remain are in locations where avalanches could bury the track or where the rotary plows are no match for the storms.

As you descend to Truckee look above the freeway. A barren ridge is mute testimony to the ravages of forest fires. In 1960 when the interstate was under construction, sparks from the equipment ignited a fire that raged uncontrolled for seven days through tens of thousands of acres. Reno was without electricity for a week when the power lines across this ridge were consumed by the flames. Now, more than two decades later, only mountain chaparral plants have returned. This is private property, and no replanting of pine seedlings has occurred. A combination of a dry slope and high altitude retards plant growth to a snail's pace. Bushes growing now sprouted from seeds that germinated after the fire. Since there are no large trees nearby to provide seeds, these shrubs will take over the slope. It will take another hundred years before some pine seedlings sprout from seeds blown in or brought by squirrels. The U.S. Forest Service land over the ridge was carefully terraced to prevent erosion and then planted with young pines, which will be ready to harvest in less than a century.

The highway descends onto a flat plain, a portion of a glacial moraine. Just before the first exit look sharp toward the south for a glimpse of the Pioneer Monument at Donner Memorial State Park. Beyond and on the north side of the interstate is the State Agricultural Inspection Station, which does what it can to prevent exotic bugs and maggots from hitchhiking into California.

Highway 89 South leads to Squaw Valley (site of the 1960 Winter Olympics) and the north shore of Lake Tahoe. At Squaw Valley a breathtaking aerial tram ride operates year round and takes passengers to High Camp. Even if you don't ski, you can dine here and enjoy the view of Lake Tahoe and its encircling mountains. The view is well worth the price of the ticket. If you wish to drive partway around the edge of Lake Tahoe, continue to Tahoe City and turn left along the north shore of the lake. You can return to Truckee and I-80 from Kings Beach via Highway 267 over Brockway Summit, elevation over 7200 feet. The entire trip is thirty-seven miles and offers any number of picnic spots, with the lake's sparkling blue water and surrounding peaks forming the backdrop.

Take the Downtown exit to explore Historic Truckee. Take the Highway 89 North exit three miles to picnic and visit the site of the Donner family's winter encampment at Alder Creek Donner Camp. Between these two exits you will see the white cupola housing Truckee's famous Rocking Stone.

Alternate Loop

OVER THE PASS ON OLD U.S. 40

Take the Soda Springs exit east for this loop over the summit on Donner Pass Highway, old U.S. 40. During summer months this scenic route has less traffic and better vistas and takes only fifteen minutes longer than the interstate between Soda Springs and Donner Lake. The loop rejoins the interstate near Donner Memorial State Park. This road is not open over the summit in winter.

The road passes summer homes clustered around the settlement of Soda Springs. The U.S. Forest Service Central Sierra Snow Laboratory is located east of Soda Springs. Since 1940 scientists at the lab have studied the Sierra Nevada snowpack. Melting mountain snow is the major source of water in California for homes, farms, industries, and hydroelectric power plants. Accurate information about the availability of water is crucial to a burgeoning state in a dry climate. The scientists have kept records of the annual snowfall since 1878. Fifty feet of snow have been known to fall in one season. When this road was the only east-west, all-year highway in northern California, imagine the difficulties faced by snowplow operators!

Glimpses of a meadow come into view south of the highway. A stream now meanders through what was Lake Van Norden, a former Pacific Gas and Electric Company reservoir. The company broke through the dam when it failed to meet earthquake-safety tests. The stream is the young South Yuba River collecting water from the mountains that encircle the meadow. The lake is reverting to a meadow similar to the one that greeted weary emigrants after their difficult summit crossing. Large numbers of small pine trees are beginning to grow out into the meadow. The lodgepole, the only two-needle pine of the Sierra, reproduces rapidly and is tolerant of a variety of soil conditions, including this soggy place.

"Where's Truckee?" Charlie Chaplin filming "The Gold Rush"
at Sugar Bowl. (*Publicity photo, United Artists Studio*)

This meadow was the site of yet another tragedy for members of the
Donner Party. Two families tried to leave in early March of 1847 and
managed to reach this spot, only to be engulfed in a late snowstorm that
lasted for a week. Rescuers appeared just before the people would have
succumbed.

As the road nears the pass you can see Sugar Bowl Ski Area's lifts and
runs, which are laid out on the slopes of Mt. Disney and Mt. Lincoln. The
bowl below these peaks receives the full blast of winter storms, and snow
depths are measured in the hundreds of inches. This area was opened in
1937 by a group of wealthy San Franciscans and investors, including Walt
Disney. When Hannes Schroll came to Cisco to compete in the 1939
World Championships, he decided to immigrate to California from his
native Austria and came to Sugar Bowl as its first ski instructor. A succession of Austrian ski instructors have maintained a Tyrolean ambiance at
the resort. The resort has also served as the outdoor set for some of
Charlie Chaplin's movies, including "The Gold Rush."

The pass is a short distance above Sugar Bowl. At the summit, the
Donner Spitze Hütte houses participants of its mountaineering school.

DONNER SUMMIT WALK

Turn right into the paved road immediately before Donner Spitze Hütte and park off the road. This is an easy, short hike, but tennis shoes or boots are recommended. About twenty-five yards from the main road, take the dirt road on the left between two iron posts; the road curves downhill around a granite knoll.

In summer every crevice around you is filled with clumps of blue or scarlet trumpet-shaped flowers whose brilliant colors dazzle the eyes. These are both pentstemons. The scarlet one was named mountain pride by John Muir. A low-growing succulent holds a cluster of tiny, yellow flowers toward the sun. What these flowers lack in size they make up for with splashy rainbow hues, nature's way of promoting their availablility to pollinating insects and hummingbirds. They grow in low mounds close to the soil or under rocky shelves in order to survive in these dry, windy heights. This ridge, although not really above timberline, has many of the species and characteristics of an alpine rock garden.

Just before the path descends steeply you will see a gnarled Sierra juniper on your right. Although only ten feet tall, this tree is much older than it looks. Despite the strong winter winds that blow across this exposed area, this juniper has lived for hundreds of years even though there is only a ribbon of bark up its trunk. Though bent and scarred, this sturdy tree clings to the rocks from which it springs and puts forth new life every summer.

Our old road continues through a wall of willows. Look carefully to the right for a large rock with a bronze plaque. This monument marks the trail of the pioneers led by Elisha Stevens who dragged their wagons over the summit on November 25, 1844. In two feet of snow, oxen slipping and sliding on the smooth granite surface, the group was making slow progress when they came upon a ten-foot-high ledge downhill from the spot where you are standing. Surely luck was with them, for they found a crack in the cliff just large enough for a single ox to pass through. The oxen were unyoked and pushed up through the crack. Then chains were attached to the oxen and let down to the wagons. With animals pulling from above and men heaving against the wheels below, each wagon was brought to higher ground. It is a tribute to the leadership skill of Elisha Stevens that an exhausted group could muster the strength to accomplish this feat.

Continue down the trail through the willow corridor. The north-facing slope above you to the right may still have snow in early summer. Here

HEMLOCK

will be your first opportunity to see the mountain hemlock, whose drooping foliage prompted John Muir to write this tribute in the 1890s.

As the juniper is the most stubborn and unshakeable of trees . . . the Mountain Hemlock (*Tsuga Mertensiana*) is the most graceful and pliant and sensitive. Until it reaches a height of fifty or sixty feet it is sumptuously clothed down to the ground with drooping branches, which are divided again and again into delicate waving sprays, grouped and arranged in ways that are indescribably beautiful, and profusely adorned with small brown cones.

The hemlock's branches bend in the slightest breeze, their suppleness insuring that young trees can survive the long hibernation under winter's heavy mantle of snow. Some young trees may bend to the ground, lying horizontal for four long months. As summer's warm winds evaporate and melt the snowy blanket, the trees spring up, shaking off their icy bonds, ready to begin a new cycle of growth.

Descend to a tunnel underneath the railroad. Pass through and look back to your right at the Chinese wall, a perfect bridge of mortarless stone constructed by the Chinese immigrants building the Central Pacific Railroad. The road you are following was part of the Dutch Flat-to-Donner Lake toll road. About a hundred yards from the railroad you may be able to find an early advertisement painted on the granite below and to the right: "Whitney Hotel—Truckee."

When climbing back up to your car you may notice yourself getting winded at this 7000-foot altitude. Walk slowly and enjoy the beauty. You may be lucky enough to see a marmot, which is a roly-poly, oversized ground squirrel. Summertime brings this slow-moving rodent out onto granite outcrops for a daily sunbath. Indians called marmots "whistle pigs" because of the sound they make to warn of intruders. Another high-pitched squeaker of the heights is the pika or rock rabbit, which collects alpine grasses for storage in an underground maze of corridors among the boulders. This little animal does not hibernate but rather lives comfortably under the snow, running back and forth to its storehouses for meals of winter salad. You may hear pikas calling, but you need practiced eyes to find them darting across their rocky domain.

Energetic hikers with sturdy shoes can take a hike up the Pacific Crest Trail to the top of Mt. Lincoln. From where you are parked, walk down the paved road about 100 yards until you see a road entering on the left. A sign for the Pacific Crest Trail is tacked on a tree. The trail follows the crests of the mountain ranges between Mexico and Canada. On a shoulder of Mt. Lincoln you cross Roller Pass, where Caleb Greenwood brought the first sixteen wagons over the summit in 1846.

Back on old U.S. 40 you cross the original Donner Pass at 7120 feet and begin a descent toward an arching cement bridge. Beyond is an official lookout with ample parking, an excellent place to enjoy the view. Below are Donner Lake and the town of Truckee. The mountains in the distance form the Carson Range in Nevada.

As you continue down the road, solitary Jeffrey pines look very much like their ponderosa cousins. Some Jeffreys grow right out of the granite. Sierra granite is subjected to extremes of temperature and moisture. In winter, water seeps into cracks in the rock, freezes, and expands; therefore, each winter the cracks grow. The sun's ultraviolet rays help decompose the granite into a sandy soil. Eventually some of this soil fills a crack and waits for a seed to blow in. The next spring, after melting snow has dampened the new soil, the seed sprouts. The grand pines have grown from seeds that found their way into cracks hundreds of years ago.

Summer travelers will find the lower portions of this road festooned with fragrant white blooms of wild lilac bushes. The blossoms of some varieties were used by Indians to make soap.

In July and August good swimming is available at the western end of Donner Lake at a public recreation beach. There is a small admission charge. Another good beach is located at the Donner Memorial State Park at the eastern end of the lake. To reach the park continue on old U.S. 40, here called Donner Pass Road.

Early auto travel over the Sierra Summit. (*Truckee Historical Society*)

Favorite Diversion

AROUND TRUCKEE

Donner Memorial Park

Take the first Truckee exit after descending from the pass, and turn right on Donner Pass Road a few hundred yards to the park entrance.

This state park offers picnic and camping sites, trails, a museum, and a swimming beach.

This park is a memorial to the Donner Party and all pioneers who made the trek west. The Emigrant Trail Museum has slide shows and exhibits that tell the Donner Party story. Dioramas depict their route and show pictures of some members of the group. One display contains a little girl's doll, a replica of five-year-old Patty Reed's most precious possession. After months with little but boiled hides for food she was rescued by her father. While she wearily trudged through deep snowdrifts,

Patty clutched her doll in her apron pocket, even though she had been forbidden to take anything with her. Both Patty and the doll survived to tell us their story.

A trail leaves the museum for the site of the Murphy family cabin. Here a bronze plaque is attached to the rock that formed one wall of the former shelter; on it the survivors and deceased of the Donner Party are listed. Of eighty-nine who had set out from Missouri in May of 1846, only forty-seven survived to see California's fabled fertile valleys.

The tale of woe is better understood when you realize that the Murphy cabin site is far removed from the Breens, who occupied Schallenberger's former hut where the Pioneer Monument stands. The Graves family was located about a quarter-mile away. The Donner family was six miles over the hill at Alder Creek. Why did they not help each other and huddle together?

The imposing Pioneer Monument east of the museum was built to commemorate all who struck out across the trackless land to reach California. Note the height of the monument's base. The snow was that deep during the winter that the Donner Party was camped here. It is easy to understand why these midwestern farmers were defeated by the quantities of snow piled up around them. The first storm was so fierce that all cattle were lost before they could be slaughtered for food. The Donners did not realize that a few miles back, in Nevada, little snow fell and game would have been plentiful. Due to the warmth radiated by the freeway and the proximity of Truckee, with its many woodburning stoves, less snow seems to accumulate here today than in the nineteenth century.

The park offers quiet picnic spots and swimming from beaches of granite sand. The beach was once a summer encampment for Nevada Indians, and their arrowheads can still be found. You often see duck families swimming by and California gulls circling overhead. Lucky autumn visitors may catch sight of America's national bird, the bald eagle, gliding over the lake in search of a fish dinner. This magnificent fisher visits this lake when the summer crowds are gone. The eagle and the local people know that fall is the best time to fish for the lake's famous Mackinaw trout.

Downtown

From the freeway take the Downtown Truckee exit and turn right. You are on a portion of the original wagon trail now called Commercial Row.

Life has never been easy in Truckee, especially in the winter. But it attracted a certain kind of hardy individual who liked the independence

McGlashan's house and cupola with the Rocking Stone. The southern orientation with its view also meant less snow accumulation (*Truckee Historical Society*)

of living so far from government and who loved the Sierra Nevada. One of those was Charles Fayette McGlashan, who became editor of the local newspaper. He was consumed by a desire to print the true story of the Donner tragedy, and in the 1880s he published *The History of the Donner Party*. He interviewed the survivors, used their recollections to describe the events leading up to the tragedy, and attempted to put the tales of cannibalism into perspective. The book is still available.

McGlashan loved the mountains. He was an avid butterfly collector and even has one type named for him. His favorite hours were spent roaming the high mountain meadows adding to his collection, which is currently on view at the courthouse in Nevada City. He built a beautiful and unusual flat-roofed house high on a hill overlooking town. Unfortunately the house burned, and the site is now occupied by a Quonset hut meeting hall for the Veterans Association. To the east of the hall, sitting atop a large rock, is a fourteen-sided white cupola that mirrored the style of McGlashan's former home. The structure surrounds one of Truckee's most curious sights, the Rocking Stone. You can walk or drive from downtown. To reach it turn left on Spring Street and left on High Street.

Local tribes have a legend about the Rocking Stone's supernatural powers. It is said that ancient people used the flattened top of the base stone to dry their meat and to keep it away from marauding animals. The food was not safe from flocks of birds, however, which swept down and stole all their food. The Indians prayed to their gods to help them. The story continues that the wind god answered by bringing a great storm that blackened the sky for days. When the storm was gone, a smaller stone was perched on top of the flat boulder. The wind god told the Indians to place their food on top of the flat rock. This they did, and when the wind god breathed, the smaller stone began to rock. From that day forward, the Indians could use this place to dry their meat, for even the wind created by bird wings would start the smaller stone to rocking, scaring the birds away. The stone has been cemented in place to prevent it from falling on the town below during an earthquake.

From this vantage point you can see the twin traces of the town's economic past, the railroad and the river. The three-story Truckee Hotel stands tall at the east end of Commercial Row. The current hotel was once the Whitney Hotel of the rocky advertisement seen on the Donner Summit Walk. While you stand by the stone, turn to **Yesterday's Voices** and read Isabella Bird's 1873 description of Truckee.

Retrace your steps to the downtown area and wander down the covered sidewalks. At the east end of Commercial Row walk left on Bridge Street and right on Church Street. Here another side of Truckee can be seen. The Community Methodist Church has stood here for over 100 years. In its earliest days it provided the women of the town with their social life. Although Truckee remained a male-dominated society, the wives of more affluent citizens held church socials, whist parties, and afternoon teas in homes decorated with silver and damask to rival any Boston parlor. Also on Church Street is the original Gray's Toll Station, a small log cabin that was moved here and renovated.

When you return to Commercial Row, walk down Jibboom Street, the back alley for the town's businesses. This street once housed an infamous red-light district and has been the scene of several Old West shootouts. At the end of Jibboom on the right, the town's original jail now houses the collections of the town's historical society.

To visit Alder Creek Donner Camp drive east on Commercial Row, which becomes Highway 89 North.

Alder Creek Donner Camp

Take the Highway 89 North exit and turn left. Drive three miles to the U.S. Forest Service picnic ground on the right. The trail around Donner Camp starts at a sign that tells the Donner's story.

Walk around the trail to the two groups of trees that protected the makeshift shelters of the two families, the final resting place for all the adults who came to this spot in 1846.

George and Jacob Donner had always farmed together, first in North Carolina and then in Tennessee. They moved on to clear new land and plant new crops in Indiana. When both brothers lost their wives they migrated again, now to Illinois. New wives were found along with new land. The farms produced well and families grew, seven babies to George and five to Jacob in nine years. When George lost his second wife bearing the last of the seven, the brothers and their families left for Texas. They did not find this arid land to their liking and returned to Illinois, where George remarried, this time to Tamsen Dozier, twenty-five years his junior. Six years and three children later, George Donner announced that the family was moving again, this time to California.

George, Jacob, and their friend James Reed were taken in by the glowing reports in Hastings's *The Emigrants' Guide to Oregon and California* of hollyhocks and sweet william blooming everywhere at Christmastime and wild clover five feet high. Harsh Illinois winters and sickness convinced them that California was the only place to spend the remaining years of their lives. But what of the rigors of the journey? These men thought they knew the answer: Hastings said his route was 200 miles shorter than any previously used.

What set the Donners and Reeds apart was their wealth and education. George and Jacob Donner were not impecunious farmers. They sold some of their land for $10,000, which Tamsen sewed into a quilt. Reed rode a beautiful stallion and had constructed what many called a "palace wagon" complete with bed and sitting room furnished with the family's heirlooms. Reed had other wagons for his provisions. The Donners also had several wagons, and the families employed young men as teamsters.

They were hampered by both inexperience in mountain travel and the size of their wagons, and when they reached the infamous Hastings cutoff, disaster struck. Those impressive wagons had to be taken apart and lowered down steep canyons, or a road wide enough had to be hacked through canyon bottoms filled with tangled underbrush. By the time they rejoined the main route again at Pilot Peak in eastern Nevada it was September, and they still faced the Forty Mile Desert.

Not until November 3 did they reach Alder Creek, where they made hasty camp when George Donner sliced his hand open while repairing a broken axle. Tamsen bound the wound and with the help of their teamsters ripped canvas from the wagons to build makeshift shelters. George, Tamsen, and their children camped under the large Jeffrey pine that still remains. Class distinctions prevailed even here, for the teamsters raised tents quite far away.

The families endured the same incredible hardships as the rest of the party six miles away at Donner Lake. Their cattle wandered off and were lost during the first great storm, and the people were reduced to eating boiled shoe leather. When rescue parties finally reached them, Jacob was dead and his wife nearly so. George miraculously still lived, although he was tormented by gangrene. Tamsen had dressed her three girls in several layers of their best pinafores and taught them to say, "We are the children of Mr. and Mrs. George Donner." She sent them ahead with rescuers, fully expecting to join them. She adamantly refused to leave her dying husband, saying that she would come only after she had buried him. He died a few days later, but we shall never know what happened to Tamsen Donner. The body of her husband, carefully wrapped in a shroud, was found by a group of soldiers in the summer of 1847. Her body was never found, and what happened remains a mystery. In 1977, 130 years after the tragedy, Ruth Whitman retraced Tamsen's trip and wrote and published a poem recreating her story. She writes for Tamsen on two dates after her children had been sent away with the rescue party.

April 10, 1847, by Alder creek

How can I store against coming loss?
what faculties of the heart
can I bring against this parting?

we traveled across the land
towards winter not towards spring

I watched the children become solemn and thin
our wagons and housewares
brittle

depleted

when I buried my boxes
my watercolors and oils my writing desk

I felt I had given all I could part with:
that was what the desert demanded of me:
then the canyons and boulders

ate at the wheels of our wagons
squeezed the life from our oxen

and we learned to part from our
livestock our friends
our comfort

how can I part with
my sustaining love
who was father

to the whole camp, orphans and families
who whistled us up at dawn

who nooned me in the shade
and fed me at sunset
the darks and lights of his eyes

playing over me like sun and clouds
on a highhearted summer afternoon:

how can I learn to sleep
without his shoulder
to bed down my griefs?

the sun stays hidden
for months the sky has wept its snow

April 12, 1847, Alder creek

Hunger. The lightness of it. I feel my legs will not
hold me up any longer. Sounds enter the senses
sharply, colors are very bright, I am filled with light,
a music that the saints sought and called God. I am
not quite in touch with the ground, I am outside my
own body. It would be easy to join the air and float
into nothingness.

Yesterday's Voices

HUNGRY AND ALONE

From the diary of Moses Schallenberger

*Moses, a young man of eighteen, was too weak to continue over
Donner Pass with the Stevens Party in 1844. He opted to remain at
the lake. Several months later his friends returned, and they constructed snowshoes for the trudge over the summit.*

The feeling of loneliness that came over me as the two men turned
away I cannot express, though it will never be forgotten. While the,
'Good-by, Mose,' so sadly and reluctantly spoken, rings in my ears to-day. I
desire to say here that both Foster and Montgomery were brave, warm-
hearted men, and it was by no fault of theirs that I was thus left alone. It

would only have made matters worse for either of them to remain with me, for the quarter of beef at the cabin would last me longer alone, and thus increase my chances of escape. While our decision was a sad one, it was the only one that could be made.

My companions had not been long out of sight before my spirits began to revive, and I began to think, like Micawber, that something might 'turn up.' So I strapped on my blankets and dried beef, shouldered my gun, and began to retrace my steps to the cabin. It had frozen during the night and this enabled me to walk on our trail without the snow-shoes. This was a great relief, but the exertion and sickness of the day before had so weakened me that I think I was never so tired in my life as when, just a little before dark, I came in sight of the cabin. The door-sill was only nine inches high, but I could not step over it without taking my hands to raise my leg. . . . As soon as I was able to crawl around the next morning I put on my snowshoes, and, taking my rifle, scoured the country thoroughly for foxes. The result was as I had expected—just as it had always been—plenty of tracks, but no fox. . . .

As soon as daylight came I was out to inspect the traps. I was anxious to see them and still I dreaded to look. After some hesitation I commenced the examination, and to my great delight I found in one of them a starved coyote. I soon had his hide off and his flesh roasted in a Dutch oven. I ate this meat, but it was horrible. I next tried boiling him, but it did not improve the flavor. I cooked him in every possible manner my imagination, spurred by hunger, could suggest, but could not get him into a condition where he could be eaten without revolting my stomach. But for three days this was all I had to eat. On the third night I caught two foxes. I roasted one of them, and the meat, though entirely devoid of fat, was delicious. I was so hungry that I could easily have eaten a fox at two meals, but I made one last me two days. . . .

Fortunately, I had a plenty of books, Dr. Townsend having brought out quite a library. I used often to read aloud, for I longed for some sound to break the oppressive stillness. For the same reason, I would talk aloud to myself. At night I built large fires and read by the light of the pine knots as late as possible, in order that I might sleep late the next morning, and thus cause the day to seem shorter. What I wanted most was enough to eat, and the next thing I tried hardest to do was to kill time. I thought the snow would never leave the ground, and the few months I had been living here seemed years.

Reprinted in *The California Trail*, by George R. Stewart, by permission of University of Nebraska Press. Copyright © 1962 by George R. Stewart.

AN ENGLISH LADY IN TRUCKEE

By Isabella Bird

*On a trip around the world to improve her health, Isabella had fasci-
nating adventures all the way.*

September 2, 1873: Shivering in the keen, frosty air near the summit
pass of the Sierras, we entered the "snow-sheds," wooden galleries,
which for about fifty miles shut out all the splendid views of the region, as
given in dioramas, not even allowing a glimpse of "the Gem of the
Sierras," the lovely Donner Lake. One of these sheds is twenty-seven
miles long. In a few hours the mercury had fallen from 103° to 29°, and
we had ascended 6,987 feet in 105 miles! After passing through the
sheds, we had several grand views of a pine forest on fire before reaching
Truckee at 11 P.M. having traveled 258 miles. Truckee, the center of the
"lumbering region" of the Sierras, is usually spoken of as "a rough mountain town," and Mr. W. had told me that all the roughs of the district congregated there, that there were nightly pistol affrays in bar-rooms, etc.,
but as he admitted that a lady was sure of respect, and Mr. G. strongly
advised me to stay and see the lakes, I got out, much dazed, and very
stupid with sleep, envying the people in the sleeping car, who were
already unconscious on their luxurious couches. The cars drew up in a
street—if street that could be called which was only a wide, cleared
space, intersected by rails, with here and there a stump, and great piles of
sawn logs bulking big in the moonlight, and a number of irregular clap-
board, steep-roofed houses, many of them with open fronts, glaring with
light and crowded with men. We had pulled up at the door of a rough
Western hotel, with a partially open front, being a bar-room crowded
with men drinking and smoking, and the space between it and the cars
was a moving mass of loafers and passengers. On the tracks, engines,
tolling heavy bells, were mightily moving, the glare from their cyclopean
eyes dulling the light of a forest which was burning fitfully on a mountain
side; and on open spaces great fires of pine logs were burning cheerily,
with groups of men round them. A band was playing noisily, and the
unholy sound of tom-toms was not far off. Mountains—the Sierras of
many a fireside dream—seemed to wall in the town, and great pines
stood out, sharp and clear cut, against a sky in which a moon and stars
were shining frostily.

From *A Lady's Life in the Rocky Mountains*, 1879. (Sausalito, Calif.: Comstock Editions, 1981.)

A TRIP TO THE SNOW

From a letter written to the San Francisco Daily Evening Bulletin,
April 3, 1878, by John Muir

More than anyone, John Muir was able to capture the essence of his beloved Sierra.

In company with a friend and his two little sons, I have just returned from a week of weathering around Tahoe, where we had glorious views of wlater . . . [water?], besides the enjoyment of a fine reviving roll in the snow, swim in the icy lake, and some rich, lusty exercise on snow-shoes [skis]. All the weather was delightfully bracing and exhilarating, though varying rapidly almost from hour to hour—snowing, blowing, clear, and cloudy, but never rigorously cold. . . .

The greater portion of the snow deposited around the lofty summits of the range falls in small, crisp flakes and broken crystals; or, when accompanied by strong winds at a low temperature, the crystals instead of being locked together in their fall to form tufted flakes, are beaten and broken into meal and fine dust. But down in the forested region about the elevation of Lake Tahoe, the greater portion comes gently to the ground, light and feathery, some of the flakes nearly an inch in diameter, and is evenly distributed and kept from drifting to any great extent beneath the shelter of the trees. Every tree is loaded with this fairy bloom, bending down the branches, and hushing every leaf. When the storm is over, and the sun shines, the snow at once begins to shift, and settle, and fall off in miniature avalanches, leaving the forest green again. The snow on the ground settles also, thawing every day, freezing every night, until it becomes a kind of coarsely granulated ice—every trace of its rayed crystalline structure destroyed. This is the present condition of most of the snow on the range. From towards midnight until midday, at this time of year, a man may walk firmly over the surface, as if on ice, provided the preceding day has been warm, and the night frosty. . . .

Only the eldest of my companions ventured with me upon the steep mountainside. This was his first experience on snow-shoes, and the several descents he made were the most remarkable specimens of locomotion that I ever had the fortune to witness. In shooting down steep declevities, the long shoes should be kept strictly parallel, and every limb immovably braced. My friend, however, launched himself in wild abandon, limbs and shoes in chaotic entanglement—now in snow, now in air, whirling over and over in rolls and somersaults that would shame the most extravagant performances of a circus acrobat. How truly original and inimitable he was. It was all refreshing, however, this downright contact with snow and sky; and on coming to rest with his runaway members deeply imbedded and far divorced, he would quietly gather himself, pick out the snow from his neck and ears, and say with preternatural solemnity, "This, Muir, is the poetry of motion."

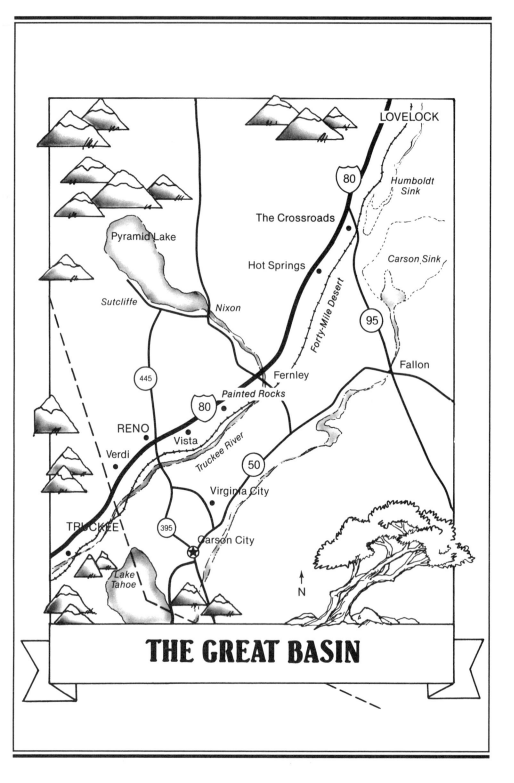

THE GREAT BASIN

7

THE GREAT BASIN
Truckee to Lovelock

Trip Planner
EXPLORING

One-third of our journey, 100 miles of desert, is covered in
this chapter. Gas stations are strategically located
every 30 miles or so.

The **East Verdi scenic view** looks down on the Emigrant
Trail and east to Reno.

The **Vista exit** allows an impressive view over the Reno
basin and the eastern side of the Sierra Nevada.

Painted Rocks is a short stop to look closely at the varied
hues of rock that have been altered by nature's
hot-water system.

Hot Springs is a desolate spot where the pioneers
obtained their last water during their forty-mile trek across
the dry desert.

The Crossroads is this book's name for the roadside rest at the intersection with Highway 95, a few miles south of Lovelock. Here you can picnic and experience the hot temperatures or cold winds of the desert.

ALTERNATE LOOP

Pyramid Lake is a highlight. The drive is in open countryside through a Paiute Indian reservation and along the Truckee River, which empties into the lake. White pelicans nest here.

FAVORITE DIVERSIONS

Verdi is an old lumbering hamlet. On the outskirts are the pioneer cemetery, the Emigrant Trail, and the road up to Dog Valley Summit.

Reno's grand old homes are found on a bluff overlooking gambling row.

The Nevada Historical Society in Reno, located near the University of Nevada, maintains a small museum which introduces you to the state's natural and historic resources.

At **Harrah's Automobile Collection in Reno** everyone finds a vehicle to admire.

Virginia City—atop a mountain lies this memory of the Comstock mining boom, where tourist attractions are plentiful. Our recommendations include a ride on the refurbished **Virginia and Truckee Railroad** and a visit to the **Chollar Mine.**

BASINS AND RANGES

As seen from the air, the mountain ranges of Nevada resemble immense caterpillars crawling from Mexico to Canada. The ranges are steep and impressive, with some summits reaching over 10,000 feet. They separate mile-high, flat valleys called *basins*. Together they make up the Basin and Range Province, which stretches 500 miles from the Sierra to the Wasatch mountains in Utah.

In his book *Basin and Range*, John McPhee expresses a feeling common to travelers: "This Nevada topography is what you see *during* mountain building. There are no foothills. It is all too young. It is live country. This is the tectonic, active, spreading, mountain-building world. To a nongeologist, it's just ranges, ranges, ranges."

The North American and Pacific plates continue to interact, as evidenced by earthquakes along the San Andreas fault. It appears, however, that this is not the only plate motion in the western United States. The crust of the North American Plate in the Great Basin has broken apart in many places. Along one side of these fault lines, the crust has been tilted steeply upward to form ranges, and on the other side the crust has sunk to become a trough or basin. Some geologists speculate that a spreading center will form in the Great Basin and that the land we recognize could become an ocean bottom.

Volcanic action has left its mark. Cone-shaped mountains and mud-flow rock are reminders of ancient volcanoes. The area of present-day volcanic activity is centered along the California border 100 miles south of Reno. Throughout the Great Basin, water heated by underground forces bubbles out as hot springs and has altered some of the rocks, producing rainbow colors. Today, water erosion is the dominant sculptor of the desert landscape. It grooves and wrinkles the mountainsides and brings down sediments that form fan-shaped deposits on the flat.

During the Ice Ages the basins filled with water and several huge lakes formed. Much of our corridor in Nevada passes through what was once Lake Lahontan, which has nearly disappeared and left Pyramid Lake as its alkaline remnant. Above the lake and on other mountainsides wave-cut terraces can be seen, some formed only 15,000 years ago.

Two rivers make a natural corridor across northern Nevada. Rising in the northeastern corner of the state, the streamlike Humboldt River meanders west through Winnemucca, turns south to flow through Love-lock, and drains into an intermittent lake called the Humboldt Sink. The Truckee River flows north and east from Lake Tahoe and through Reno before it turns north to empty into its sink, Pyramid Lake. A waterless area of alkali flats and sandy hummocks fills the stretch between the Humboldt Sink and the big bend of the Truckee where it turns north-ward. This barren stretch became known to the emigrants as the dreaded Forty-Mile Desert.

The Sierra Nevada rain shadow dictates the climate of the Great Basin. Whereas the slope west of Donner Summit may get over forty inches of moisture per year, the high desert may receive under ten inches. The Sierra not only limits the precipitation but it also walls off the moderating influences of coastal breezes. The high desert is a land of climatic extremes. Cold winter days of minus-twenty degrees precede blistering summers; snowcapped mountains loom over cracked soils in the basins; dry gullies suddenly fill with flash floods after raging thunderstorms.

Plants and animals surviving in the desert deserve the utmost respect. It takes special adaptations to withstand the heat and dessicating winds. Plants survive extremes of temperature and moisture in a variety of ways. The leaves of perennials are small, furry, or scaly and sometimes are coated with a waxy substance. Roots go deep. Seeds can lie dormant for decades waiting for lifegiving rains; when the rains come, the desert becomes a carpet of colors.

Because of the climate, vegetation is sparse in Nevada, which gives erosion a free hand. Much of the basin-and-range terrain is spotted with the dominant shrub that gave Nevada its nickname, the Sagebrush State. Its silvery leaves have a spicy aroma reminiscent of the kitchen herb, but sagebrush is from a different plant family. These shrubs are widely scattered over the desert to allow each plant to obtain sufficient water and nutriment.

Few trees grow in the high desert, not only because of the lack of moisture but also because of intensive lumbering a century ago. Bristlecone pines remain in a few places at timberline. Near the Sierra Crest and down the eastern slope, second-growth Jeffrey pines tower above the sagebrush. Farther into the Great Basin trees diminish in number and size. Dotted on the hillsides in areas of twelve inches of annual precipitation, groupings of trees in the *pinyon-juniper woodland* community offer

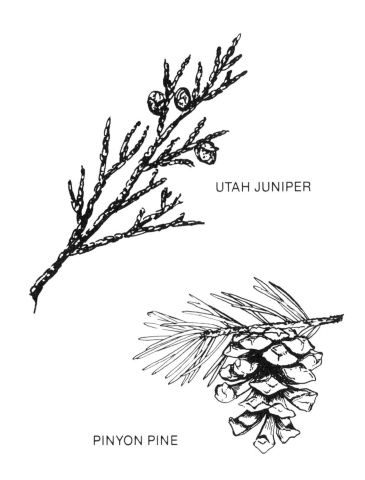

UTAH JUNIPER

PINYON PINE

shelter to desert animals. Often seen together, neither tree is much more than twenty feet tall. High up in the canyons quaking aspen turn stream-sides to gold in October. Along the year-round rivers, willows and stately cottonwood trees predominate, providing shade and security for mag-pies, orioles, warblers, grosbeaks, and flycatchers.

In the basins where the annual rainfall is below six inches, plants grow in soils that would be the despair of any gardener—clay, salts, sand, and stony "desert varnish." The *shadscale scrub* community is composed of thorny gray bushes with names like goosefoot and bud-sage.

Interspersed is greasewood, which can easily be confused with sage-brush. Around the edges of the salt flats and the intermittent lakes is the *alkali sink* community of pickleweed and saltbushes.

Never famous for its welcoming scenery, Nevada has the distinction of being the driest state with the most desert area. Reaching the Humboldt River in 1849, an emigrant reported, "The heat is fiery, intense, sultry, oppressive, suffocating, parching, and scorching the earth, air, water, and everything green—Californians included." But ask any old-time prospector or weather-worn rancher about his terrain, and his love of these open spaces shines through.

ALL THAT GLITTERS

Driving across Nevada it is difficult to imagine that people were able to live here before the age of paved roads and piped water. Yet people set-tled in this region 10,000 years ago when Ice-Age lakes and a wetter cli-mate provided abundant fish and game. As climatic conditions changed, these early inhabitants came to depend less on hunting and more on gathering. They found protection from searing summer heat and win-ter's cold in caves or in huts made from willow branches.

The Washoe tribe settled on the eastern slope of the Sierra and around Reno. Of a different language group were the Paiutes, who lived to the east. They lived in small bands and were known by the foods that sus-tained them. One group, the Cui-ui Eaters, lived by Pyramid Lake and ate fish of that name. The Cattail-Eaters lived in the marshy areas sur-rounding Humboldt and Carson sinks. Having no agriculture, the tribe-lets moved from place to place seeking sagebrush for firewood, rabbits to snare, and seeds to gather. Each fall they climbed the foothills in search of pinyon nuts, which were roasted or made into a substantial protein-rich gruel.

Fifty years after the Revolutionary War, when most Americans were clustered along the Atlantic seaboard, trappers such as Jedediah Smith began exploring the Far West. In 1829 Canadian Peter Ogden trapped along the Humboldt River, and fifteen years later John C. Fremont explored the Great Basin looking for a route to the Pacific Ocean.

It took the Stevens emigrant group to discover the most direct route across Nevada to the Sierra and on to California. They met a Paiute who drew pictures in the sand showing a river that would lead them to a pass over the mountains. They heard his name as Truckee and gave his name to the river they followed. Two years later the Donner Party followed the route that was becoming clearly marked with parallel wagon ruts.

By 1848 several hundred weary pioneers had crossed the waterless Forty-Mile Desert. News of gold in California brought thousands more. Nevada's sinks and sands were disheartening barriers standing between emigrants and imagined fortunes.

While the California gold rush was on, Nevada remained but a desert to be crossed, just part of the vast Utah Territory. Then in 1859, on a mountainside southeast of Reno, several poor prospectors dug into blue muck, which turned out to be silver ore. The Comstock Lode had been discovered. They sold their claim to entrepreneurs who hired mining experts and miners to dig tunnels deep into the mountain, and Virginia City was born. Machinery, men, and capital poured into Nevada from California. In return, the Comstock's silver and gold were processed into ingots and shipped to California. A disconcerted Nevadan, realizing that the Comstock rivaled the wealth of Aztecs and Incas, wrote, "Let San Franciscans, when disposed to sneer at the feeble Sagebrush State, remember she is feeble only because she suffered the rich currents in her veins to be transfused into the bloodless arteries of their city."

Nevada didn't give up her wealth easily. It was extracted only after arduous digging in hot, deep tunnels. Fatigue, solitude, and boredom led to wild abandon when miners came to town. Reckless spending and gambling and boisterous social outlets helped formulate the Nevada personality. Many old-timers were individualists willing to contend with physical hardships in pursuit of elusive goals but unwilling to put up with governmental restrictions. Their attitude finds expression today in the "sagebrush rebellion," a protest against federal land ownership and restrictions aimed at preventing overgrazing.

Impatience with government restrictions made life difficult for federal officials sent west to manage the new territory in the 1850s. Mark Twain wrote, "The new officers were 'emigrants,' and that was no title to anybody's affection or admiration either." This state of affairs ended in 1864 when Nevada became a state, supporting the Union in the Civil War.

Four years later the Central Pacific Railroad struck east over the granite barrier and began its final rush to Promontory Point in Utah. Central Pacific engineers laid out their route along the old Emigrant Trail. The all-powerful railroad held a land auction at the end of the track construction in 1868 and named the town Reno after a Union army officer. Once the transcontinental track was completed, instant towns sprang up to serve the needs of engines for water and wood and of weary passengers for hot meals. Reno, Lovelock, Winnemucca, and Elko are still serving the needs of travelers.

By the 1890s the Comstock Lode began to peter out, and Nevadans turned to cattle ranching. The state's fortunes waxed and waned during the rest of the nineteenth century, dependent upon wildly fluctuating prices for hay, cattle, sheep, and minerals.

Lack of water slowed Nevada's agricultural growth until substantial irrigation projects were begun in this century. The dream of bringing the desert to life was realized with the leadership of Nevada Congressman Francis Newlands. He used his influence in Congress to enact the Federal Reclamation Act of 1902. Not surprisingly, the first water project diverted the Truckee River to the arid lands east of Reno.

Since World War II, Nevada has again found a fortune in silver, this time in the form of coins jingling on gaming tables and streaming into and out of the one-armed bandits, making tourism the state's major industry. The state's future, by necessity, will be determined by decisions portioning the limited water supply among the gaming towns, agricultural areas, and natural lakes and rivers.

Exploring

TRUCKEE TO LOVELOCK

Just where does the traveler first encounter the Great Basin? Hydrologists concerned with the watershed include the land draining the hills and valleys east of Donner Summit. Botanists note the decreasing vegetation near Reno. To many the bowl in which Truckee lies gives the first impression of the wide open spaces to come, and our text begins here.

The distance from Truckee to Reno is thirty-four miles. Just east of Truckee is the flat plain of Martis Valley, created when lake basins were filled with gravel deposited by the melting glaciers. A century ago the entire area was heavily lumbered. Sagebrush and yellow, fragrant antelope brush bloom among second-growth Jeffrey pines. Now this sparsely vegetated region contains three reservoirs—Stampede, Prosser, and Boca—all used to provide water for Reno and for the desert farms to the east. Water behind the dams has covered much of the evidence of the Emigrant Trail. What's left of the trail and what was once the two-lane, unpaved transcontinental route is now a dirt road leading through the mountains north of the freeway to Dog Valley Summit. The Verdi **Favorite Diversion** explores a short section of this trail.

Leaving Martis Valley, the interstate first meets the Truckee River where it makes a sharp bend through a volcanic obstacle of basaltic lava flows. The river has wended its way from Lake Tahoe, some twenty miles to the southwest. The interstate now follows the Truckee as it twists and turns between rock walls and through glacial deposits. Keep a tally of how many times you cross the river before it leaves the highway east of Reno to flow into its sink at Pyramid Lake.

Just before the turnoff to Boca Reservoir, note the scars from a fire that blackened 26,000 acres in 1977, which was caused by sparks from railroad engines. Thanks to contributions from garden clubs and youth groups to the Penny Pines Plantation project, replanting on the other side of the ridge has begun. The dam of Boca Reservoir, built in 1939, can be seen beyond the fire-scarred hillside. A century ago, ice from the original lake was cut, stored in sawdust and shipped to the Central Valley to be packed around fruits and vegetables on their way—perhaps over the same route—to eastern markets. The advent of refrigerated railroad cars retired the ice lake. Now sailors, campers, and anglers find the lake a fine summer haunt.

A right turn at the Boca exit leads to the scattered houses of Hirshdale lying along old U.S. 40. Past the settlement, the road dead-ends in an old car graveyard. What treasures are to be found off the interstate!

If you would like to study a bit of volcanic geology, watch your mileage at the Boca exit. In just over three miles stop at the unmarked dirt pullout just before the Toiyabe National Forest sign, or as you drive by turn your attention up the hillside to your left.

On the north side of the highway the roadcut displays a channel filled with mudflow material and reddish basaltic rock. Because volcanic eruptions tend to cause rainstorms, the water mixes with the flow material to become a slurry, much like what pours from a cement mixer. At the top of the ridge are "hoodoos," rock colonnades that have been protected by an umbrella of stronger rock. Toward the river are scattered Jeffrey pines, and Utah junipers can be spotted on distant mountains. In autumn mountain mahogany can easily be identified by its featherlike, silvery seeds. Black cottonwoods line the riverbanks below.

After Floriston, as the highway descends toward Reno, a sinuous flume hangs from the rock cliffs above the river. This wooden canal transports water two miles down to Farad, where it powers a small hydroelectric plant to generate enough electricity for a community of 3000 people. Constructed originally to power pumps draining the underground tunnels of the Comstock mines, the Farad Station is now part of the Sierra Pacific Power Company. Shortly after Farad you leave California.

Nevada! Some travelers are relieved to have made it to the gambling state. Others dread the long drive ahead across the desert. The highway department has placed mileage markers, and each exit is numbered by the miles from the California border. Drivers can calculate their gas mileage and measure the width of the state.

In a short distance is the exit to Verdi, a small town nestled against the mountains. Leave the interstate on Business 80 to take the **Favorite Diversion** to the old cemetery and Dog Valley Summit.

Boomtown is on a river terrace bluff above Verdi and next to a classic western ranch with its peacefully grazing, white-faced Hereford cattle. Boomtown is a monument to the gas-engine era. Large, bright, and brash, it has grown from a truckstop to a hotel/restaurant/casino complex all housed behind the facade of a western town. Flashing lights have supplanted the flash of cowboy gunfire.

EAST VERDI SCENIC VIEW

Take a moment to stop at this scenic view. The two concrete bridge abutments have been brought here to stand as proud reminders of the Northern Lincoln Highway. Step out of the car and look into the valley below, where emigrant wagon tracks are clearly visible along with a yellow historical marker.

The surrounding plain is filled with large boulders and smaller stratified rock washed down by melting Sierra glaciers. The mountains to the south separate Reno from Lake Tahoe. Called the Carson Range, it is a volcanic spur of the Sierra. Gaze around at the pines, the last big conifers to be seen for many miles. Here on the outskirts of Reno the Great Basin has truly begun.

As you approach Reno, several exits from the interstate lead to **Favorite Diversions** in Reno and Virginia City. Take West 4th Street, exit 8, for the pleasant drive into downtown Reno on Mayberry Drive. Virginia Street leads south to the casino action and north to the University of Nevada and to the Nevada Historical Society. Highway 395 leads south to Virginia City. In Sparks, Rock Boulevard takes off to the south to Glendale and a left turn for Harrah's Automobile Collection. Pyramid Way is the turn for the Pyramid Lake **Alternate Loop**.

Although Sparks seems like a continuation of casinoland, it is actually a separate community named after Governor John Sparks. It was settled early in this century as the repair center and switching yard for the railroad. The many warehouses and trucking facilities built along the interstate attest to Nevada's attractive tax structure. The awesome hole in the ground north of the freeway is not for excess inventory from the warehouses; the apartments have a cliff-edge view of a gravel pit.

Note the stress on agriculture, industry, and transportation. (*Nevada Historical Society*)

VISTA EXIT

Take the Vista exit to enjoy the wide-ranging view to the west. The ring of mountains around Reno captures summer air and winter fog, both of which can result in severe smog. Below, the pioneer trail circled to the south to avoid the marshy meadows. Dotting the hillsides are pinyon and juniper trees. Take a minute to look at the sign replicating the Great Seal of Nevada. It illustrates the many ways Nevadans have made their living from the land.

The Truckee River and the railroad become our companions once again. For the pioneers the river was a blessing—a source of fresh, cold water after forty miles of hot and dusty desert. But it was also cursed loudly and vociferously. Between Wadsworth and Reno some parties were forced to cross its rocky bottom more than thirty times, making every step painful. Tempers flared as cold, wet people and weary animals struggled forward.

The Truckee River canyon highlights various geological features. On the north is the Pah Pah Range and to the south across the river is the Virginia Range. Both show evidence of volcanic activity in the not-so-distant past. A finger of prehistoric Lake Lahontan once touched these hillsides. You can see wave-cut terraces along the hills between Patrick and Mustang exits. Similar lines can be seen all the way to Winnemucca, giving the sense that you are driving on a lake bottom. The exit to Patrick recalls Senator Pat McCarran, whose family ranch lies near the river.

The Tracy-Clark exit leads to two industrial concerns. Just at the exit is a ranch with horses for rent. The Tracy Station of the Sierra Pacific Power Company imports natural gas and oil to heat water for operating the turbines. The resulting electricity flows into a power system for communities east of the Sierra. Tours for small groups can be arranged.

An installation of the Eagle Pitcher Company peeks out from a screen of cottonwood trees. It processes diatomaceous earth, which is the white, glassy skeletal remains of microscopic organisms. The factory crushes and dries the earth for use as filters and absorbents. Check with the manager for tour possibilities.

The river's meander is defined by vegetation along its banks. Leafless branches of riparian trees compose a lacy pattern of subtle pinks, greens, yellows, and reds. They blend softly with the palette of colors from mineral and rock deposits on the hillsides. Magpies live in these colorful plant tunnels. With their black bills, they are cousins of the yellow-billed magpie of California's Central Valley.

The Thisbe-Derby Dam exit frontage road leads to a historic marker celebrating the Federal Reclamation Act of 1902. Nearby, a system of dams and canals was constructed to divert Truckee water for agriculture. The small concrete dam is just out of sight, but the diversion canal is seen on the hill above. It slopes toward Fernley and Fallon, towns that sprouted as farmers arrived to tame the alkali sands. The desert "soil" proved far more cooperative when manure, gypsum, and alum were added. Today's fields of alfalfa and hay provide feed for the cattle industry.

PAINTED ROCKS

Take the Orchard exit offramp, and park at the two stone pillars that have stood guard for decades. These big rock-candy monuments are our preamble to the painted rocks along the freeway ahead. Except for the creamy white quartz, all the rocks of the pillars are volcanic. The green, purple, and pink colors are caused by the action of hot solutions that have chemically altered the rock. Iron oxide is the usual coloring agent. When you can see crystals, as in the dark-gray speckled specimen, the rock has not been altered. (By the way, the golden flecks in the quartz are only "fool's gold.")

Back on the freeway, scan the hillside above the Painted Rock exit for evidence of prospectors' mining holes. Gold has been mined in the district, but not very successfully.

Wadsworth lies just north of the highway on old U.S. 40. It was a prosperous community until the railroad relocated and moved buildings and people to Sparks in 1904. Highway 447 leads north to the Paiute Indian Reservation and to Pyramid Lake sixteen miles away. The **Alternate Loop** returns to the interstate here.

The big bend of the Truckee River offered water for exhausted and thirsty pioneers after forty miles of waterless travel. Feelings of relief poured from Elisha Brooks upon reaching this spot in 1852: "We beheld the green banks and crystal clear waters of the Truckee River by the morning sun; and it was to us the River of Life." The river yielded salmon trout, a true delight after months of a skimpy diet of beans, bacon, fried dough, and more beans. Emigrants were reminded of home by the sight of cottonwoods after more than a thousand miles of treeless travel. The ones you see have replaced the giants cut by early settlers.

For several miles past the Nevada Cement Plant the highway passes sand dunes remaining from Lake Lahontan. Shifting sand made these last miles of desert pure torture for the pioneers, who were forced to push and pull the wagons forward. Bennett Clark wrote of his 1849 crossing:

> About 2 O'clock we struck the heavy sand 10 miles from the Trucky River, & had the utmost difficulty in getting our stock thro—stopping every few yards to rest. . . . All along the desert from the very start, even the waysides was strewed with the dead bodies of oxen, mules and horses and the stench was horrible. All our traveling experience furnishes no parallel to this.

The interstate follows the right-of-way of the Central Pacific Railroad. The tracks were laid near the ruts of the pioneer trail and across the "fearful crossing" of the Forty-Mile Desert. Though not much of the wagon trail can be seen from the freeway, rest assured that the ghosts of pioneers who died along this tortuous stretch are less than a mile away.

Desert driving elicits strong complaints, which range from the awful heat to the tedium of staring at gray, stunted shrubs dotting the drab landscape. Also, to paraphrase an eminent American leader, "Once you've seen one mountain, you've seen them all!" Perhaps the challenge posed by these comments can be met within this book's covers, and the trip will seem shorter with new mind-images for company.

And thus the hardest travail of the pioneers' trip was ending, just as your desert journey is beginning. Prepared? Water to drink and perhaps some for the car? Repair tools, tire chains, compass, and a detailed map if you dare to leave the pavement? Today the 365-mile trip from Wadsworth to the Utah border can be made in a quick six hours any time of day or night in all seasons. Westward-bound wagons took over three weeks to cross this same distance. Not only was the trip across the desert long but it was also made at the worst time of year. Because the pioneers could not start across the midwestern plains until spring when the land was dried out, the grass was greening, and the rivers were receding, they did not reach Nevada until the hot, dry summer. Water was scarce and in places poisonous, and flies and dust made everyone miserable.

Families wealthy enough to have begun the trip with "palace wagons" were often forced by the end of the desert march to part with most of their prize possessions. Until a few years ago the trail was littered with pottery, iron parts, pieces of furniture, and even bones. Treasure hunters have taken everything. Along this stretch 900 graves have been found, grim reminders of the toll the desert extracted from the weak, sick, unprepared, or unlucky.

"If I never see another sagebrush. . . ." (*The Denver Public Library, Western History Department*)

Beyond Fernley the interstate leads to the intersection with Highway 95, which crosses the Carson Sink north of Fallon. The Trinity Mountains are to the west of the freeway and the Hot Springs Mountains off to the east. On the hillsides look for the impressive shorelines of Lake Lahontan. Imagine that your car is a boat traversing the enormous lake and that the mountaintops have become islands and peninsulas.

Just past Fernley an alkali sink playa is filled intermittently with water. The golden-brown grasses and small plants ringing the borders of this alkaline area are similar to the salt-tolerant plants of ocean marshes. Wading sandpipers can be sighted as well as avocets, with their reddish heads and black-and-white striped wings. Environmental detectives might observe if this water is too salty to form ice when the outside temperature is below freezing.

On either side of the road are curious sand hummocks, memorably tedious to the horse-powered pioneer wagons. Tentacles of sagebrush and greasewood roots hold the mounds of sand in place.

HOT SPRINGS

The midway point of the Forty-Mile Desert is at the Hot Springs/ Nightengale exit. Disgruntled pioneers called it the "spring of false hope" when they stopped here to marshall their dwindling strength. If they could return to this spot, consider their surprise at coming across a modern food-processing factory that uses the water that sickened their families and their oxen to produce heat for dehydrating onions!

Stop at the office of Geothermal Food Processors to ask permission to walk up the slope about 100 yards to the site of the springs. They are no longer filled with water, but the channels constructed by the pioneers remain. These small containments spread out the boiling water so that it could cool. It was barely potable even then, and animals were known to have died from it. Mark Twain commented that he tried molasses and pickles to improve the taste! Looking south from the springs you can barely see a yellow Emigrant Trail marker. Seek out the route the pioneers took as they marched doggedly ahead.

Eight miles past Hot Springs, the highway crests a hill. To the northeast a reddish, mineralized mountain oversees the desert. Between you and the mountain lies the outflow area of the Humboldt Sink, dry as a bone at times and a shallow lake at others. Farther to the east below the mountains on the horizon is the Carson Sink.

Near mile marker 75, ten miles past the hot springs, brownish, pyramid-shaped rock pillars dot the landscape between I-80 and the sink. These are tufa pinnacles, similar to the impressive formations on the edges of Pyramid Lake. Algae reacting with water bubbling up from hot springs results in precipitation of minerals. The surrounding countryside supports spiny, drought-tolerant plants of the shadscale community and grasses imported by cattle ranchers. Rabbit brush forms dried arrangements along the edge of the road, where more moisture is available. In and among the plants the purplish surface is the wind-and-sun phenomena called desert varnish.

THE CROSSROADS

Exit 83 is the end of our trip. It is a pleasant oasis complete with shade, picnic tables, barbecue grills, wheelchair-accessible bathrooms, and historic markers.

The roadside rest is located at a crossroads of history, as the future of each pioneer party was determined by the choices made at this point. Should they continue south forty miles across the alkali flats of the Carson Sink to the Carson River and hence over the Sierra to Placerville? Or should they travel southwest forty miles to follow the Truckee River? Before 1849 most parties selected the Truckee route.

A state historic marker points out the shores of prehistoric Lake Lahontan and caves where the Archaic or Lovelock Culture set up housekeeping over 10,000 years ago. An old Paiute legend described these people as small, red-haired, freckled cannibals. The Paiutes claim to have driven the ancients into a cave and told them that unless they stopped eating their neighbors the cave would be their grave. Receiving no promises, the Paiutes heaped driftwood at the entrance and cremated the cannibals.

Within view two miles north of the rest area lies a low gravel ridge or bar composed of Lake Lahontan terrace and beach deposits. Hidden from view on the other side is Humboldt Lake, at times filled with water, and Big Meadows near Lovelock, where the pioneers cut what grass they could and filled their wagons for the forbidding trip ahead. The Humboldt River will remain in sight for the eastbound traveler for the next 300 miles. An ancient river on the plain, it will meander three times that

The 1870s marked the change from wagon trails to iron rails. (*Southern Pacific Railroad and the California State Railroad museum, Sacramento*)

distance. The interstate takes advantage of the work of the ages by following the river's route through numerous mountain ranges.

Our journey is at an end. For those heading to California, however, the adventure is just beginning. To the west lie reminders of pioneer hardships, sites of gold and silver mines, the grandeur of the Sierra, green and golden foothills, the fertile Central Valley, and the magnificent views of the San Francisco Bay.

Alternate Loop

PYRAMID LAKE

In Sparks take the Pyramid Lake exit to Highway 445. At the lake follow along the south shore east to Nixon, then south on Highway 447 to rejoin the interstate at Wadsworth. The drive adds twenty-five miles on well-maintained paved roads that cross rangelands and open desert.

North of Reno Highway 445 cuts through a low pass in the hills. After several miles of new ranchettes, the countryside becomes dotted with junipers, pinyon pines, range cattle, and fences constructed of branches. Be on the lookout for the Wild Horse and Burro Placement Center, where about 1000 horses and burros await adoption. Open weekdays, it is a must stop for animal lovers. These wild animals have multiplied so fast that they are consuming much of the feed on the range. Beautiful as horses are when they race across the desert with manes flowing, they eat much of the scarce grass needed for cattle, sheep, and native animals. A roundup for the horses and burros is a mini-drama of the New West. Portable corrals are constructed and animals are herded into them by helicopters.

The Paiute Indian Reservation begins nine miles farther on. Set aside in 1859, it encompasses the area surrounding Pyramid Lake. Fishing and off-road travel are controlled by the Tribal Authority.

Stop at the roadside rest at the crest of the hill overlooking the lake. There is a sense of unreality about Pyramid Lake—such a vast body of water surrounded by desolate mountains and contorted stone sculptures along the shore. Compare your reaction to John C. Fremont's when he encountered the lake in 1844 while on a government exploring trip. He recorded that it "broke upon my eyes like an ocean." He went on that he named the lake for a shoreline rock that was "a pretty exact outline of the great Pyramid of Cheops."

The lake is one of the few remnants of Ice-Age Lake Lahontan. It is approximately 30 miles long, up to 11 miles wide, and 300 feet deep. Kaleidoscopic water colors give the appearance of a map colored sea green, cyanide blue, brownish yellow, and glassy pink. The colors can be accounted for partly by inorganic particles suspended in the water to which seasonal plankton blooms are added. Formations along the shore are tufa, precipitated deposits of calcium carbonate. Algae growing in and around hot springs assist in the precipitation.

The large island near the eastern shore is Anaho Island. An Indian legend relates that here a giant basket was placed over an erring Indian woman. She turned to stone, but her breath remained visible as the steam from the island's hot springs.

Evidence abounds that Pyramid Lake was once much larger; note the old beaches and terraces on the hillsides. Part of the reason for its shrinking is climatic change. In this arid land, nineteen times more water can evaporate than falls as rain. In addition, eighty years of siphoning off Truckee River water for irrigation and for use by Reno's growing population has reduced natural inflow, and the lake is now ninety feet lower than when Fremont arrived.

Pyramid is a paradise for birds. Anaho Island—closed to tourists—continues to be one of the nation's largest breeding areas for white pelicans, with a nesting population of about 8000 birds. The birds are safe

The Great Stone Mother, a tufa formation at Pyramid Lake. The legend of the Paiute Tribes is that the First Mother and First Father originally lived in the area now occupied by Pyramid Lake, and there raised a family. The sons became the heads of the Tribes and eventually began to war with one another. When the Great Mother could not persuade them to cease warring she was greatly grieved, and, taking her basket, sat upon the hillside and wept. Her tears at last filled the valley and created what we now know as Pyramid Lake. In time she was turned to stone, but the Lake her tears created continues to fill the valley. The Tribes believe that as long as the Great Stone Mother guards the Lake, its waters will continue, and her children will have a home near its shores under her protection. (*Nevada Historical Society*)

from predators on their island, but should the water level drop another twenty feet the island will become a peninsula, allowing access to coyotes and other predatory animals. There is also a small colony of California gulls that may have flown here from Ocean Beach in San Francisco. Bird lovers may see great blue herons and double-crested cormorants glide across the sky.

The lake has long been a favorite for outings. A 1940 guidebook had this to say: "Discriminating people of the Truckee Meadows [Reno] bring out-of-state visitors to this lake on their first trip into the environs, for its color and the color of the surrounding terrain is breath-taking. The shores are popular for steak-parties at sunset, particularly at the time of the full moon, for the gamut from red to dark purple is then complete."

At the lake's shore, a short detour north leads to Sutcliffe, a stage stop and later a fishing resort visited by such celebrities as Clark Gable and Herbert Hoover. Fishing continues to be popular, especially for the native cutthroat trout, which have been known to weigh in at forty pounds. Sutcliffe has a motel, restaurant, and a fish hatchery that is open to visitors. Nine miles past Sutcliffe is Warrior Point Recreational Facility, with forty campsites operated by Washoe County Parks.

If you go to Sutcliffe, return to the intersection with Highway 445 and continue along the south side of the lake to Nixon. The abandoned rail line seen from the road was constructed in 1912 by Southern Pacific and ran from Fernley to northeastern California, carrying both lumber and passengers. As you enter Nixon the fanciful stone building near the intersection is an unfinished Paiute museum.

The Truckee River, or what's left of it, flows into the lake at Nixon. If the water level continues to sink, the water will become more salty, the fish will be unable to survive, the birds will lose their food sources, and some of the Paiutes will lose their livelihood, which is based on fishing and tourism.

Take Highway 447 south to Wadsworth and stop at the historic marker eleven miles from Nixon. Here you can recreate a historic western battle. In the 1860s friction increased between the settlers in the Comstock area and the Paiutes. The Paiutes were beginning to feel the pinch of losing access to their homeland as well as competition for deer and other animals necessary for their survival. Provoked by attacks on their women, the Paiutes killed four white men. Frightened, the settlers called together a volunteer army. The motley army was led into a clever trap while riding down the Truckee River valley, and seventy were killed. Fear spread and settlers from as far as California joined U.S. Army soldiers to quell the insurrection in a second, one-sided battle. The federal government granted the defeated Paiutes the land around the lake after many years of negotiating. The poignant words of the Paiute chieftain recounting the losses and hardships suffered by his people are quoted in **Yesterday's Voices**.

Three miles after the marker note the sign for Captain Dave Numana's Hapa-Agai Hatchery, operated by Tribal Enterprises. The hatchery raises the sweet-flavored sucker fish, which has been a staple of the Paiute diet. Tours are available. In a few miles the road rejoins the interstate at the big bend of the Truckee at Wadsworth.

Favorite Diversions

VERDI

Take Business 80 in the western outskirts of Verdi.

Verdi (like the opera composer) nestles into a verdant valley between forested mountains and treeless hills. The town began as a timber center in the last century when wood was vital for progress. It was needed for railroad ties, for steam-engine fuel, as support timbers in mining tunnels, to build flumes, and for home heating and cooking. One wonders why Verdi did not remain a thriving metropolis when the timber industry waned. It certainly has positive attributes, being situated on a river within the cooler pine belt and only ten miles from Reno. New mobile-home parks are evidence that it is again growing, but as a bedroom community.

Verdi's most exciting historical moment was the Great Train Robbery of 1870, just a year and a half after rail service began. Six robbers "kidnapped" the locomotive, mail, and express cars and escaped with $41,000. God-fearing citizens pointed out that "crime doesn't pay" when the six were captured in a week.

As you pass a house here and there while driving into town, note the roadside sign, obviously written by an open-space fan: "Congested area—no firearms." Crystal Park, located on the Truckee River just after the bridge, is a lovely spot for a picnic or a little overdue fishing.

Turn left on Bridge Street, which leads to public riding stables and the Donner Trail Dinner House (open all year; closed on Monday and Tuesday; expensive). It used to be a dude ranch, popular when Nevada was the country's divorce capital. Eastern socialites, including Nelson Rockefeller's first wife, spent their six weeks of necessary residence here while waiting for a quickie divorce.

Take the right-hand fork in the road just past the dinner house. The Crystal Peak Cemetery lies at the top of the short hill, where some gravestones date back to the 1860s. If a wire fence fifty feet to the left of the cemetery entrance is broken down, cross through and follow the fence around two corners of the cemetery. Diagonally across from the entrance gate stands a lone pine (gentle Jeffrey or prickly ponderosa?). In front of the tree is a yellow marker proclaiming the presence of the Emigrant Trail. Look for the ruts most resembling the wagon trail. How far apart were the wheels? Close scrutiny reveals scratches on several rocks embedded in the trail that may have been made by iron-rimmed wagon wheels. While you stand among the desert plants, smell the aroma of sage.

A mini-adventure beckons from this point. Continue driving west. Within a couple of blocks look sharply to the south for an iron obelisk protected on all sides by cyclone fencing. Here you will be able to stand with a foot in two states. The monument was put in place in 1872 by A.W. Von Schmidt, astronomer and surveyor from San Francisco. He noted that this point is 170 miles and 43 chains (a chain is 66 feet) from the Oregon border.

Von Schmidt was not the first to pass this way. In 1845 aged Caleb Greenwood opened this route for wagons while leading an early pioneer group to California. Nearly every subsequent pioneer party used it, preferring its two summits over the mountain to the rocks and icy water of the Truckee River. In 1846 Heinrich Lienhard wrote in his diary:

> Here we left Truckee River and ascended the mountain, through thick forest, across difficult, rocky mountain slope. We were in constant fear that the wheels of our wagon would strike against the giant firs on the lower side of the road.

Proceeding up the grade you will travel the main transcontinental route in use until the 1920s, when the Truckee River highway was hacked out of the rock. Dog Valley Summit is reached in two and one-half miles, some of which is gravel. At the summit the left fork stays on the ridge, eventually coming to Boca and Stampede reservoirs. It is passable only in summer, and even then, four-wheel vehicles are advised. Park at the summit and walk west a few hundred feet to gaze into the valley below. Now grazing land within a national forest, Dog Valley seems a green jewel amid the pines. The historic Henness Pass wagon road led past the valley on its way to Nevada City.

Retracing your route to Verdi, you might wish to stop for refreshment at the Verdi Inn, a roadhouse since the 1920s. Its current owner displays her fine collection of antique dolls and liqueur bottles along the walls of this inn. Colorful fish swim in an aquarium separating the bar and the dining room.

RENO

Leave Interstate 80 at West 4th Street. In a short distance turn right on Mayberry Drive, which leads into town.

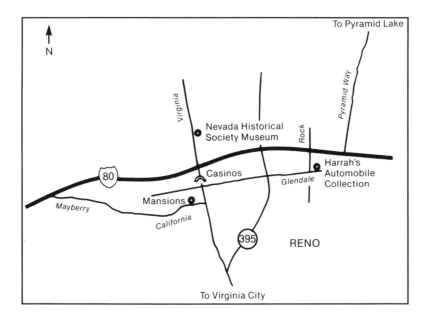

Washoe Indians congregated in this valley where Reno was to grow. Abundant food was available in this sagebrush plain through which the Truckee River flowed. Marshes along the river provided homes for birds and materials for shelter.

Few pioneers lingered in the valley, so anxious were they to sample the proverbial wealth of California. The score or so who stayed in Truckee Meadows grazed cattle and cut the luxurious marsh grasses. Various trails led through the marshy meadows to routes over the Sierra. To save a few miles and a wet crossing of the Truckee River, entrepreneurs Charles Fuller and Myron Lake built a bridge and provided minimal accommodations. A bonanza came with the discovery of the Comstock Lode when beef, butter, and supply animals came into great demand. Some years later as railroad track was nearing the crossroad along the Truckee, Lake schemed with Charles Crocker, the construction superintendent. The result was an auction at "the end of the track." Downtown properties went for as much as $1000. With the anticipation that a short railroad line was in the works to Virginia City, the settlement became a bustling frontier town. For reasons hidden by the years, the town was named after a young Union general, Jesse Lee Reno, who had been killed in the Civil War. He had no direct association with the town or its founders.

Life in Reno in the latter decades of the nineteenth century was spent in making money, grousing about taxes, and ignoring provisions for

A snowy December evening in the 1920s soon after the transcontinental highway was opened. (*Nevada Historical Society*)

parks and museums. Locals played politics, and Reno became the county seat but was not destined to become the glorious capital of the Silver State.

Reno's Grand Old Homes

Mayberry Drive is built upon the Emigrant Trail; it becomes California Street, which dead-ends at South Virginia Street. Along California Street you pass stately mansions standing in splendor on a bluff. Newly rich Nevadans at the turn of the century must have impressed even themselves with their copies of architectural styles from around the world.

Turn left on South Virginia Street. The bridge over the Truckee is near the site of the wagon crossing. You are now on casino row, the center of "the biggest little city." Once a cow town, now tourists are corralled as they take advantage of the gaming that was legalized in 1931. A helpful hint: the big casinos are so anxious to get customers that they are usually pleased to cash checks—no doubt hoping that most of the cash will be spent at the gaming tables. The visitor center is just a block west on Sierra Street, not far from the river. Stop by for a copy of the walking tour to the elegant mansions, which was prepared by the Junior League of Reno.

Nevada Historical Society

Drive north on Virginia Street, crossing over the interstate and passing the University of Nevada.

At the north end of the campus is a complex of educational and cultural facilities, including the Lawlor Events Center, a planetarium, and the Nevada Historical Society. All are accessible from North Virginia Street. The pleasant museum attracts school groups as well as leisurely visitors. Carefully prepared dioramas follow Nevada's history from prehistoric times to the present. Especially interesting are the Emigrant Trail "debris," bleached by the hot desert sun, and the display of Washoe basketry. Materials relating to Nevada's history are watched over by research librarians happy to answer your questions. The society is open Wednesday through Sunday from 10 A.M. to 5 P.M; docent tours are available.

Harrah's Automobile Collection

Great fun for all ages, this not-to-be-missed exhibit is located in big warehouses. Harrah's Casino offers a shuttle on antique vehicles from its downtown casino. There is an admission charge. Within a few years a museum will be constructed near the casino to house 300 of the most special vehicles.

Wealthy casino owner Bill Harrah built this collection, because he felt that the automobile made a significant contribution to our country's rise as a world power. As Detroit had made no move to build a hall of fame to these mechanical heroes, he created this monument as a labor of love, sparing no expense.

Over 1200 vehicles are displayed in shiny, mint condition, everything from 1892 "speedsters" to a sleek DeLorean. Also on display is a Bugatti Royale coupe, appraised at over two million dollars. Visitors can admire a Model A like the one from grandma's first date or revel in the sleek design of racing machines. See James Dean's "cool" black '49 Mercury and study model changes of Fords and Packards over the decades. Notice how features like tires became stronger and wider as vehicles became heavier and more versatile.

An unexpected jackpot tucked away to the right of the entrance is the one-room Lyon Pony Express museum with its flintlocks, arrow collections, player piano, shiny pumper fire engine, and guess-the-name rock collection.

VIRGINIA CITY

From Reno take Highway 395 south ten miles; turn east on Highway 340 (the Geiger Grade) for fourteen miles. The drive is on good but steep paved roads and takes about an hour from Reno. Virginia City is a city in name only and has only limited overnight accommodations. There is a public swimming pool.

A summer day's excursion into the high desert mountains to the site of the Comstock mining boom provides a "bonanza" of memories and activities. Victorian buildings and mine tailings give testimony to the glory days. Spectacular views of the Sierra contrast with vistas of smooth basins and ranges. For those seeking active entertainment, try the ride on an old "puffer" train and walk into the mountain at a historic mine.

Two Geiger Grades have been named after the nineteenth-century road builder. Today's road seems much safer than the former steep, dusty track that can still be seen and is used by adventurers with four-wheel-drive vehicles. Driving to the summit brings travelers in close contact with mountain vegetation. Small, single-needled pinyon pines (in early summer laden with yellow pollen) alternate with scale-leafed junipers. Notice the substantial pine roots along sandy roadcuts—it's a long way down to water.

Five miles up the grade, an overlook offers fantastic vistas. Do stop and get your bearings. Across the valley the runs of two ski areas, Mt. Rose and Slide Mountain, cut down the steep Sierra slopes. Carson City, the state capital, lies to the south down the valley. The brilliantly colored rock walls of the overlook are constructed from nearby andesite, a volcanic rock.

Our road crests a summit at nearly 6800 feet. Summertime temperatures here stay a pleasant ten degrees cooler than Reno. A state historical marker indicates the site of "Lousetown," an unattractive-sounding community. Also mentioned is an ice project—not ice to cool tea or martinis, but to provide a tolerable working environment for miners who toiled underground.

The terrain around Virginia City is volcanic and is marked by cinder cones such as Sugarloaf, which you see to the east as you enter town. The precious minerals exist because of the effects of volcanic heat and the movement of molten materials toward the earth's surface. These subterranean pressures push hot water into cracks and fissures, including mining tunnels. The heat down under can reach the intolerable temperature of 140 degrees. Mine owners were forced to build ice-cooled rooms where miners could cool down between short shifts below.

Virginia City in 1936. Mine tailings are just behind the church steeples. (*Nevada Historical Society*)

Between 1859 when the Comstock Lode was discovered and 1879, Virginia City, or Washoe as it was called, grew to over 30,000 residents, becoming the biggest little town in Nevada. People lived in chaos, dust, and at times in snowdrifts. One year after the discovery, the instant city boasted of one hotel, nine restaurants, forty-two saloons, one bath house, ten laundries, one tailor and dressmaker, two barbers, one dentist, seven cobblers, ten stables, seven blacksmiths, one surveyor, five brokers, and thirty-eight stores. Miners brought a confusion of languages and at first were not concerned about amenities. Women and children slowly trickled in, and some semblance of social order began, including the construction of a school, a union hall, an opera house, and several churches.

Your first view of Virginia City, known as one of the bawdiest towns of the Old West, is incongruous. A church steeple is the only indication that a settlement lies over the hill. More to tourists' expectations is the map to "Cat Houses of Nevada" gracing the wall of a historic bar.

On the way into town, stop at the visitor center on C Street and see the short audio-visual presentation. Also pick up a copy of the driving/ walking tour printed by the U.S. Heritage Conservation and Recreation Service.

Tourists strolling along Virginia City's six-block main street often decry the hillocks of ugly, yellow mine tailings that dot the landscape. Most folks who live and work here accept the debris as a fact of life. As a woman working at a tourist attraction was heard to say, "Without mining there wouldn't be a town."

The Virginia and Truckee Railroad

For a ride on the Virginia (City) and Truckee (River) Steam Railroad, leave C Street at Taylor and walk downhill two blocks to the F Street terminal.

For a fee visitors ride behind the lovingly renovated steam engine. On the way passengers are treated to commentary by an old-time conductor. Afterwards, chances are that the engineer will let the young at heart climb the steps of the engine to see the controls and feel the intense heat of the firebox.

Shrewd financiers set the wheels of Virginia City railroading in motion. Three men associated with the Bank of California saw an opportunity: the need to get lumber and supplies up the mountain and ore downhill faster and cheaper than the muleskinners could do the job. William Ralston, bank cashier; D. O. Mills, president; and William Sharon, the bank's Nevada representative, put together the scheme, invested little of their own money, and went on to make fortunes off their little V & T line.

Twenty-one miles of track were laid in 1869 of the route that would eventually connect Virginia City to Carson City and Reno. Much of the work was done by Chinese laborers who had just finished building the Central Pacific Railroad. When the first train arrived in nearby Gold Hill, Sharon made sure that beer flowed and champagne corks popped. Miners blew whistles from every steam mill and hoist, and engine whistles added to the cacophony. The citizenry of Virginia City loved it. The local paper reported, "Our people spend all their holidays riding over the new track." In the heyday of the little line, forty-five trains ran daily. It shut down officially in 1950, leaving behind a ghost town since revived by tourism.

Chollar Mine

Continue past the V & T terminal, cross the tracks, and turn left, following the signs to the mine a block ahead.

A tour of the only "real" mine open to visitors takes under an hour. There is a small admission charge.

This mine goes back to the beginning of the boom, and it ranks in wealth among the top five Comstock mines. It was worked until 1942, when the federal government closed down all "unessential mining" during World War II. In the past few years, as the price of gold and silver has risen, fortune hunters have begun mining the tailings.

Visitors don rubber boots before entering the damp mine tunnel. The 425-foot tunnel leads to a room-sized cavern where the silver-bearing blue muck can be seen and felt. Massive timbers shoring up the walls and ceiling use a geometric design developed in Virginia City. The wood once graced hillsides of the Sierra and came here via the V & T rail line.

When the guide turns off the electricity and lights a candle, you are transported back to the working conditions of the nineteenth century. Intolerable heat, foul air, dust from the drilling, water dripping, and exhausting hours were a miner's life.

Adolph Sutro, whose Cliff House graced the San Francisco shoreline, made his fortune in Virginia City. He dreamed that a tunnel could be dug from the Carson River below the lode to the mine tunnels to drain the hot water from the mines. The miners became Sutro's allies and invested in his project. Backers of the railroad saw potential competition, for the tunnel could also be used to transport ore. They countered Sutro at every turn. Fortunately for the railroad, Sutro's tunnel took thirteen years to finance and build. By that time the boom was nearing its end. Still, it proved profitable for its originator. Today the only obvious evidence of the tunnel is a cement-covered entrance three miles east of Dayton near the Carson River.

The railroad, the mine, and the tunnel give witness to human perseverence when wealth, elusive as it may be, seems close at hand. Dreaming of the big strike, fortune seekers poured into Virginia City and other spots where precious metals were rumored to line the streets.

Mark Twain, who lived in Virginia City for a time and was caught up in this scramble, later wrote: "I confess, without shame, that I expected to find masses of silver lying all about the ground. I expected to see it glittering in the sun on the mountain summits. I said nothing about this, for some instinct told me that I might possibly have an exaggerated idea about it. . . ." Needless to say, he did.

Yesterday's Voices

EXODUS TO WASHOE

By J. Ross Browne

The lust for riches inspires exaggeration and rationalizes strange behavior. Washoe was another term for the Comstock Lode.

As I live, it is a cry of Silver! Silver in WASHOE! Not gold, now, you silly men of Gold Bluff, you Kern Riverites, you daring explorers of British Columbia! But SILVER—solid, pure SILVER! Beds of it ten thousand feet deep! Acres of it! miles of it! hundreds of millions of dollars poking their backs up out of the earth ready to be pocketed!. . . "Sir," said my informant to me, in strict confidence, no later than this morning, "you may rely upon it, for I am personally acquainted with a brother of the gentleman whose most intimate friend saw the man whose partner has just come over the mountains, and he says there never was the like on the face of the earth! The ledges are ten thousand feet deep—solid masses of silver. Let us be off! Now is the time! A pack-mule, pick and shovel, hammer, and frying-pan will do. You need nothing more. HURRAH FOR WASHOE!". . .

A short distance beyond Gold Hill we came in sight of the great mining capital of Washoe, the far-famed Virginia City. . . .

On a slope of mountains speckled with snow, sage-brushes, and mounds of upturned earth, without any apparent beginning or end, congruity or regard for the eternal fitness of things, lay outspread the wondrous city of Virginia.

Frame shanties, pitched together as if by accident; tents of canvas, of blankets, of brush, of potato-sacks and old shirts, with empty whisky-barrels for chimneys; smoky hovels of mud and stone; coyote holes in the mountain side forcibly seized and held by men; pits and shafts with smoke issuing from every crevice; piles of goods and rubbish on craggy points, in the hollows, on the rocks, in the mud, in the snow, everywhere, scattered broadcast in pell-mell confusion, as if the clouds had suddenly burst overhead and rained down the dregs of all the flimsy, rickety, filthy little hovels and rubbish of merchandise that had ever undergone the process of evaporation from the earth since the days of Noah. The intervals of space, which may or may not have been streets, were dotted over with human beings of such sort, variety, and numbers, that the famous ant-hills of Africa were as nothing in the comparison. To say that they were rough, muddy, unkempt, and unwashed would be but faintly expressive of their actual appearance; they were all this by reason of exposure to the weather; but they seemed to have caught the very diabolical tint and grime of the whole place. Here and there, to be sure, a San Francisco dandy of the "boiled-shirt" and "stove-pipe" pattern loomed up in proud consciousness of the triumphs of art under adverse circumstances, but they were merely peacocks in the barn-yard.

PAIUTE CHIEF TELLS IT LIKE IT WAS

From the Official Report by Colonel Frederick W. Lander

An American army colonel reported back to Washington in 1860 on his meeting with "Winnemucka, chief of the Humboldt river Pah-Utes." Regardless of the language problem, the chief poured out his feelings about white domination. The experiences of his people help explain the cause of the Indian War of 1860 between the Paiutes and the whites.

Winnemucka [Numaga] said he would look hard at me and when the sun was low would be ready to talk. The council, which was held at sunset, lasted over an hour and was quite an interesting one.

I told the Chief that I came to hear him say all he had to tell the great Father of the whites. I would listen with attention, but that I was only a listener. I could make him no promises. When the great Father heard from his children, the Pah-Utes, he would then know what to do. Perhaps he might be very angry because his people had been killed. He might send many warriors to fight the Indians and kill them, the Chief must talk plain, he must hide nothing, I should listen to him with open ears.

His reply was characteristic of the better class Indians of the plains. He said that when he asked me to wait until night before he would talk it was not because he liked the darkness. His heart was very open, it was like the sunshine, but some clouds had been before him, many of his young men had been killed, and he saw in my train men who had killed them, his breath was hot, it might have burnt my ears had he spoken too soon, now he had sat upon my blanket, had eaten of my meat and at last had smoked the pipe, and was quiet so that he could talk calmly.

At the expiration of perhaps two minutes, he threw of [off] his blanket and hunting shirt and commenced a harangue or speech of which the following is as near a translation as could probably be made. During this display which in tone, enunciation and jesture might be styled oratorical, he sometimes used broken English as if doutful [doubtful] of the ability of the interpreter to convey his exact meaning. He especially said in rough English, "Irishman come—Dutchman come—American man come—China-John come,—digum hole,—findum money heap,—good money find um,—Pah-Utes money—no give'um Pah-Ute money,—" (and then he stooped down and scraped together a little pile of earth which he covered closely with one hand while he held out the other hand empty and with open palm, as showing how the miners did and said,) "white man put him hand over money, and no give Pah-Utes any money,—give'um Pah-Utes heap God-dam,—'hook him,—beat him,—kill him. Big Father help Dutchman,—help Irishman,—help American man,—help China-John man,—why no help keep Pah-Ute man.? Pah-Ute man heap good long time,—no give 'um nothing'—Pah-Ute man no kill'um whites,—white man kill'um Pah-Utes, —Pah-Utes heap fight'um,—Soldier man come,—Winnemucka no sabe! Winnemucka fight—Winnemucka die, no care no more.—" The fierce denunciation with which these broken sentences were delivered,—the wild reckless manner of the chief and the deep mournful ejaculations of the warriors who surrounded him, when testifying their concurrence in his expressions, deprived this language of the ridiculous character which it may seem to bear when written. . . .

Reprinted in *The Paiutes of Pyramid Lake* by Ruth Hermann. (San Jose, Calif.: Harlan Young Press, 1972.)

MORNIN' ON THE DESERT

Anonymous

This poem was found written on the door of an old cabin in Nevada. Do we enjoy hustle and bustle as much as the freedom this person found in isolation?

Mornin' on the desert, and the wind is blowin' free,
And it's ours, jest for the breathin', so let's fill up, you and me.
No more stuffy cities, where you have to pay to breathe,
Where the helpless human creatures move and throng the[y] strive
    and seethe.

Mornin' on the desert, and the air is like a wine,
And it seems like all creation has been made for me and mine.
No house to stop my vision, save a neighbor's miles away,
And the little dobe shanty that belong to me and May.

Lonesome? Not a minute! Why I've got these mountains here,
That was put here just to please me, with their blush and frown and
   cheer.

They're wating when the summer sun gets too sizzlin' hot
An' we jest go campin' in 'em with a pan and coffee pot.
Mornin' on the desert—I can smell the sagebrush smoke,
I hate to see it burnin', but the land must sure be broke.
Ain't it jest a pity that wherever man may live,
He tears up much that's beautiful that the good God has to give?

"Sagebrush ain't so pretty?" Well, all eyes don't see the same.
Have you ever saw the moonlight turn it to a silvery flame?
An' that greasewood thicket yonder—Well, it smells jest awful sweet
When the night wind has been shakin' it—for its smell is hard to beat.
Lonesome? Well, I guess not! I've been lonesome in a town,
But I sure do love the desert with its stretches wide and brown.
All day through the sagebrush here the wind is blowin' free,
An' it's ours jest for the breathin', so let's fill up, you and me.

Reprinted in *Book of Nevada Poems*. (Reno: Nevada Federation of Womens' Clubs, 1927.)

LUPINE

NATURAL COMMUNITIES EASTWARD ALONG
THE INTERSTATE 80 CORRIDOR
in generally ascending elevation with reference by chapter

Coastal California Life Region

- *Ocean Marine*—Pacific Shore (Chap. 1)
  bull kelp
- *Intertidal*—Pacific Shore (Chap. 1)
  Rocky Marine
    orange and yellow sponge, red urchin,
      abalone, 21-leg star, feather boa kelp
  Main Tidepools
    sea lettuce, abalone, purple urchin, ochre star
  Uppermost Tidepools
    rockweed, mussel, gooseneck barnacle, anemone
  High-Tide Splash
    intestine alga, periwinkle, acorn barnacle
- *Coastal Strand*—Pacific Shore (Chap. 1)
  Salt-Spray Cliff
    maritime plantain, sea pink
  Inland Dune
    silver beachweed, sand verbena, dune sagebrush
  Upper Beach
    silver beachweed, sea rocket (introduced),
      dune grass (introduced)
- *Bay Marine*—Bay (Chap. 2)
  feather boa kelp
- *Salt Marsh*—Bay (Chap. 2)
  cordgrass, pickleweed, salt grass, sticky gum plant
- *Freshwater Marsh*—Pacific Shore (Chap. 1), Inner Coast (Chap. 3),
    Central Valley (Chap. 4), Lower Sierra (Chap. 5),
      Upper Sierra (Chap. 6)
        cattail, tule, willow
- *Coast Riparian Forest*—Pacific Shore (Chap. 1)
  Oregon alder, coastal willow
- *Coastal Scrub and Grassland*—Pacific Shore (Chap. 1), Bay (Chap. 2)
  coyote brush, bush lupine, coast bunchgrass (needlegrass)
- *Closed-Cone Conifer Forest*—Pacific Shore (Chap. 1)
  bishop pine, tanoak, huckleberry

- *Redwood Forest*—Pacific Shore (Chap. 1)
    coast redwood, redwood sorrel
- *Coastal Woodland*—Pacific Shore (Chap. 1)
    coast live oak, bay laurel
- *Canyon Forest or Mixed Evergreen Forest*—Pacific Shore, (Chap. 1)
    Inner Coast (Chap. 3), Lower Sierra (Chap. 5)
        canyon live oak, Douglas fir, madrone
- *Chaparral*—Pacific Shore (Chap. 1), Inner Coast (Chap. 3),
    Lower Sierra (Chap. 5)
        chamise, manzanita, ceanothus
- *Valley Grassland and Vernal Pools*—Inner Coast (Chap. 3),
    Central Valley (Chap. 4), Lower Sierra (Chap. 5)
        needlegrass, goldfields, meadowfoam,
            occasional valley oaks

Interior California Life Region

- *Lowland Riparian Forest*—Central Valley (Chap. 4)
    Fremont cottonwood, river willow
- *Foothill Oak Woodland*—Inner Coast (Chap. 3), Lower Sierra (Chap. 5)
        digger pine, blue oak
- *Lower Mountain Riparian*—Lower Sierra (Chap. 5)
    white alder, Oregon ash
- *Ponderosa Forest*—Lower Sierra (Chap. 5)
    ponderosa pine, sugar pine, Kellogg oak, white fir,
        incense cedar
- *Mountain Chaparral*—Lower Sierra (Chap. 5), Upper Sierra (Chap. 6)
    bitter cherry, manzanita, ceanothus, huckleberry oak
- *Upper Mountain Riparian*—Upper Sierra (Chap. 6)
    mountain alder, creek dogwood, black cottonwood, willow
- *Lodgepole/Red Fir Forest*—Upper Sierra (Chap. 6)
    lodgepole pine, red fir, Sierra juniper and
        Jeffrey pine (dry sites)
- *Subalpine Forest*—Upper Sierra (Chap. 6)
    mountain hemlock, whitebark pine (some lodgepole)
- *Alpine Rock Garden*—Upper Sierra (Chap. 6)
    dwarf willow, cushion buckwheat, tundra-type plants

Great Basin Life Region

- *Jeffrey Forest*—Upper Sierra (Chap. 6), Great Basin (Chap. 7)
    Jeffrey pine, sagebrush, antelope bush,
        mountain mahogany
- *Pinyon-Juniper Woodland*—Great Basin (Chap. 7)
    one-needled pinyon, Utah juniper
- *Great Basin Sagebrush*—Great Basin (Chap. 7)
    sagebrush, antelope bush
- *Shadscale Scrub*—Great Basin (Chap. 7)
    spiny sagebrush, winterfat, saltbush, hopsage
- *Alkali Sink*—Great Basin (Chap. 7)
    pickleweed, saltbush
- *Bristlecone Forest*—Great Basin (not seen on our route) (Chap. 7)
    bristlecone pine, limber pine, mountain mahogany

READ ON

General History

Bronson, William. *The Earth Shook, the Sky Burned*. New York: Doubleday, 1959.

Farquhar, Francis P. *History of the Sierra Nevada*. Berkeley: University of California Press, 1965.

Holliday, J.S. *The World Rushed In*. New York: Simon and Schuster, 1981.

Hoover, Mildred, and Hero and Ethel Rensch (revised by William N. Abeloe). *Historic Spots in California*. 3d ed. Stanford Calif.: Stanford University Press, 1966.

Hunt, Thomas H. *Ghost Trails to California: A Pictorial Journey from the Rockies to the Gold Country*. Palo Alto, Calif.: American West Publishing Co., 1974.

Jackson, Joseph Henry. *Anybody's Gold, The Story of California's Mining Towns*. San Francisco: Chronicle Books, 1970.

Kroeber, Theodora. *Ishi in Two Worlds: A Biography of the Last Wild Indian in North America*. Berkeley: University of California Press, 1961.

Sauer, Carl. *Man in Nature: American Days Before the Whiteman*. Berkeley: Turtle Island Foundation, 1975.

Stewart, George R. *The California Trail, an Epic with Many Heroes*. Omaha: University of Nebraska Press, 1962.

Stewart, George R. *Ordeal by Hunger*. New York: Pocket Books, 1936.

Sunset Editors. *Gold Rush Country*. 4th ed. Menlo Park, Calif.: Sunset-Lane Publishers, 1972.

Vale, Thomas R., and Geraldine Vale. *U.S. 40 Today: Thirty Years of Landscape Change in America*. Madison: The University of Wisconsin Press, 1983.

Regional Histories

Brown, Juanita K. *Nuggets of Nevada County History*. Nevada City, Calif.: Nevada County Historical Society, 1983.

Curran, Harold. *Fearful Crossing: The Central Overland Trail Through Nevada*. Reno: Great Basin Press, 1982.

Lord, Paul A., Jr., ed. *Fire and Ice, A Portrait of Truckee*. Truckee, Calif.: Truckee Donner Historical Society, 1981.

McGlashan, M. Nona. *Give Me a Mountain Meadow, The Life of Charles Fayette McGlashan (1847-1931)*. Fresno, Calif.: Pioneer Publishing Co., 1977.

Margolin, Malcolm. *The Ohlone Way, Indian Life in the San Francisco-Monterey Bay Area*. Berkeley: Heyday Books, 1978.

Meschery, Joanne. *Truckee, An Illustrated History of the Town and Its Surroundings*. Truckee, Calif.: Rocking Stone Press, 1978.

The Nevada Emigrant Trail Marking Committee. *The Overland Emigrant Trail to California: A Guide to Trail Markers Placed in Western Nevada and the Sierra Nevada Mountains in California*. Reno: Nevada Historical Society, 1975 (revised 1980).

Sutherland, Barbara, and James Fife. *Donner Memorial State Park Teacher's Handbook*. California State Parks System, 1982.

Townley, John M. *Tough Little Town on the Truckee: Reno to 1900*. Reno: The Great Basin Studies Center, 1983.

Wheat, Margaret M. *Survival Arts of the Primitive Paiutes*. Reno: University of Nevada Press, 1967.

Wiley, Bert. *The Overland Emigrant Trail to California*. Privately published, 1979.

Natural History

Bakker, Elna. *An Island Called California: An Ecological Introduction to Its Natural Communities*. Berkeley: University of California Press, 1971.

Crittenden, Mabel, and Dorothy Telfer. *Wildflowers of the West*. Millbrae, Calif.: Celestial Arts, 1975.

Doss, Margot P. *A Walker's Yearbook*. San Francisco: Novato, Calif.: Presidio Press, 1983.

Gere, James M., and Haresh C. Shah. *Terra Non Firma, Understanding and Preparing for Earthquakes*. Stanford, Calif.: Stanford Alumni Association, 1984.

Gilliam, Harold. *Weather of the San Francisco Bay Region*. Berkeley: University of California Press, 1962.

Hill, Mary. *Geology of the Sierra Nevada*. Berkeley: University of California Press, 1975.

Howard, Arthur D. *Geologic History of Middle California*. Berkeley: University of California Press, 1979.

Iacopi, Robert, ed. *Earthquake Country: California*. Menlo Park, Calif.: Sunset-Lane Books, 1971.

McPhee, John. *Basin and Range*. New York: Farrar, Straus & Giroux, 1981.

Muir, John. *The Mountains of California*. Berkeley: Ten Speed Press, 1977 (originally published in 1894).

Smith, Arthur C. *Introduction to the Natural History of the San Francisco Bay Region*. Berkeley: University of California Press, 1959.

Storer, Tracy, and Robert Usinger. *Sierra Nevada Natural History—An Illustrated Handbook*. Berkeley: University of California Press, 1970.

Watts, Tom. *Pacific Coast Tree Finder*. Berkeley: Nature Study Guild, 1973.

Webster, Paul. *The Mighty Sierra: Portrait of a Mountain World*. Palo Alto, Calif.: American West Publishing Co., 1972.

Wheeler, Sessions S. *The Desert Lake: The Story of Nevada's Pyramid Lake*. Caldwell, Idaho: Caxton Printers, 1974.

Literature

Bird, Isabella. *A Lady's Life in the Rocky Mountains*. Sausalito, Calif.: Comstock Editions, 1977 (originally published in 1879).

Bergon, Frank, ed. *The Wilderness Reader*. New York: The New American Library, 1980.

Caughey, John, and Laree Caughey, compilers. *California Heritage, An Anthology of History and Literature*. Itasca, Ill.: F.E. Peacock, 1971.

Galloway, David. *Tamsen, A Novel of the Tragic Journey of the Donner Party and the Heroism of an Extraordinary Woman*. New York: Harcourt, Brace, Jovanovich, 1983.

Kingston, Maxine Hong. *China Men*. New York: Ballantine, 1981.

Muir, John, ed. *West of the Rocky Mountains*. Philadelphia: Running Press, 1976 (originally published in 1888).

Norris, Frank. *The Octopus*. New York: The New American Library, 1981 (originally published in 1901).

Reid, Robert, compiler. *A Treasury of the Sierra Nevada*. Berkeley: Wilderness Press, 1982.

Stone, Irving. *Men to Match My Mountains*. New York: Berkley Publishers, 1982.

Twain, Mark. *Roughing It*. New York: New American Library, 1962 (originally published in 1872).

Whitman, Ruth. *Tamsen Donner: A Woman's Journey*. Cambridge, Mass.: Alice James Books, 1977.

Index

UNUSUAL BOOKS THAT FOCUS ON OUR WESTERN HERITAGE

Quantity

_____ **ADVENTURES ON & OFF INTERSTATE 80.** $12.95.

_____ **OPAL: THE JOURNAL OF AN UNDERSTANDING HEART.** Opal Whiteley; adapted by Jane Boulton. The perceptive diary of a young girl who lived in Oregon lumber camps at the turn of the century. Opal poetically describes her personal magical world of farm and forest. 190 pages. Elegant cloth edition. $12.95.

_____ **PASSING FARMS: ENDURING VALUES.** Yvonne Jacobson. Introduction by Wallace Stegner. An insider's look at the history of California's Santa Clara Valley, now better known as Silicon Valley. 270 pages. 140 rare photographs. Cloth edition. $39.50.

_____ **THE NEW BOOK OF CALIFORNIA TOMORROW: REFLECTIONS AND PROJECTIONS FROM THE GOLDEN STATE.** Edited by John Hart. A wide-ranging annotated anthology of "the best of _California Tomorrow,_" which mirrors the past 25 years of the environmental issues and provides a basis for rational planning. 450 pages. Paperback. $12.95.

_____ **THE URBAN EDGE: DESIGNS FOR THE CALIFORNIA COAST.** Edited by Dewey Schwartzenburg. This splendid volume from the State Coastal Conservancy offers guidelines for development that meet aesthetic, economic, environmental, and social needs. 128 pages. Paperback. $10.00.

_____ **DOCTOR NELLIE.** The autobiography of Helen MacKnight Doyle. This touching memoir chronicles her courage in transcending life on the frontier to become one of the first woman doctors trained in San Francisco and to practice in the Owens Valley. 365 pages. Elegant cloth edition. $17.95.

_____ **LIFE ON TWO LEVELS.** Josephine Whitney Duveneck. The inspirational autobiography of a woman of wealth from the East Coast who poured her life and love into making California a better home for people of many races and backgrounds. 382 pages. Cloth. $13.95.

_____ **THE LOST CEMENT MINE.** James W. A. Wright. One of the oldest and most elusive gold deposits is "the lost cement mine." This colorful history with illustrations and maps assists the reader in tracking this treasure in the high Sierra. 95 pages. Paperback. $7.95.

_____ **MAMMOTH LAKES SIERRA: A HANDBOOK FOR ROADSIDE AND TRAIL.** Edited by Genny Smith. A guide to the eastern Sierra Nevada describing points of interest, trails, natural history, and early events. 162 pages. Paperback. $7.95.

See other side for order form.

To: **William Kaufmann, Inc.**
   95 First St.
   Los Altos, California 94022

Please send me the books noted on the reverse. Enclosed is a check for full payment. I understand that I can return the books within 30 days for a full refund.

$ _____ Total for books

$ _____ Sales tax for California residents

$ _____ Postage and handling. $1.50 first book/50¢ for each additional book. (Book rate)

$ _____ Total amount of check

Name _____

Address _____

City _____ State _____ Zip _____

These publishers are pleased to assist nonprofit organizations. Inquiries about quantity discounts and special mailings are invited.

Person to contact _____

Organization _____ Phone (   ) _____